Incest and Agency in Elizabeth's England

Incest and Agency in Elizabeth's England

Maureen Quilligan

PENN

UNIVERSITY OF PENNSYLVANIA PRESS

Philadelphia

10 9 8 7 6 5 4 3 2 1

Published by
University of Pennsylvania Press
Philadelphia, Pennsylvania 19104–4011

Library of Congress Cataloging-in-Publication Data

Quilligan, Maureen, 1944–
    Incest and agency in Elizabeth's England / Maureen Quilligan.
        p.   cm.
    ISBN 0-8122-3863-X (cloth : alk. paper) ; ISBN 0-8122-1905-8 (pbk. : alk. paper)
    Includes bibliographical references and index.
    1. English literature—Early modern, 1500–1700—History and criticism.
2. Incest in literature. 3. Feminism and literature—England—History—16th century.
4. Women and literature—England—History—16th century. I. Title
PR428.I57 Q55   2005
820.9'3552—22

2004065102

to
Nancy J. Vickers
In honor of the friendship that first began rewriting
the Renaissance almost thirty year ago
In anticipation of recreations to come

Contents

I

Halting the Traffic in Women:
Theoretical Foundations

WE HAVE BEEN TAUGHT BY feminist scholarship that women are constrained by family structures; we have taken this as a foundational principle of arguments for the liberation of women, at least in part because we have so poorly understood the activities women have actually undertaken within kinship structures in traditional societies. If, however, we understand that traditional family and kinship structures may be radically different from our own, we may see how family rank could work to empower highly placed women rather than to limit them. In the sixteenth century the family dynasty became far more pivotal in political arrangements in absolutist Europe than it had been throughout the cloistered Middle Ages, a development that would make the Renaissance aristocratic family a potential site of real agency for women.

Before scrutinizing at a theoretical level exactly how and why traditional kinship structure might endow elite females with agency by means of an endogamous halt in what we have come to call "the traffic in women," it will be helpful to look at a specific example of the incest taboo in a text which is central to the culture of the Renaissance. No text can be more canonical than *King Lear*; more important, the play clearly lays out for us the tragedy which occurs when proper intergenerational relations are not observed. *King Lear* outlines the profound dangers to the culture when men and women fail to abide by the law against incest.

The Cultural Paradigm: Cordelia's Silence

In the opening scene of *King Lear*, Cordelia's refusal to speak demonstrates by *negative* example how authoritative female speech in the Renaissance is linked with, indeed may be enabled by, the discourse of incest. Unlike her

voluble sisters Goneril and Regan, who claim to love their father inordi-
nately, Cordelia refuses to trespass beyond the natural bond of a daughter
to a parent. When Lear orders her to prove that she loves him more than
her sisters do (and they have just said they love him more than they love
their husbands), her unwillingness to answer affirms her appropriate and
natural position as a woman, daughter, and potential wife. Asked if she has
nothing to add to her terse reply, her first response is the single word
"Nothing." If this looks to the modern eye like a radical defiance of patriarchal authority, the modern eye is fooled by its own assumptions. Indeed,
after her sisters have professed an all-transcending love for their father (if
they really meant what they said, their feelings would be incestuous),
Cordelia speaks to (and for) the Renaissance audience: "What shall Cordelia speak? Love, and be silent" (I.i.64). Cordelia here enunciates the
silence which is the most appropriate kind of speech for a dutiful woman.

Prodding her to greater eloquence about an entirely inappropriate
love for him, King Lear tells her to "Speak again." In her answer, she makes
a noteworthy parallel between her taciturnity and the proper distinctions
of love relationships.

Unhappy that I am, I cannot heave
My heart into my mouth. I love your Majesty
According to my bond, no more nor less. (I.i.93–94)

Cordelia here stresses her "bond," which naturally limits her love for her
father. When Lear further pleads that she "mend" her speech "a little," she
answers only to point out the transgression against matrimonial norms that
her sisters have hypocritically committed for their own venal purposes.

Why have my sisters husbands, if they say
They love you all? (I.i.101–2)

Incest haunts this play's subplot: Gloucester's eyes are gouged out on
stage, and his Oedipus-like punishment betrays the presence of familial
transgression within the play. But while in its opening scene, Cordelia
does not accuse her sisters (or her father) of anything but a hypocritical
language of incest, she *is* implying that Goneril and Regan are transgressing (or would be if they weren't lying) their own proper and natural
"bonds" by saying they love their father more than their husbands. Cordelia's complaint against her sisters, moreover, succinctly outlines what the
incest taboo is culturally meant to accomplish, that is (according to Claude
Lévi-Strauss) to extend patriarchal alliances across social groups by making

a bond between men, here the daughter's father and her husband. Cordelia sums up the proper traffic:

Happily, when I shall wed,
That lord whose hand must take my plight shall carry
Half my love with him, half my care and duty.
Sure I shall never marry like my sisters,
To love my father all. (I.i.106–10)

The rights and affections between the two men (father and husband) meet, as they should, in the woman: she becomes the bond between them. Cordelia thus identifies her sisters' unnatural infractions as a monstrous transgression against the necessary traffic in women.[1]

It is possible to trace Lear's tragedy to his disastrous interruption of the normal patterns of inheritance by daughters (who traditionally get equal portions), and to his incestuous preference for his youngest daughter (on whose "kind nursery" he intends to rely, thus making her into a caregiving mother). We must, however, postpone until a later chapter a fuller discussion of this play.[2] The important point here is that Cordelia's predicament offers us with admirable clarity the cultural paradigm in Renaissance society within which any attempt to claim female agency had to work. Cordelia's stance in the opening scene as *silent* daughter formulaically explicates what the ideal woman was perceived to be. Her silence *is* her cultural obedience and equals her refusal to claim agency for herself. Anthropological theory, as we shall see, has struggled to articulate how the necessary passivity of female desire translates into lack of access to speech. Lévi-Strauss famously leaves the female ability to manipulate language as the foundation of a great mystery. Cordelia's insistence on her own "silence" categorically underscores the connection between speechlessness and an acceptance of the female's nature to be traded out. The ideal woman in the patriarchal society of the English Renaissance is chaste, obedient, and most of all *silent*.

We must be careful not to be misled into thinking Cordelia's defiance of her father means that she is claiming agency for herself. She may seem to be doing just that, especially to post-nineteenth-century audiences, and thus to be the most independent and "modern" of the sisters. However, we must pay the closest possible attention to what she actually says: she mouths a thoroughly conservative statement of what women should do in her society. They should have no independent desires; they should provide the bond between men. They should remain chaste, silent, and obedient.

The bond must be appropriate, neither too endogamous (by marrying her husband's brother, Gertrude—like Catherine of Aragon—turns Hamlet's Denmark into "a couch for luxury and damnéd incest"), nor too exogamous (Brabantio cannot believe his mild, quiet, "still" daughter Desdemona would "fall in love with what she feared to look on!"—the Moor Othello—"in spite of nature, of years, of country, credit, everything").

Although they seem defiant to us, Desdemona and Cordelia closely follow the models of proper conduct for Renaissance womanhood. Compare Desdemona's and Cordelia's defenses of their seeming disobedience. Desdemona explains to Brabantio:

My noble father, I do perceive I have a divided duty.
To you I am bound for life and education.
My life and education both do learn me
How to respect you. You are the lord of duty,
I am hitherto your daughter. But here's my husband,
And so much duty as my mother showed
To you, preferring you to her father,
So much I challenge that I may profess
Due to the Moor my lord. (*Othello*, I.3.180–88)

Cordelia sounds the same:

                    Good my lord,
You have begot me, bred me, loved me,
I return those duties back as are right fit—
Obey you, love you, and most honour you.
Why have my sisters husbands if they say
They love you all? (*Lear*, I.i.97–102)

Asked by Emilia to "Speak again . . . O sweet mistress, speak!" to accuse her murderer ("Who has done this deed?"), Desdemona softly answers, "Nobody." Asked by Lear, "What is't thou sayest?—Her voice was ever soft, / Gentle, and low, an excellent thing in women," Cordelia's lips are still. She begins *Lear* by choosing silence. After she accuses her sisters, contrasting their unnatural and hypocritical hyperbole with her own sense of the boundaries to the duty she owes her father, she is banished from the stage. She marries and leaves the country. (Significantly, she is the only daughter with marriage proposals from *outside* the kingdom—France and Burgundy—as if these foreign marriage partners were there to underscore the exogamy she prefers.) Thereafter, she speaks very little. Cordelia's taciturnity thus marks at the opening of the play an association of appropriate

female silence with a woman's perfect and passive willingness to be exchanged. In the contrast between Cordelia's onstage taciturnity (followed
by her off-stage silence) and the garrulous horror with which her sisters'
swell into perverted authority, *King Lear*—and the culture of which it is a
part—imagines female agency as a monstrous growth predicated on incestuous female desire. Cordelia's return at the head of a foreign army in act
IV insists further on the problematic association of female agency with
incest, for she invades the kingdom less as her husband's wife than as her
father's daughter. Indeed, as Richard McCabe has usefully pointed out,
"Once she appears to love [Lear] 'all,' his vision of future bliss excludes all
thought of [her husband] France." Lear dreams of a paradise for two even
in prison, "we two alone," singing like birds in a cage.[3] His boast, "Have
I caught you now?" reminds us of his desire for his daughter's nursery at
the play's opening.

Shakespeare's two quietest heroines articulate by their silence the
symmetrical boundaries stabilized by the incest taboo. Judith Butler has
recently pointed out the parallel nature of the interdiction against excessive endogamy and exogamy in the incest taboo: "there must be exogamy.
But there must also be a limit to exogamy; that is, marriage must be
outside the clan but not outside a certain racial self-understanding. . . .
Cornered . . . between a compulsory heterosexuality and a prohibited
miscegenation, something called culture, saturated with the anxiety and
identity of dominant European whiteness, reproduces itself in and as uni-
versality itself."[4] Between them, Cordelia and Desdemona articulate the
parallel nature of their predicaments. Cordelia is finally punished for acced-
ing to her father's incestuous desires; Desdemona is punished for going
beyond the cultural boundary of color-based racial difference, which is (I
would argue) historically instantiated in the play itself, when Othello is
taught how to speak its discourse. Strangely we misread both heroines'
crises because we do not listen to what they are actually saying: each
announces the most conservative obedience to the traffic in women.

In a later text of the high Renaissance canon, the first female to speak
embodies a trinity of incest, femaleness, and evil in a single figure. She is
Sin in *Paradise Lost*. From this female monster, we learn that it was at the
moment at which Satan first thought of rebelling against the patriarchal
God that he gave birth to Sin. She would become first his incestuous
daughter, and then herself an incestuous mother, raped by her son Death.
She with her son comes to earth after the fall to remake God's entire creation. That very fall was caused by Adam's incestuous preference for the

creature born from his body over his obedience to God. Like that of Sin, Eve's sexual partner is the male from whose body she has been born. Milton too makes an important connection between the incestuous daughter and the manipulation of verbal signs; in a pun on her very name, Milton has Sin explain that the host of heaven "Called me Sin and for a Sign portentous held me." Thus, like Shakespeare, Milton associates the daughter's responsiveness to incestuous desire with her position within a system of signs.

Even an author so putatively supportive of female agency as Edmund Spenser felt compelled to twin his female warrior hero Britomart with Argante, her double, a dark shadow of the virtuous female who chases after her, and whose darkness must be challenged—if only in a brief episode in the epic—by the chaste Palladine. Spenser introduces the giantess Argante as one who had committed incest *in the womb* with her twin brother, Ollyphant.[5] While Spenser's text may have directly influenced Milton's Sin, what is more significant here is the shared emphasis among these and so many other canonical works of the period; the emphasis insists upon the remarkable cultural resonance throughout Renaissance culture (including Jacobean tragedies like *The Duchess of Malfi*) of associations between female agency and incestuous desire.

As the instance of Cordelia's striking wordlessness in *King Lear*'s opening scene makes evident, the fundamental source of authority denied the obedient woman is language that leads to action. Indeed, Goneril and Regan's protestations of what would be (were it real) an incestuous love for their father are couched in terms that call direct attention to the relationship of eloquence to deed. By insisting on how incapable speech is of delivering meaning, Goneril's hyperbole paradoxically makes a grand rhetorical display of rhetoric's failure adequately to represent reality. Ordered by her father to "speak first," she swears that her feelings are too large for words to compass:

> Sir I love you more than word can wield the matter;
> Dearer than eyesight, space and liberty.
> Beyond what can be valued, rich or rare;
> No less than life, with grace, health, beauty, honor,
> As much as child e'er loved, or father found;
> A love that makes breath poor and speech unable:
> Beyond all manner of so much I love you. (I.i.56–62)

The "eyesight" that Goneril claims means less to her than her love for her father becomes, of course, a spectacularly literalized coordinate of loyal relations between father and child in the more explicitly Oedipal subplot of Gloucester's blinding. Here, it signals the incestuous bent of Goneril's speechifying. Regan goes on to outdo her sister in professional doublespeak

I find she names my very deed of love;
Only she comes too short, that I profess
Myself an enemy to all other joys
Which the most precious square of sense professes,
And find I am alone felicitate in your dear Highness' love. (I.i.74–78)

That silence should be the mark, as *King Lear* seems to indicate, of the willingly exchanged woman, while transgressive polysyllabic garrulousness marks the endogamously invested daughter, says a great deal about the perceived (and for some, dangerous) potential for female eloquence and authority at this cultural moment. Suzanne Hull has tabulated the large number of books aimed specifically at a female readership during the period whose purpose was to teach women to be (as Hull titles her study) *chaste, silent, and obedient.* Hull's point is that each of these three injunctions enjoins the other two, silence being the signal hallmark of both chastity and obedience.[6] Patricia Parker has further argued for the crucial conjuncture of society's association of verbal excess with female excess during the period. Her study of rhetorical handbooks reveals how extremes of rhetorical display were seen to threaten with the same transgressive immoderation as female sexuality: both had to be controlled with analogical means of restraint.[7]

My purpose in the following chapters is certainly not to question the centrality of the incest taboo throughout human societies. Rather, my aim is to understand the remarkable presence in the Renaissance of what we may call incest schemes in the books of a small number of women who did manage to claim an active female authority by writing in high canonical genres—what we would call "literature"—and who, even more transgressively at the time, often sought publication in print. By looking at these historical texts in all their specificity, I hope to be able to contribute something new to the conversation about female agency, which has taken place, at least at the theoretical level, with a set of assumptions based upon distinctly modern social arrangements. While modern anthropological theory about woman's agency has deeply informed my understanding of why some Renaissance women writers wrote as they did, I argue that the historical texts themselves have some corrections to offer modern theorizing.

Indeed, my attempt to understand the scandalous anomaly of an

instantiating act of incest in the work of a writer who has been called
France's first professional woman of letters, is what originally compelled
me to notice how certain other key premodern women writers re-create
scenes of endogamy, subsequently using these narratives for their own
empowerment. As far as we know, the first history of women by a European woman is Christine de Pizan's *Livre de la cité des dames* (1405). This
early fifteenth-century allegory builds its city of ladies with a foundation
stone of legendary mother-son incest. Is it an accident that the first
printed work by Queen Elizabeth I's hand was a translation she had done
at age eleven of Marguerite de Navarre's *Miroir de l'âme pécheresse* (first
published in 1531), a poem which uses the notion of "holy" incest as its
prevailing trope? Is there no connection between the fact that Mary
Wroth, the author of the first sonnet cycle and prose romance printed in
English by a woman, carried on an endogamous (if not legally incestuous) illegitimate relationship with her first cousin and the fact that she
described that relationship—under the guise of her two lovers, Pamphilia
and Amphilanthus—in both the sonnets and the prose volume? Is it an
accident that Sir Philip Sidney and his sister Mary Herbert, the Countess
of Pembroke, translated the Psalms together and that the sister finished
the brother's work by revising it for publication? Does the importance of
the brother-sister tie have anything to tell us about the reason Elizabeth
Cary may have chosen to write about a woman who defies her husband's
sexual demands because he had murdered her brother? May not Isabella
Whitney have cast one of her most important long poems as a fictive
legacy to her brother because such a relationship resonated with the
power of endogamous female agency? As such women sought positions
of authority within the highest canons of literature, they would appear to
be speaking directly to the thematics of endogamy they found there,
manipulating this discourse to their own purposes of self-authorization as
female storytellers.

In the chapters that follow, I have attempted to keep these female-
authored texts in dialogue with better-known texts by men, rather than
cordoning them off into what Myra Jehlen long ago called the "no-man's
land" of a problematically univocal female tradition. The dialogue allows
us to interrogate the long border that not so much lies between the two
traditions as forms their common ground.[8] As we shall see, this approach
not only has the salutary effect of keeping the texts inside the cultural conversation of which they were an integral part, but also offers altered perspectives on canonical texts by Sidney, Spenser, Shakespeare, and Milton.

The result may prove a useful estrangement of texts that we have told ourselves we already know very well, a not insignificant benefit of any critical practice that insists on reading in concert writing by both men and women.

I begin the discussion with the special instance of Elizabeth I—whose continued unmarried state was the foundation for an "unnatural" female agency enabled by her endogamous halt of the proper traffic in women. From that perspective I then consider Sir Philip Sidney's peculiarly familiar challenge to Elizabeth's power to make her own decision about marriage. Through their complex relationship with the queen, the Sidney family gained a social status out of all proportion to their actual wealth, and that relationship continues, as the next chapter explores, in Sidney's sister's writing, evident in the ways in which she connects her authority to her brother in her literary work, particularly in her address to the queen.

I turn then to Edmund Spenser, who once served as secretary to Sidney's uncle, the Earl of Leicester; Spenser disguises his criticism of the queen's endogamous, unmarried virginity in the character of Britomart, the cross-dressed female knight at the heroic center of nearly three books of *The Faerie Queene*. A rereading of the discourse of incest in Spenser's allegory leads me to a way of understanding the remarkable revision of both Sidney's and Spenser's romances in Mary Wroth's *Urania*. That Wroth is Sir Philip Sidney's niece and was sexually involved with her first cousin, the Countess of Pembroke's son, is the test case for my argument. The study concludes with a fuller discussion of the relation of Cordelia and incest in Shakespeare's *King Lear*, followed by a brief analysis of Milton's meditations on female agency and the problem of incest in *Paradise Lost*.

The Incest Taboo in Anthropological Theory

While the utility of any theory rests with its local applications, the association of transgressive women with transgressive uses of language runs deeper than practices particular to the Renaissance. The interdiction against incest is a constant in all human societies, pivotal at all periods and in all places, however mutually exclusive the specific tabooed permutations and sexual combinations may have been from one culture to the next. Anthropological theory has been well organized to ask at this most generalized level what is achieved by the social process of interdicting certain sexual liaisons and authorizing others.[9] The theory has been less interested in articulating the power of female speech to interrupt the social controls placed upon female desire—and Lévi-Strauss's account is a good place to begin to see this difficulty, as well as its dismissal.

As he concludes his seminal work, *Elementary Structures of Kinship*, Lévi-Strauss points out the endemically problematic position of women tabooed by the incest prohibition. This discussion is, in fact, the only time that he takes into account how the tabooed women might themselves experience their functional status as passive objects to be traded in the system of exchanges just analyzed.

> The total relationship of exchange which constitutes marriage is not established between a man and a woman where each owes and receives something, but between two groups of men, and the woman figures only as one of the objects in the exchange, not as one of the partners between whom the exchange takes place. This remains true even when the girl's feelings are taken into consideration, as, moreover, is usually the case. In acquiescing to the proposed union, she precipitates or allows the exchange to take place; she cannot alter its nature. This view must be kept in all strictness, even with regard to our own society, where marriage appears to be a contract between persons. Set going by the marriage of a man and a woman, with its aspects set out in the marriage service, this cycle of reciprocity is only a secondary mode of a wider cycle of reciprocity, which pledges the union of a man and a woman who is either someone's daughter or sister, by the union of the daughter or sister of that man or another man with the first man in question.[10]

Although Lévi-Strauss observes here that a girl might have some feelings about the particulars of the exchange, he emphatically insists that she cannot change its nature, which is to be, in Eve Kosofsky Sedgwick's useful shorthand, a "homosocial connection," a bond not between a man and a woman but "between men."[11] As he ends his book, however, Lévi-Strauss has glimpsed the problem that the potential agency of women poses for the system under analysis. It is significant that he presents this problem in terms of a woman's relationship to *language*. True to his structuralist position at the time, Lévi-Strauss is arguing that the system of exchange of women, enforced by the incest taboo, works like a language. He understands as similar the semiotic function of language and the "elementary structures of kinship," because, as he argues, both are means of social communication bound by discoverable rules. Having pointed out that the incest taboo often operates, along with other taboos, against the misuse of language, he proposes that, in the system of exchange which creates culture, "women themselves are treated as signs, which are misused when not put to the use reserved to signs, which is to be communicated."

He is quick to grant, however, that in reality women are more than signs because they make and use signs themselves:

even in a man's world [a woman] is still a person, and since in so far as she is defined as a sign she must be recognized as a generator of signs. In the matrimonial dialogue of men, woman is never purely what is spoken about; for if women in general represent a certain category of signs, destined to certain kinds of communication, each woman preserves a particular value arising from her talent . . . for taking her part in a duet. In contrast to words, which have wholly become signs, woman has remained at once a sign and a value. This explains why the relations between the sexes have preserved that affective richness, ardor and mystery which doubtless originally permeated the universe of human communications. (496)

While Lévi-Strauss never explores the implications of the fact that a woman's value-endowed ability to speak, that is, to manipulate signs herself, may come into conflict with her function as a sign in the system of the traffic in women, it is clear that female semiotic agency is potentially *very* problematic to this system. The implications have been the focus of much feminist anthropology of recent decades.

Gayle Rubin's greatest quarrel was with Lévi-Strauss's failure to follow the implications of the end of his own text: "Why is he not, at this point, denouncing what kinship systems do to women instead of presenting one of the greatest rip-offs of all time as the root of romance?"[12] Rubin's move against Lévi-Strauss—rhetorically highlighted by the drop in diction—was programmatic: she did not query his peculiar emphasis on female speech and the concomitant issue of silence, but stressed how his interests in understanding the traffic in women as an exchange of rights and privileges only among men worked to deny women any agency. Her insight into his critical practice illuminated its blindness to the way the system itself institutes different statuses for males and females. Thus Rubin was following Lévi-Strauss in her understanding of the "traffic," the process by which men reciprocally trade women among themselves in the founding act of civilization. But she goes on to ask questions Lévi-Strauss does not: how profoundly asymmetrical does this traffic make the different rights men and women have in themselves? Rubin moved the discussion from the fact that men trade women among themselves, to the fact that it is men who trade and women who are traded: a male has the right in himself to trade and a female has no right in herself. According to Rubin, systems underwritten by the incest taboo and that traffic in women do not merely exchange women. They exchange sexual access, genealogical status, lineage names and ancestors, rights and people—men, women, and children—in concrete social relationships. These relationships always include certain rights for men, others for women. "Exchange of women" is a shorthand for expressing that the social relations of a kinship system specify that men have certain rights to their female kin and that women do not have the same rights either to themselves or to their male kin. In this sense, the exchange of women is a profound perception of a system in which women do not have full rights to themselves. (177)

Another way of putting this insight—and indeed the way that Lévi-Strauss glanced at the problem of female agency at the end of his book—is to say that men may use women as signs in the semiotic system of kinship, but women cannot speak for themselves in the kinship system. In that system, women are only signs—a function with which their own ability to use language may well come into conflict, as Cordelia's silence exemplifies. Or as Milton's incestuous daughter Sin announces when the angels recognize her as a "sign."

Rubin's critique of Lévi-Strauss was empowered by her inexplicit recognition that the issue of female *agency*, including a female's use of language—is what is at stake in the suppression of female *desire*. Thus she mounted her argument against Lévi-Strauss's anthropological understanding of the workings of the incest taboo by appealing to the status of that taboo in psychoanalysis and outlining the familiar process by which the Oedipal complex creates differently gendered—and heterosexually desiring—others. Following Lacan's rereading of Freud, Rubin laid out a similar set of exchanges, in which the male, in possession of the phallus (which names a specifically male privilege but also is the privileged signifier of subjectivity), is able to pass the phallus on to another male through a female. (The phallus is passed to the son through the mother, but also passed through women in exchanges between men.) In this exchange, the female is only a passive conduit for that power, able to pass it along to another male but unable to possess it herself.

This position as agencyless conduit is, as it were, what Cordelia asserts as her place: the limit of her bond to her father is that she will form the bond between her father and her husband. For her sisters to insist that they love their father all is for them to ignore their already-married status, to ignore the fact that the phallus has already passed through them, connecting Lear and their husbands. The play, of course, acknowledges this connection when Lear disowns Cordelia by appealing not to Goneril and Regan but to their husbands: "Cornwall and Albany, / With my two daughters' dowers digest the third" (I.i.129–30). When Goneril and Regan speak of their all-engulfing love for their father, it is as if they've forgotten that they have already been exchanged; they speak as if it were possible to double back, so to speak, as if by their rhetoric they could win for themselves the greatest portion of Lear's wealth, as if they could have the phallus—that is, their father's power—descend to them without passing it on to their husbands. The proof of their evil is that they desire to usurp that interdicted phallic power from both father and husbands. Their adulterous lust for the bastard Edmund underscores the illegitimacy of their desires, which become incestuous when Edmund dallies with both of them as sisters.

Rubin's concluding argument was that what is ultimately interdicted by the incest taboo is active female desire itself, rather than any particular categories of unallowable sexual couplings. Freud argued that

> the turning away from her mother is an extremely important step in the course of the little girl's development. It is more than a mere change of object . . . hand in hand with it there is to be observed a marked lowering of the active sexual impulses and a rise of the passive ones. . . . The transition to the father object is accomplished with the help of the passive trends in so far as they have escaped catastrophe. The path to the development of femininity now lies open to the girl.[13]

Rubin stresses that this presumed passivity is a renunciation of the girl's active desire: "What is important in Freud's schema however is not the geography of desire but its self-confidence" (195). Deprived of the agency which derives from faith in one's self, the girl "has become a little woman—feminine, passive, heterosexual" (196).

Theoretically, there are three ways to halt the traffic in women. One is incest, where women make an erotic choice within their own close kin. Two is celibacy, either personal spinsterhood or institutional vocation, the latter when a woman enters a religious order (here, however, the halt is at least named with the terms borrowed from intimate family positions; nuns are traditionally called "sisters"). And, as adumbrated by Rubin, there is a third way out of the traffic—a choice that would in theory root out all kinship system—and that is a lesbian desire that does not comply with the compulsory heterosexuality required by the exchange of women. Rubin's emphasis on the potentially active status of the woman who evades the rules and is capable of making her own choices, ought to suggest the power of the first means for agency. If the declaration of agency allows an evasion of the traffic in women, a different way of achieving this cessation is to refuse to be traded out and, instead, actively to choose an endogamous male as partner. Rubin did not take up the question of the function of the incest taboo at the level of language—which is, of course, the place where Lacan found Lévi-Strauss most interesting. But because what is important about this agency is its transgression of the tabooed woman's *passivity*, it is important to glance, however briefly, at the question of the construction of female identity within language.

What Lacanian theory seems in part to have accomplished is to provide an answer to Lévi-Strauss's ultimate conundrum about women's semiotic abilities; it does so by uncovering what Lacan calls the "impossibility" of women in the very nature of language itself.

That the woman should be inscribed in an order of exchange of which she is the object, is what makes for the fundamentally conflictual, and, I would say, insoluble character of her position: the symbolic order literally submits her, it transcends her. . . . There is for her something insurmountable, something unacceptable, in the fact of being placed as an object in a symbolic order to which, at the same time, she is subjected just as much as the man.[14]

Jacqueline Rose points out that Lacan eventually moved away from the Lévi-Straussian notion of exchange articulated above and developed a more complicated model for the subject's simultaneous acquisition of language and sexual identity. As Rose puts it, Lacan shifted from seeing the problem as one of a "process of exchange (women as objects) to the construction of woman as a category within language" (47).[15] This move, of course, binds even more intimately the limits placed on female agency to the question of language, and makes even more problematic a woman's access to language as a means of representing her own activity (as distinct from male agency). Specifically, Rose takes issue with Rubin's appeal to Lacan as a way of reappropriating the Oedipal conflict to an anthropological function: she points out that Rubin's use of Lacan loses sight of such fundamental psychoanalytic concepts as the unconscious and slights the long and nuanced process of the formation of sexual identity, "reducing relations . . . to quite literal . . . acts of exchange."[16] But Rose ultimately agrees with Rubin that Lacan's formulations—like Lévi-Strauss's —are complicit with the male-biased system he is describing.

Rose is equally critical of the kinds of emphases given Lacan's thought by French feminists such as Luce Irigaray, who attempt to blaze a pathway out of the impasse into which the Lacanian logic of language places the female. In this argument, the female is seen as outside any language predicated on the male body, that is, on the presence or absence of a penis/phallus. Instead the woman has access to an alternate version of verbal activity—an *écriture feminine*—a feminine writing which works differently as a means of representation from male language because it relies on a pre-Oedipal (and preverbal) relationship to the maternal body. Thus Irigaray writes: "Woman is never far from the 'mother.' I do not mean the role but the 'mother' as no-name and as a source of goods. There is always at least a little good mother milk left in her. She writes with white ink." Irigaray further pinpoints the problem as one of "woman's 'improper' access to representation, her entry into a specular and speculative economy that affords her instincts no signs, no symbols or emblems, or methods of writing that could figure her instincts."[17] In essence, this is to say no more than what Cordelia's silence indicated: the proper passivity of the obedient good woman requires no access to the system of representation which is language.

In *This Sex Which Is Not One*, Irigaray meditates on the different language women might speak together by using phrases like "The Mechanics of Fluids," puns like "When Our Lips Speak Together," a labile communication which is never univocal: "Woman never speaks the same way. What she emits is flowing, fluctuating. Blurring. And she is not listened to, unless proper meaning (meaning of the proper) is lost. Whence the resistances to that voice that overflows the "subject.""[18]

In a similar manner, Julia Kristeva suggests that there is a compensatory countering to this denial of access. While the gendering of different subjects is not her main concern, Kristeva grants women a unique and particular language among themselves:

Women doubtless reproduce among themselves the strange gamut of forgotten body relationships with their mothers. Complicity in the unspoken connivance of the inexpressible, of a wink, a tone of voice, a gesture, a tinge, a scent. . . . No communication between individuals but connection between atoms, molecules, wisps of words, droplets of sentences. The community of women is a community of dolphins.[19]

Kaja Silverman has usefully criticized the theoretical positing of a separate language for women by pointing out how such female speech, predicated on the plenitude of the mother/infant couple, puts the fully functioning adult mother inside the enclosure experienced by the child, and thereby denies to the mother her adult verbal sophistication, substituting instead a magic language reminiscent of the babble of the infant. Silverman asks:

Are we to understand the mother as somehow representing . . . forces antipathetic to language and identity? . . . What occurs here is [that] once again the child's discursive exteriority—its emergency from the maternal enclosure—can be established only by placing the mother herself inside that enclosure, by relegating her to the interior or the chora or—what is the same thing—by stripping her of all linguistic capabilities."[20]

Seen from the point of view of Silverman's critique, such imagining of a different language as Irigaray and Kristeva propose ends where Lévi-Strauss's does: denying to women the ability to manipulate the fully articulated system of signs with which men communicate with each other, thereby silencing them. More crucially for a critical practice attempting to retrieve the history of female cultural activity in all its verbal sophistication, these prophetic calls by utopian French feminists for future *écriture féminine* are deeply problematic for understanding the historical practice of premodern women writers. If such poststructuralist female writing is destined to happen only in the future, how does scholarship evaluate the writing that women have already done centuries earlier?

There is—or it is at least theoretically possible that there should be—a more immediate way than sexual or semiotic separatism out of the silencing system of exchanges whereby women in the late Middle Ages and Renaissance came to write. In theory, a woman could declare access to the representational system simply by refusing to be traded out of it. One type of refusal results in celibacy, that is, in the subjugation of sexual desire entirely: this choice is the institutional foundation upon which such writers as Hildegard of Bingen and Julian of Norwich may be said to have built their authorship. If not in celibacy or homosexuality, the transgressive refusal to be exogamously traded results in something that resembles incest.[21]

Silverman suggests this alternative when she calls for the articulation of a multiform female desire,

desire which challenges dominance from within representation and meaning, rather than from the place of a mutely resistant biology or sexual "essence." Once we have recognized that unconscious desire is far from monolithic . . . then it becomes possible to think of all sorts of discursive and relational strategies for activating the fantasmatic scene which corresponds to maternal desire, one which the symbolic does its best to cordon off and render inactive by denying it representational support. (124)

Silverman's phrase "maternal desire" is here strangely ambiguous. Does it refer to the child's desire for the mother, or to the mother's desire for her child, or both? Christine de Pizan had excused Semiramis from just such a desire for her son, a desire which Christine's male precursors Dante and Boccaccio had made the foundational horror of the *Commedia* and *De mulieribus claris*.

Lévi-Strauss acknowledged the desire against which all the varieties of the marriage exchanges that he had traced through a good quarter of the globe were set to work:

> To this very day, mankind has always dreamed of seizing and fixing that fleeting moment when it was permissible to believe that the law of exchange could be evaded, that one could gain without losing, enjoy without sharing . . . [it would be] . . . primitive happiness at a time when the confusion of languages made words into common property, the . . . bliss of . . . heaven where women will no longer be exchanged . . . a world in which one might *keep to oneself*. (497)

That is the bliss enjoyed by Adam in Eden, of course. He keeps to himself the being made from his body, Eve, and therefore in a way practices a form of strangely *maternal* incest. Should it surprise us to realize that a female's version of this paradisal dream is no different?

When Gayle Rubin proposed a different way out of the bind imposed by the traffic in women, she emphasized that the traffic not only regulates the circulation of women, it enjoins upon both men and women an "obligatory heterosexuality." Therefore to choose a same-sex partner would be, at least theoretically, the same as choosing radical endogamy.[22] Eve Sedgwick opened an entire field of enquiry when she asked a fundamental question about Rubin's argument: what is the function of the fundamental asymmetry that has been constructed historically between the ways women bond and the ways men bond? Pointing to germinal work by Carroll Smith-Rosenberg that demonstrates how only in the nineteenth century was female homosexuality constructed as something different from and outside the normal range of female-to-female relationships, Sedgwick theorizes that "the diacritical opposition between the 'homosocial' and the 'homosexual' seems to be much less thorough and dichotomous for women, in our society, than for men" (2). According to her argument, this difference produces a crucial "asymmetry" in the way male and female sexuality gets constructed by a patriarchal system that relies on the traffic in women: male homosocial relations require an intermediary, the female, through whom the men may form a bond that is thereby differentiated from a homosexual relationship—which is defined as inimical to proper homosocial relations between men. What Sedgwick does here is to reformulate in reverse Rubin's articulation of the traffic: male homosociality needs the trafficked female to disguise the important part homosexuality plays in heterosexuality.

Much significant critical work has grown out of this recognition that the opposition between male homosociality and male homosexuality hides the important fact that male homosexuality is a necessary component of patriarchy.[23] Among a number of other critics, Jonathan Goldberg, in *Sodometries* and elsewhere, applies Sedgwick's argument to discussions of early modern subjectivity, querying the virtually universal assumption among scholars of the period that desire in the Renaissance is always defined as heterosexual desire.[24] Goldberg does the useful service of reminding us that the desire an entire culture claimed to have felt for their virgin queen, Elizabeth I of England, may have had much to do with the fact that what she offered was a desire which participated in the sodomitical, that is, desire not in service of dynastic marriage. At least part of Elizabeth's allure for her male contemporaries may therefore have been exerted by the androgyny of her self-presentations (39–45).[25]

One of the most important critiques of exchange theory is Judith Butler's, who in an early text, *Gender Trouble*, read Gayle Rubin against Michel Foucault's argument that a taboo or repressive law actually generates what it interdicts.[26] Butler thus argues that homosexual desire is, in fact, *created* by the incest taboo: "If we apply the Foucaultian critique of the repressive hypothesis to the incest taboo, then it would appear that the law produces both the sanctioned heterosexuality and transgressive homosexuality. Both are indeed effects" (94)

Butler's purpose is to understand the elision of female homosexual desire in current gender theory and to construct out of her critique the possibility of understanding gender as "performativity"—that is, the stylized repetition of defining bodily acts over time. In her critique of poststructuralist psychoanalytic feminist theory, she did not stop to consider what part transgressive incest plays in this circuit, possibly because incest is that which is explicitly prohibited and needs no comment. Her psychoanalytic emphasis defined incestuous desire as only that which the child feels for a parent, only as intergenerational, never what one might feel for a peer member of another interdicted group (siblings or cousins).

With the publication of *Antigone's Claim: Kinship Between Life and Death*, Butler does take up the question of incestuous desire in Antigone's love for her brother Polyneices—and also for her father Oedipus, who is (because they share Jocasta as mother) one of her half-brothers. Butler reads Lacan against Hegel in an attempt to undermine Lacan's claim that female identity lies in the linguistic experience of the Oedipal complex, so that femaleness, as we have seen, is denied legitimate access to the modes of representation within language. In the process of doing so, she makes Antigone into "not quite a queer heroine," whose incestuous desire for her brother and her corresponding punishment by being entombed alive emblematizes a "heterosexual fatality.[27] Never fully theorizing how queerness might be able to map so easily over incest, Butler nonetheless makes Antigone into a character for questioning the heterosexual traffic.

Antigone, who concludes the oedipal drama [in that hers is the last play in the Theban cycle], fails to produce heterosexual closure for that drama, and . . . this may intimate the direction for psychoanalytic theory that takes Antigone as its point of departure. Certainly, she does not achieve another sexuality, one that is *not* heterosexuality, but she does seem to deinstitute heterosexuality by refusing to do what is necessary to stay alive for Haemon, by refusing to become a mother and a wife, by scandalizing the public with her wavering gender, by embracing death as her bridal chamber. (76)

Butler's argument here broaches the magnitude of retheorizing female sexuality around the incest taboo. In some sense, Butler can be said to be doing to Sophocles' cycle of plays what, as we shall see in the next section, Annette Weiner has done for the Trobriand Islands: revisiting a space which famously had been theorized to see only male agency at work, and where female subjectivity remained invisible, at least to the male-authored theory. The revision of these theories by focusing on Antigone's agency—and, as we shall see, on the actual objects transferred among women in the Trobriand Islands—radically changes both psychoanalysis and anthropology. This book is not the place to do the theoretical work necessary to see how these interesting parallels might play out in anthropology and psychoanalysis themselves. Suffice it to say that the present argument can only claim to be an articulation of some of the challenges offered to theory by newly crucial historical materials.

Because she uses only the male-oriented understanding of the "traffic in women," Eve Sedgwick's understanding of the homosocial space in which Shakespeare's sonnets circulated among men in the early modern period makes female agency in that genre impossible to articulate. Lorna Hutson, for example, examines the difficulties facing the Renaissance poet Aemila Lanyer, who attempted to use sonnet discourse to address female patrons. She outlines the impasse: "A female author cannot mirror the virtue of a female patron if the space of the . . . mutually authenticating gaze . . . is actually a *homosocial space*—a space of discursive and political opportunity conceivable only between men."[28] So restricting had this theory of exclusive homosociality come to seem as a means of enabling any understanding of how women actually came to write during the Renaissance that critic Karen Newman suggested doing away with it altogether: "we have exhausted the usefulness of the 'traffic in women' paradigm as it is currently used in feminist analysis. . . . [R]eading woman repeatedly as the object of male exchange constructs a victim's discourse that risks reinscribing the very sexual politics it ostensibly seeks to expose and change."[29] What Newman proposed instead, as a means of liberating our analysis of women's cultural achievements, was a turn to a more philosophical discourse, one that seeks to understand the mutual constitution of the object and the subject. She suggested a revision of Hegel by way of Theodor Adorno that would posit a more equal relation between subject and object (subject and subject or object and object) as "distinction without domination" (50).[30]

Another Renaissance scholar, Naomi Miller, has taken Sedgwick's idea of "homosociality" in a very different direction, using a degendered form of it to outline a program of female homosocial relations in the period, as they were represented specifically by women writers. Sedgwick had argued for the theoretical *asymmetry* between male and female homosexuality, in which male homosexuality was visible and distinctly different from what she calls male "homosociality," while women's homosexuality was invisible and hence indistinguishable from whatever else women might do with women (all of which activity is sexually and socially insignificant). Miller simply ignores Sedgwick's distinction, borrowing the idea of "homosociality" and applying it to women. In the process she ends up making an argument quite similar, as we shall see, to Annette Weiner's understanding of the work women do collectively to keep female circuits of mutual relations alive. Unlike the foregoing critics, who are dealing with male authors, Miller has formulated a critical history of female writing practice, specifically to describe the narratives of Lady Mary Wroth.[31] In contrast to Sedgwick, Miller understands *all* female homosocial relations to be subversive, socially suspect, and under constant scrutiny and social repression. Thus, without emphasizing it, Miller suggests a most important fact about the traffic in women: while lesbianism is relatively invisible in the early modern period because it is folded into female homosocial relations, those homosocial relations between women are *themselves* interdicted at the time as potentially subversive. Miller focuses on groupings of women (like the gossips' feasts) that, from a theoretical position, Irigaray has heralded as revolutionary. Miller's wonderfully productive misappropriation of Sedgewick's insight hints that the asymmetry Sedgwick outlines may work both ways: because it is not posited as antithetical to female homosociality, female homosexuality simply evaporates and becomes culturally less visible. In contrast, because male homosexuality *is* posited as inimical to male heterosexuality, it is rendered visible, its scandalous visibility as sodometry disguising the functional part it plays in patriarchy. In essence, female same sex desire fades into invisibility by virtue of the fact that the culture has no reason to see how female homosexuality might conflict with proper female homosociality, because there *is* no socially acceptable female homosociality. All bonds between women are either socially suspect and/or beneath notice (invisible). If what is tabooed by the culture is the entire range of female homosocial bondings, there is no need to interdict, as a special case, female-to-female sexual desire. Only when female homosocial bonding becomes historically legitimate and powerful does the asymmetry fade and female homosexuality begin to precipitate out as a different element.

It thus should come as no surprise that looking at the start of the women's movement in the nineteenth century Carroll Smith-Rosenberg should find evidence of self-described (and culturally condemned) homosexuality among women. When suffragism appears to be gaining social legitimacy and power, female homosexuality becomes fully visible and is seen as something very different from "legitimate" female-to-female homosocial relations.[32] As Valerie Traub has demonstrated, while it is difficult to find evidence of lesbian desire in male representations of the Renaissance, it is not impossible, and she has found a number of artfully rich expressions of it throughout the culture for those who have eyes to see it. The connection between female homosociality and homosexuality, however, can work in reverse: at the end of the seventeenth century, Traub argues, the figure of the tribade "perverts" the idea of chaste female friendship, so that both become "visible" and therefore explicitly interdicted.[33] Traub brilliantly ties this transformation to the changing economic nature of the family in English society, without explicitly arguing that what has changed is the fundamental kinship structure of the culture.[34]

Rubin's argument about compulsory heterosexuality has clearly been very fruitful for empowering scholarship which seeks to discover the "invisible" parameters of female desire at earlier historical periods. Save for Naomi Miller's unacknowledged transcendence of the detailed difference between male and female homosociality in Sedgwick's argument, the theory about the traffic in women has not, however, been notable for allowing insight into Renaissance women's writing. While Newman is clearly right to pressure the problematic status of objects and subjects in the classical Maussian notion of exchange theory, and Kathy Psomiades has recently begun to uncover the Victorian economics behind the nineteenth-century anthropological studies underlying this theory, the "traffic in women" has had its usefulness as well as its limitations. It may have still more to offer us, especially if we understand, as some feminist anthropologists have begun to argue, that in the traffic women have their own objects to "trade," objects they circulate among themselves.[35] Karen Newman, indeed, is most insightful about the theoretical machinery of the traffic in her dismissal of one of the possible escape routes from it. As she so succinctly puts it, "Logically . . . in Lévi-Strauss's system, the result of women's subjectivity would be incest" (43). Newman herself seems simply to reject out of hand the clear theoretical implication of her remark. Yet what if we were to entertain its possibilities? What does it mean to equate female subjectivity with incest? Is there anything we can learn from leaving open this radical theoretical possibility? Does seeing incest as a positive means for gaining female agency help us in any way to read texts by Renaissance women writers? The responses to these questions have some surprising anthropological answers.

Feminist Anthropology: Revising Exchange Theory

Recently, feminist anthropologists have begun a major reassessment and revaluation of Marcel Mauss's basic tenet about the fundamental reciprocity required by the exchange of objects. In *The Gender of the Gift: Problems with Women and Problems with Society in Melanesia*, for example, Marilyn Strathern has offered a thoroughgoing critique of arguments relying on Mauss, insisting that a misemphasis occurs when insufficient attention is paid to the status of women as *gifts*; unlike commodities, gifts circulate as persons, with full personal agency.[36] She says that only when one misrecognizes women as mere objects (and not as the fully agented "gifts" they are) can the traffic be said to work against their full personhood, denying them active social agency. The status of the object in modern society is radically different from its status in premodern societies, where it has not been objectified as a commodity. As "objects," Melanesian women have agency.

Useful though Strathern's distinctions may be in qualifying the oppression women suffer through being exchanged, her argument does not help us to understand what women might be doing within their own homosocial groups, when they are interacting there together: is their activity simply neutral, of no use to the processes of civilization (as Lévi-Strauss would have us understand)? Or might it instead comprise a huge area of human experience heretofore overlooked by the theory of the traffic in women?

More crucially for a wholesale revision of the theory, anthropologist Annette Weiner has revisited those Trobriand Islanders on the basis of whose customs Malinowski and Mauss first argued for the notion of the gift and its required reciprocity, work Lévi-Strauss relied on so heavily in his articulation of kinship structure. Weiner has recently argued that the Malinowski and Mauss studies left out a signal component of economic exchanges: the objects managed by the women themselves. In a sequence of critical books seeking to articulate the positive and active parts women play in the social exchanges that constitute culture, Weiner offers a fundamental critique. *Reciprocity* is *not* the driving force behind exchange, she argues; rather, it is the desire to *retain* what she calls "inalienable possessions." If so, the fundamental building block of human culture would be not, as Lévi-Strauss has it, the traffic in women, but what Weiner titles the "paradox of keeping-while-giving."[37] This paradox allows Weiner to understand and give weight to the part women play in the creation of social value. For it is women who are assigned care for those objects that are never intended to circulate—never to become part of the cycles of reciprocity and exchange—which the women themselves usually have made out of textiles. Women's value is associated with a kinship of continuity, specifically with ancestors; that is, it is associated with those vital objects that assure social identity because they embody the social group's cohesion and history. Essentially heirlooms, these objects are not for trade, but for keeping within the family, passed down through the generations. In the process of reconfiguring exchange theory by placing women actively into the mix, Weiner argues for a powerful connection that she calls "sibling intimacy."

Bother-sister incest existed as a portentous political option either as an actual genealogically correct marriage or as a prerogative of the first sister and bother clan ancestors. Sister-brother incest is at once sacred and profane, politically dynamic and rigorously disguised, the ultimate solution to legitimacy and the most feared compromise. Reductionist rules of its prohibition linked as they are to the rules of reciprocity can never expose the vast reproductive power in sibling intimacy even in societies where sibling incest is rigorously taboo. The sibling taboo is bound up with the same paradoxical dynamics and motivation that so haunt and shape the problem of keeping-while-giving. (16–17)

By announcing its centrality to a properly understood process of exchange, she comes close to outlining the way in which a categorical transgression of the incest taboo allows the articulation of female agency.

When a woman marries, the full range of her reproductive powers is far too essential to be lost to her brother and the other members of her natal group. Whereas in most cases, a woman's biological procreative role is established within her marriage, thereby sexually upholding the sibling sexual relations taboo, her other productive and reproductive roles—those usually omitted in kinship theory—remain clearly tied to the relation between herself and her brother. Even when the sibling taboo is rigorously upheld, the desire for and possibilities of sibling intimacy are present, giving women as sisters a unique kind of power. . . . [T]he intimacy of sister and brother directly affects a woman's presence in economic, cosmological, and political affairs. (72–73)

While Weiner here implies that our modern Western overemphasis on sexual intercourse as the only true sexual function has blinded us to the sexual activities that tie brother to sister, it is also important to note that she does not exclude actual sexual congress from her definition of sibling intimacy, but reminds us that, throughout diverse cultures, there is usually a myth of brother-sister intercourse at the origin of a powerful family. Of course, ancient mythologies of dynastic gods and folklore heroes almost inevitably originate in (often twin) brother-sister incest. (Examples would include sibling gods of creation such as Cronus and Rhea, Osiris and Isis, or founding sibling lovers like Freyr and Freya, Siegmund and Sieglinde, Arthur and Morgan le Fay.)

Weiner's arguments are important for two reasons: (1) she demonstrates how any attempt to retrieve active female agency within the traffic necessarily uncovers transgression of the incest taboo; and (2) she explicitly argues how the theory of exchange which strips it to mere reciprocity (among men) works to deny women their socially valuable endeavors. Her work makes clear not only the systemic but also the actual necessity of reconfiguring the use of the incest taboo in order to account for women's real function in society. When women are not entirely traded out, that is, when they remain in relation to their natal families, especially their brothers, their endogamous position may allow them to exercise immense political power.

Weiner's argument about the naturalness of sibling intimacy, implicit in the noncirculation of "inalienable possessions," takes into account gift-giving among women. By placing a very different status on these objects, her observations bring into view a new social arena of human activity. What she adds to the theory of the traffic in women is the fundamentally important component of a particular kind of action/stasis: as her subtitle makes clear, this activity is marked by "the paradox of keeping-while-giving." Weiner's observation thus locates female power in the halt, as it were, of the flow of traffic. The argument corrects what she views as a masculinist bias, implicitly imported from the West and imposed onto the materials that Malinowski and Mauss necessarily misrepresented (and that Lévi-Strauss elevated to the status of an elegantly abstracted theory). Weiner's critique helps us see that placing some real value on the objects which women circulate among themselves within a family over genera-tions allows us to calibrate an increase in that family's prestige: when the inalienable possessions do not have to be traded out but may circulate among women in the family, the family stands to gain over time an ever-increasing degree of prestige, and expansion of property.

In Polynesia, many forms of cloth made by women are highly prized and often guarded as inalienable possessions, so that each one takes on its own subjective identity. But keeping these possessions inalienable while giving others away in exchange develops into a demanding economic and political commitment. . . . The enhancement of a person's or a group's social identity is dependent upon strategies of conserving such possessions, be they names, myths, sacred cloaks, or bones, that distinguish the difference between one person or group and another. Grand displays of expenditures give the illusion that everyone shares in a ruler's largess, as any medieval nobleman or a Trobriand chief knows full well, but the political impact of these events resides in what has been kept. (47–48)

Weiner makes clear that cloth is a particularly appropriate posses-sion for figuring the ligatures of generational connectedness. Not only is cloth a typical production of women throughout human history, it is, in its specific physical nature, an apt symbol for the interweave of social connections.

Cloth is not an actual human physical substance, but rather a kind of sym-bolic skin, that is most often used as a wrapping or covering. . . . Cloth, unlike hard materials, is able to represent the more realistic paradox of how permanence in social, political, and ancestral relationships is sought after despite the precari-ousness of these relationships to loss, decay, and death. (58–59)

When the eleven-year-old princess Elizabeth Tudor offered a gift to a kinswoman, her stepmother Katherine Parr, it was in the form of her translation of Marguerite de Navarre's poem on holy incest, *Le Miroir de l'âme pécheresse*. Even more important from an anthropological point of view, however, it was presented within a cloth "sleeve" that Elizabeth had apparently embroidered herself. This presentation conforms very suggestively to Weiner's view of the function of objects as gifts, a view that challenges the traditional theory of the traffic in women. As an object circulated intimately among women—and moreover as an embroidered cloth object—Elizabeth's translation of Navarre's text functions as a particularly meaningful example of contemporary female homosocial relations. So too, in terms of its bizarre discursive contents (the poem uses "holy incest" as its foundational metaphor), the text itself asks us to make a core revision of the theory about the traffic in women, so as to understand how Elizabeth's teenaged discursive activity may have been engaged by Marguerite's use of incest.[38]

In a sense, the entire argument of *Incest and Agency* is my attempt to account fully, both theoretically and historically, for this odd embroidered object given to a stepmother by a princess herself tainted with incest charges, a book covered by a woven cloth containing a translation of a poem on incest—a poem written by one of the most illustrious women in Europe, herself the sister of Francis I, then king of France. The transmission of this "text"—a metaphor derived oddly enough from textile as if the volume was doubly a woven gift—has much to tell us about female agency at the time. So too, a similar seventeenth-century female-to-female gift of an incest narrative makes Elizabeth's text less of an oddity. Mary Wroth entitles her romance about incest with the name of the woman who would have been her "sister-in-law" had she been allowed to marry a lover who was her first cousin.

Arguments like Weiner's that locate one arena for female agency within the family (through the female's means of aggrandizing that family's prestige within a traditional hierarchy) may elucidate an interesting suggestion of Catherine Gallagher's about female authority in the later seventeenth century. Questioning why so many women writers of the English seventeenth century were Tories, upholding an absolutist attitude toward politics, Gallagher guesses that the doctrine of the *roi absolu* made it possible for women to imagine a *moi absolue*. Hence absolutist theory would cohere with feminist resistance to male subjection.[39] Using Weiner's perspective, however, we can posit a more fundamental link between absolutist theories of social hierarchy and female agency in traditional societies: female agency empowers and is empowered by an endogamous assertion of family prestige. When Rosemary Kegl, for instance, notes in Margaret Cavendish's *Blazing World* a curious refusal to see the value of the work that Cavendish's women printers did when they published her corpus, she assumes that Cavendish felt a need to limit a "sort of activity" that "might be recognized *as* intellectual." But, as the citations Kegl draws out of Cavendish's work reveal, Cavendish's snobbery reflects less any devaluing of intellectual work than it does her positive understanding of her own rank and family: Cavendish's bizarre and unwomanly "humor" for intellectual work was actually nurtured by her natal family, and when further indulged by her aristocratic husband, she was able to import into her marriage an identity as an author already forged within her birth family.[40]

If we understand the existence of such an arena for female agency within traditional societies, we may perhaps no longer need to be so uncomfortable with the fact that women of earlier historical periods seldom conformed to our own democratic brand of feminist politics. Again, a more objective scrutiny of the specific affordances allowed to women in these earlier historical periods—very different from, if not utterly alien to us politically—may lead to a reassessment of what our bias has forced upon our reading of the male traditions that we have for so long seen as the beginning of our modernity.

Postcolonial theory has enabled us to grasp the ways in which the native "other" is different from, and not less than, the metropolitan "same": our own modernizing colonization of earlier historical periods may be said to have functioned in the same way in some feminist arguments: in their transhistorical genius, earlier men are like "us" today, but—so the argument goes—less talented women, forever embedded in their historical moment, are not like "us."[41] My response is that neither early modern men nor early modern women transcend their moments; both are very different from us and it is easier to recognize these differences, and so to see what we may have imposed on male texts when we juxtapose them with texts by women.

In Weiner's concern to trace the nature of the value women have traditionally possessed through their closer relationship to ancestors (not only in nonliterate Oceania but throughout all human culture), she understandably does not address the issue of what happens when a Western woman encroaches upon a male domain by taking up the pen to write. To put such a transgression in comparable terms within the Trobriand Islanders' experience, we would need to posit a case in which a woman gained her authority not in the traditional female way, by making gifts of dried banana skins, but by trading in yams, the wealth-making objects that males trade. For her to do so would be to risk a staggering cross-domain transgression. And this transgression is what a woman risked when she wrote and published during the early modern period in Europe.[42]

To see female authorship in this way makes the transgression appear as the fundamentally radical act that it is. A woman's writing is not only a transgression of the female role, but also an incursion into an exclusively male domain, and as such a disruption of the whole cultural system at its core. It should not be surprising, then, that the literary signal of this challenging disruption—and also, possibly, the attempt by the female author to make her incursion appear more legitimate—may include some indicator of a legitimate halt in the traffic in women, some allowable endogamy, as it were, that is at least akin to the "keeping-while-giving" with which Weiner's evidence would seem to ally women and their power.

The Canonical Challenge: Christine's Cornerstone

Such a line of reasoning helps to make sense of Christine de Pizan's opening gesture in the *Livre de la cité des dames*, a move that specifically grounds her text in incest. Saying so makes Christine's gesture no less scandalous, of course, and it is important to acknowledge that to cause scandal within the male domain was not only inevitable but also pivotal for Christine's purposes.

The example of Christine's text is not accidental; rather, it is foundational, in many senses of the term, for a tradition of premodern female letters. The *Book of the City of Ladies* is, so far as we yet know, the first history of women authored by a European woman. Written in 1405, and with a large manuscript circulation throughout the fifteenth century, it was also translated into English in 1521. Indeed, books by Christine were among the first to be printed by Caxton, and she has as an author an illustrious representation among English incunabula.[43] Elizabeth I of England could have read the *Book of the City of Ladies* in English in the 1521 imprint or in any number of French manuscripts in the royal collection at a time when she would have had access to them. When Elizabeth was a girl, her father Henry VIII may even have commissioned tapestries to be made from the narratives of the *Livre de la cité des dames* for hanging in her room at

Hatfield House. Earlier, in Renaissance France, Marguerite de Navarre may well have read the *Cité* too (a manuscript copy was in the library at Blois, which she would have used as a young girl), and Christine's rewriting of Boccaccio may well be an inspiration for Marguerite's own version of Boccaccian tales.[44]

Given that the *Cité des dames* is so pivotal an ur-text for any possible female tradition of writerly authority, it is all the more striking that incest plays so foundational a role in the text. As I have argued elsewhere, Christine's decision to make the first story in her allegory the mother-son incest of Semiramis, queen of the Assyrians, is an audacious move in itself, and one by which the author stages her difference from her precursors Boccaccio and Dante, both of whom had condemned Semiramis.[45] In a profound sense, Christine chooses to begin with a scandalously positive interpretation of the story of Semiramis in order to establish her own authority against the male tradition she has inherited. As a medieval writer, Christine is tied more explicitly to that inherited tradition than the Renaissance authors who will be the main focus of these studies, but it is nonetheless instructive to consider how an earlier female writer uses an incest narrative to rewrite tradition and to establish an authorial place for herself.

Dante paired Semiramis with Dido in the second circle of the *Inferno* as a quintessential image of female lust, writing that it was she who made lust licit in her law: "che libito fé licito in sua legge" (*Inferno*, V.57). By decreeing her own law ("sua legge"), Dante's Semiramis corrupted the notion of the "natural" law that underpins the exchange of women. Following Dante in *De mulieribus claris*, Boccaccio narrates the Semiramis story second, following that of Eve; for him she is an exemplum of a heroic woman warrior queen whose exploits (she had conquered Ethiopia and India and restored the city of Babylon) would have been worthy of a great man were it not that she stained everything by committing mother-son incest.

But with one wicked sin this woman stained all these accomplishments . . . which are not only praiseworthy for a woman but would be marvelous even for a vigorous man. It is believed that this unhappy woman, constantly burning with carnal desire, gave herself to many men. Among her lovers, and this is something more beastly than human, was her own son Ninus, a very handsome young man. As if he had changed his sex with his mother, Ninus rotted away idly in bed, while she sweated in arms against her enemies.[46]

According to Boccaccio, in order to cover her crime Semiramis decreed a notorious law (*legem . . . insignem*) which allowed her subjects to pleasure themselves however they wished. Such "lawlessness" is Boccaccio's equivalent of Dante's illicit "legge," and the repetition of the issue of legality reemphasizes the rule-bound nature of the incest taboo that protects the laws of necessary exchange. Incest de-sexes both Ninus and Semiramis, turning Ninus into an idle woman and his mother into a warrior. Boccaccio then goes on to report strangely enough that some authorities say that Semiramis invented chastity belts and that others record a variety of ways in which she came to a bad end: "Either because he could not bear seeing his mother with many other lovers, or because he thought her dishonor brought him shame, or perhaps because he feared that children might be born to succeed to the throne, Ninus killed the wicked queen in anger" (7).

In her version, Christine depicts a Semiramis every bit as heroic and martially powerful as Boccaccio's. But there is a profound difference: the queen's mother-son incest does not appear to bother Christine and is certainly not grounds for condemnation. She grants that Semiramis took her son as a lover; she also acknowledges that the act was transgressive. But, for Christine, it was not dishonorable. "It is quite true that many people reproach her—and if she had lived under our law, rightfully so—because she took as husband a son she had had with Ninus her lord."[47] However, the fact that Semiramis did not live under the same law as later Europeans appears to be reason enough for Christine to refuse to be scandalized by the queen's incestuous act. Apparently for Christine there is another law by which Semiramis's actions are understandable. Whereas Dante inveighs against Semiramis's illicit law, and Boccaccio denounces her for decreeing laws of her own, Christine takes a temporal position: Semiramis is outside the law because she is *before* it. Her act has priority over it.

Indeed, Christine proceeds with an attempt to understand what legitimate reasons Semiramis, an otherwise honorable woman, might have had to behave in such way. Unlike Boccaccio, who merely lists multiple (and mutually exclusive motives) for Ninus's execution of his mother, Christine provides cogent insight into the motives Semiramis might have had for the incest. (They are like the motives that keep any dynastic power endogamous—from the Egyptian pharaohs to the Hapsburgs.) First, Semiramis worried that had her son married elsewhere, there would have been another queen to vie with her in rule. And second, she believed that no other man, except her son, was worthy to have her as a wife. In this latter supposition, Christine comes close to formulating one of the kinship rules that at certain times in history, according to Lévi-Strauss, actually mandated incest. For example, Lévi-Straus describes how in parts of the Indian subcontinent caste rules were so strong that occasionally there would be no appropriate partner for an individual. As a result the person was, of necessity, allowed to marry into his or her endogamous group, after the lifting of the usual interdictions.[48] Of course Christine also has on her side the tradition of biblical history, which held that for Adam and for Noah (after the flood) incest was allowable as a necessary way to reconstitute the human race.[49] Christine would seem to be arguing that the incest taboo is not natural, but cultural and temporally relative, and that its rules change with history. Most importantly for us, she imagines the first act of building her city of ladies—which is simultaneously a construction of literary authority for herself and for all other women—as a story which refuses to condemn mother-son incest. Semiramis lived prior to the "written" law—"la loi escripte"—and she appropriately inaugurates a text that resolutely refuses to confine women to a non-public, non-self-owning silence. Christine does not see women as relegated to the status of signs; they are for her—in a multitude of ways—the makers of signs. In Christine's version, Semiramis's incest with her son stalls the movement of the traffic at the place where a woman speaks an actively transgressive desire at the *most* tabooed conjuncture possible—mother-son incest.

Thus, while Christine's two precursors, Dante and Boccaccio, initiate their texts with legends that dramatize a fundamentally originary and deadly dangerous Oedipal event, Christine's initial legend explicitly writes that anxiety out of her "city." By justifying Semiramis's taking her son as her lover, Christine would appear to be saying that the castration anxiety that so unsettled Boccaccio ("As if he had changed his sex with his mother, Ninus rotted away...") is, in terms of the foundation of women's history, ultimately insignificant. Her gesture anticipates with uncanny prolepsis Hélène Cixous's dismissal in her influential essay, "The Laugh of the Medusa." Cixous also theorizes that fears of castration may simply not be at issue for women.

Too bad for them [men] if they fall apart upon discovering that women aren't men, or that the mother doesn't have one [a phallus]. But isn't this fear convenient for them? Wouldn't the worst be, is the worst, in truth, that women aren't castrated, that they have only to stop listening to the Sirens . . . for history to change its meaning. You only have to look at the Medusa straight on to see her. . . . She's beautiful and she's laughing.[50]

As Gayle Rubin sagely pointed out, the homosocial system of ex-changing women no longer organizes our society as it did under the sys-tems analyzed by Lévi-Strauss. Gift exchanges are no longer at issue, and our commercial and moral transactions have become infinitely more com-plex than any simplified theory about the exchange of women can explain.[51]

> The organization of sex and gender once had functions other than itself—it orga-nized society. Now, it only organizes and reproduces itself. The kinds of relation-ships of sexuality established in the dim human past still dominate our sexual lives, our ideas about men and women, and the ways we raise our children. But they lack the functional load they once carried. (199)

Rubin claims that not only *must* the kinship system change (and indeed the make-up of the family has gone through a set of radical changes in the past half-century), it will change. Part of that change may be because the system no longer organizes an entire social cosmos, it is finally possi-ble to see and analyze its operations, to make the system an object of study. To focus that study on the operations of the exchange of women during the Renaissance in England is to view from a new perspective not only the most notorious case of incest in Western European royalty, but to see how instances of incest—that is, the halt in the orderly traffic in women—can provide an enabling condition for female agency.

Thus the next chapter will argue that because Henry VIII decided that he had committed incest when he married his brother's wife, Catherine of Aragon, he ironically freed to reign as the virgin Gloriana, Queen Eliza-beth I, the tainted daughter of his second wife Anne Boleyn (whom he had executed for alleged incest with her brother). The empowering result of this single protracted bit of incest history, complicated in and of itself, will not explicate all our considerations about the traffic in women in English Renaissance culture. But it is a paradigmatic case, and will be a good place to begin.

2

Elizabeth I
(with a Note on Marguerite de Navarre)

THE ENGLISH REFORMATION was a very different affair from continental forms of the movement, for it took shape as an act of royal will. Henry VIII broke from the Catholic Church specifically over an issue of incest. Catherine of Aragon's failure to produce a male heir was proof to Henry that he had sinned by marrying Catherine, who had been his deceased elder brother Arthur's wife. Henry argued that the pope had clearly had no authority to grant the dispensation of the taboo which had years earlier allowed Henry to marry within the prohibited degrees. The current pope (who happened to be Catherine's nephew) refused to grant Henry a divorce from her on the grounds of incestuous consanguinity, and ruled that the earlier papal dispensation made their marriage entirely legal. In response to this impasse, and in order to insure the Tudor dynasty's survival through the birth of a male heir, Henry dissolved England's relationship to the Roman Catholic Church, assumed control over the church himself, and married Anne Boleyn, then pregnant with Elizabeth—who Henry, of course, hoped would be a boy.[1]

But by doing so Henry ironically compounded his incest problems, for in marrying Anne he was marrying a woman with whose older sister he had had an affair. By the rules of the day that relationship made his second marriage just as incestuous as the first.[2] Henry clearly assumed his relationship to the Boleyn sisters fell under the Church's incest rules. Even before the break with the Roman church was final, Henry had asked the pope for a second dispensation, this time to marry the woman whose older sister had been his mistress. The pope had easily fulfilled *this* request, because he clearly had no intention of granting the dispensation that would render it useful—the divorce from Catharine of Aragon.[3]

Henry's prior relationship with Mary Boleyn was part of the grounds on which, a mere three years later, the Anglican archbishop Thomas

Cranmer justified granting Henry a divorce from Anne. The point is not so much that by all these legal and ecclesiastical maneuvers, Henry revealed his hypocrisy (and confusion), but that he knew his relationship with Anne Boleyn fell within the interdicted degrees of incest just as much as had his marriage to Catherine. Elizabeth Tudor was thus the product of a marriage that her father had already acknowledged to be tainted by incest. When Anne, pregnant for the second time, produced a stillborn male, repeating Catherine of Aragon's pattern, Henry claimed to have seen the same hand of God raised against him once more. He executed Elizabeth's mother, accusing Anne of, among other crimes, acts of incest with her brother George, whom he also executed. Meanwhile, he admitted in the bill of divorce that he himself had committed incest with Anne by having had prior intercourse with her sister Mary.[4]

Princess Elizabeth was thus, quite officially and notoriously, the child of an incestuous mother; less officially, the daughter of an incestuous father, and as such the product of a doubly incestuous union. Her peculiar and tainted status makes her reign as an autonomous female monarch a particularly interesting case. Because of these problematically incestuous origins, Marc Shell has suggested that Elizabeth's translation, at age eleven, of a French poem that deals with incest shows her profound concern for the confusions of intimate familial relations.[5] The various contexts of this poem, which was reprinted, as we shall see, four times during her reign as queen, have much to tell us about the evolving discourse of incestuous eroticism underlying Elizabeth's famed virginity. The decision to translate and first publish the text may not have been eleven-year-old Elizabeth's, but as queen she clearly allowed the poem's subsequent reprintings. It thus makes the poem a pivotal part of Elizabeth's sense of her own *oeuvre*.

But first it is important to emphasize that Elizabeth would never have had the choice to rule as a legendary Virgin Queen if her father had taken his patriarchal duties toward her more seriously and, rather than bastardizing her at the age of three, had formed, and actively pursued to fruition, marriage alliances for her. Declared illegitimate, with her mother executed for treason, herself the damaged goods produced by an incestuous union, Elizabeth was never as useful as a princess without these drawbacks would have been in the dynastic traffic in women taking place during the three reigns that preceded hers. Neither her father nor her brother—who dying at sixteen never married—nor her elder sister Mary ever succeeded in trading her out in an advantageous marriage. (Equally illegitimate, Mary Tudor was not married off by her father or her brother either; she found herself a husband after she became queen.)

Wallace MacCaffrey points out that at age five (after her mother had been executed and she bastardized), Elizabeth was in fact "ticketed," first for one of the Hapsburg princes and later for a Valois son. "None of the overtures came to anything," MacCaffrey admits, "but they made it clear that [Elizabeth's and Mary's] technical illegitimacy was not to disqualify the royal girls for the traditional role of princesses in the diplomacy of Europe."[6] Nevertheless, Mary remained single until she gave herself away in marriage to Philip II of Spain, and did so against the clamorous (and prescient) objections of her people. It was an act of agency that her younger sister Elizabeth never dared to demonstrate—although Philip II himself would have been very willing to marry Elizabeth after Mary's death, if for no other reason than to keep up the English alliance. Coincidentally, had his plan succeeded, Elizabeth would have been committing the same kind of incest for which Henry VIII had divorced Catherine and executed Anne (marrying a sibling's spouse); but as Philip had already ignored the incest taint in Mary's case, presumably such concerns would not have troubled him.[7]

During the six-year reign of her brother Edward, Elizabeth was wooed by the powerful Thomas Seymour, who as the widower of Katherine Parr, her stepmother, would also have been contracting a legally incestuous marriage had he managed to wed Elizabeth. He was executed for treason because of the clandestine nature of these arrangements as well as for other plotting; the teenaged Elizabeth saved herself by vigorously denying any collusion in plans for a marriage between them.[8] Throughout Mary's reign, Elizabeth's marriage to one candidate or another was often discussed as a means to ensure the continuing Roman Catholicism of England should Mary die without issue and Elizabeth inherit the throne. Various Catholic grooms were proposed, but again the marriages were never pursued with any success.

Although Elizabeth had many more suitors after she ascended the throne, none of the suits ever came to fruition. Doubtless, there were particular reasons in each case for the failure, but the overall pattern demonstrates the nonexogamous status of both Tudor daughters. In very large part Elizabeth's and Mary's positions as unmarried and therefore potentially autonomous virgin princesses at their accessions (Mary at thirty-seven and Elizabeth at twenty-five) were owing to their complicated backgrounds, of which their illegitimacy, with its basis in incest, was a fundamental element. Indeed, with uncanny specificity, the situation of the two Tudor queens demonstrates in Renaissance history what incest narratives demarcate in theory: the potential for active female agency. When she remains untraded, for whatever reason, a woman is freer to choose her own desire actively. That Mary chose to marry, and that Elizabeth did not, should not cloud our perception of the analogous agency they shared at their accessions to the English throne.

It is also significant that when Mary Tudor did exercise her anomalous right to select her own mate, she chose a husband from her mother's family. Philip was her first cousin twice removed; as ancestors they shared Ferdinand and Isabella, who were Mary's maternal grandparents and Philip's maternal great-grandparents. Mary's mother Catherine of Aragon and Philip's grandmother Joanna La Loca were sisters. Philip in fact called his wife Mary his "aunt" (she was his father's first cousin), and for her part Mary called her husband's father, Emperor Charles V, who had proposed the match, "the father of her soul and of her body."[9] In some sense, then, Mary was (metaphorically) marrying *within* her Spanish mother's family. (Philip was, of course, a Hapsburg, a family that had amassed, and was to continue to maintain, imperial status in Europe through centuries of careful close-kin marriage alliances.)

The case of Elizabeth (and of her sister Mary) offers a clear articulation of the theory of incest and agency: at the place of "halt," the female who is not traded out by a male family member may then turn inward to a nonexogamous arena in which she can exercise some, if not total, control. She may thereby claim an active agency for herself. In part, Mary's subsequent failure as an autonomous ruler was that by choosing Philip, a man who was in her eyes a kinsman (the son of the loyal cousin who had attempted to protect her mother Catherine of Aragon, his own aunt), she had chosen a man who in the eyes of her common English subjects was alien, a foreigner. The Hapsburg strategy of close-kin family rule did not appear to work, although of course, had Mary and Philip had a child, he or she would have ruled England (and Elizabeth would probably never have come to the throne). That Elizabeth ultimately chose not to marry anyone, foreign or native, may have owed a great deal to the lesson her sister's disastrous marriage taught her. But her choice also meant that she became her own patriarch, as it were, and so maintained the open discursive space for herself that being an endogamously withheld woman provided. Her culturally vaunted virginity is the historical result of her status as an untraded woman. It is important to stress that what is at issue in Elizabeth's case is not so much incest seen as an act of sexual congress between near family members (or "consanguine" partners by reason of their affinity, as in the case of Henry and Mary and Anne Boleyn), but as the action which produced the most spectacularly scandalous halt of the traffic in women known at the time. It is the halt that institutes a place and a time for autonomous female agency.

Elizabeth had of course said from her youth that she would never marry; early in her reign she defined her endogamous position as a single person. Her "spinsterhood" developed culturally into her iconic position as virgin wife and mother of the family of England. Herself nursed by the nation, married to the nation, and mother to the nation, she came to enjoy a metaphorically incestuous relationship with the country that she governed. It was a metaphor with which she was very familiar.

The origin of this familial language for political relations is the central point of this chapter. Mary Tudor felt, and often said, that she had "married" England before she married Philip. So Elizabeth Tudor was certainly not the first English queen to use rhetoric of metaphorical "marriage to the kingdom." But more specifically, as Marc Shell has provocatively argued, Elizabeth first made use of this slippery familial metaphor in her translation of the French poem on incest, the *Miroir de l'âme pécheresse* by Marguerite de Navarre, royal sister of Francis I.[10] In this poem, Marguerite portrays the relationship between the soul and God in terms of the trope of "holy incest." The God she loves is her brother, father, spouse, and son; her soul is sister, mother, spouse, and child to Him. Why the eleven-year-old Elizabeth should have translated this particular poem to give as a gift to her stepmother Katherine Parr, will ultimately remain a matter for speculation. But the choice does not even need to be Elizabeth's own in order for it to be interesting, or indeed, significant as a demonstration of the connections between incest and the demarcation of a heretofore unacknowledged arena of female desire and authority.[11]

Marguerite's *Miroir de l'âme pécheresse* is a pivotal text in its own right, important not only because of the author's royal authority as the sister of Francis I, but also for the impact that its publication, if not its strangely overlooked theology, had on the politics of the early wars of religion in France.[12] Successive publications of Elizabeth's translation extended the life of this text for another sixty years, so that it reiterates, throughout a long and pivotal period of Renaissance culture, the conjuncture of royal female authority and the trope of incest. Published first in England in 1548, then again in 1569–70, then in two separate editions in 1582, and for the last time in 1590, editions of Elizabeth's *Glass of a Sinful Soul* span virtually her entire life. In their different presentations decade after decade, the texts have much to tell us about how Elizabeth's discourse of incest could be put to different uses throughout her long reign. Along with the autograph manuscript itself, presently at the Bodleian Library in Oxford, the material states of the successive editions reveal a great deal about the culture's changing attitudes toward female agency.[13]

Marguerite de Navarre's 1533 *Miroir*

First published in 1531, Marguerite's *Miroir de l'âme pécheresse*, for all its startling use of the trope of holy incest, caused absolutely no stir. But when it was republished in 1533 the book was censured by the Sorbonne and publicly burned. Pressed by Marguerite's brother, Francis I, to explain why they had censured it, the assembled faculties of the university scurried to outdo each other in proving that none of them had ever even read it. The official excuse to Francis was that the poem had been interdicted on a mere technicality: it had not been registered prior to publication, as required by law. However, after the subsequent "affaire des placards" had hardened Francis I's opinion against the reformists who had pasted broadsides on the walls of his court, attacking the orthodox theology of communion, the printer of the 1533 *Miroir* was executed.[14] As Pierre Jourda points out, the man was condemned to death not because of what the judgment called "his scandalous blasphemies" in printing the placards, but because he had printed the *Miroir*. Thus, however much the Sorbonne may have argued that the condemnation was not specific to Marguerite's theology—indeed, the faculties of the Sorbonne had been forced by the threat of Francis's anger to praise her orthodoxy—it would appear that the book itself was the culprit. Jourda suggests that the difference in the censors' treatment of the 1531 imprint and the 1533 version may have been due to Marguerite's including in the later edition a psalm translated by Clément Marot (Jourda, 179n), to whom, apparently, Marguerite had suggested the idea of the translation.[15] Although we will never know for sure just what it was that the Sorbonne found so offensive about the 1533 *Miroir*, it will be useful to consider, for a moment, how the printing of a poem that uses "holy incest" as a central trope might be connected to Marguerite's subversive reformist sympathies, and how those sympathies might connect to Marot's act of translating the psalm.

The makeup of the 1533 book suggests the importance of these questions. Why should Marguerite suggest a translation to Marot, and would her doing so be seen as offensive in itself? Why should Marguerite decide (if indeed it were her decision) to include the psalm with a second printing of her poem? How might translating the psalms and imagining the legitimacy of incestuous relations come together as part of a coherent attack on Roman Catholic orthodoxy—as at least the Sorbonne's initial response suggests was the case? To pose such questions will allow us to see not only how incest discourse oddly empowers female agency, but also in what historically specific and local ways the discourse of incest spoke to the religious crises of the 1530s that led to the Reformation in Northern Europe.

It is impossible to overstress the importance of the appearance of the first psalm translated by Marot in Marguerite's 1533 edition of the *Miroir*, for thus began their early association in what turned out to be a fundamental mode of radical Protestant practice. It is nevertheless difficult to claim that Marot's psalm itself instigated the Sorbonne's attack on Marguerite's book, because it was not until six years later, in 1539, when Jean Calvin included thirteen of Marot's translations in his first collection of French psalms with German music, that the Psalms might have been perceived to be the basis for Huguenot liturgical practice—as they shortly thereafter certainly became.[16] Nor could the mere translation of the text into French have been at issue, for, as Michel Jeanneret points out, there had been many Catholic-inspired translations before Marot's (33–50). Both Marot and Marguerite were such public figures in and of themselves that nothing more than their own notoriety may have been necessary to raise the ire of the Sorbonne. But it is entirely possible that at least one member of the faculty had actually read Marguerite's text and knew from reading it that her theology was deeply suspect. While the subject matter of incest itself could have been scandalous, there might also have been in Marguerite's agenda a deeper challenge to the Church than any of the contemporary actors might consciously have realized. The Sorbonne was right—Marguerite's metaphor profoundly subverts the Church's authority.

That incest is the central trope of the poem becomes immediately clear; it is the first major metaphor in the meditation by the soul on the affective intimacy that binds it to God. The introduction of the trope presents the multiple incestuous relations of the soul to God as a solution to specific theological problems, such as false doctrine about communion ("bad bread"); the trope also offers the same answer to the soul's panicked recognition that no intermediary is potent enough to work the soul's desire for salvation. The familial metaphor of incest thus provides, from the outset, a response to a desire for an unmediated relationship to God, one that bypasses church-authorized intercessors.

Car trop estoit ma paoure ame repue
De mauluais pain, et damnnable doctrine:
En deprisant secours et medicine.

Et quand aussi l'eusse voulu querir
Nul ne congnois, qu'eusse peu requerir:
Car il n'y a homme, ny sainct, ny ange,
Par qui le cueur iamais d'ung pecheur change.
Las bon IESVS, voyant ma cecité
Et que secours en ma necessité
Ne puis auoir d'aulcune creature:
De mon salut auéz faict l'ouerture
Quelle bonté, mais quelle grand'doulceur:
Est il pere à fille, ou frere à soeur,
Qui vn tel tour iamais eust voulu faire.
. . .
Bien suffiroit saillant de tel danger,
De me traicter ainsi qu'vng estranger.
Mais mon ame traictéz (si dire j'ouse)
Comme mere, fille, soeur, et espouse. (132–72)[17]

Here is the young Elizabeth's translation:

Oftentimes have I broken with Thy covenant, for my poor soul was too much fed
with the ill bread and damnable doctrine, I despising succor and physic such as
would have helped me. And if I had been willing to look for it, I know no man
whom I had required, for there is neither man, saint nor angel for whom the heart
of a sinner will change.

Alas, good Jesus! Thou seeing my blindness and that at my need I could have
no succor of men, then didst Thou open the way of my salvation. O what goodness and sweetness! Is there any father to the daughter, or else brother to the sister, which would ever do as He hath done?
. . .
For it should suffice me (I coming out of such a danger) to be ordered like a
stranger; but Thou dost handle my soul (if so I durst say) as a mother, daughter,
sister, and wife.[18]

Doing away with any priestly intermediary between the soul and God,
the relational intimacy of the metaphor insists upon the soul's multiple
but consistently gendered intrafamilial relationship to the deity. To make
the relationship even more intimate, the worshiper is now able to celebrate her love of God in her mother tongue (in the new French translation of David's psalm), thereby claiming for herself David's (royal) position
of familiar connection to God. Marguerite's style of address produces a
remarkably intense intimacy and immediacy. Elizabeth's lexical choices
in her translation make the intimacy even more immediate: where Marguerite uses the verb "traictez" in describing how the soul might expect
and accept a limited, formal connection to God, Elizabeth translates it as

"ordered" ("it should suffice me . . . to be ordered like a stranger"); when the same verb is used to describe the far greater intimacy God offers, Elizabeth renders it with the English word "handle," adding the immediacy of touch to the contact ("Thou dost handle my soul . . . as a mother, daughter, sister, and wife").[19]

By substituting incestuous intimacy for false "bread" and "doctrine," and by specifically referring to the nature of that bread, the poem's argument implicitly makes the familial metaphor a correction for problems posed by the orthodox ideology of communion. The contiguity suggests that had any professor at the Sorbonne in fact read the poem, he would have been right to consider it heretical on the question of the Eucharist. (It was a placard specifically casting doubts on the orthodox view of transubstantiation that caused Francis I's rage at and subsequent execution of the reformers.)

Nothing could insist more immediately on the soul's direct relationship to God than such a familial metaphor. But, one might still ask, why use a language of incest in particular? While the metaphor borrows a traditional Marian language of address (she was, after all, God's mother as well as daughter), the answer lies partly in the specifics of Marguerite's historical situation. She owed her impunity from charges of heresy to her close relationship to her brother the king. That she was well aware of the power of this position she made clear in a famous remark to the Duke de Montmorency, the champion of a priest who had criticized her and as a result had been admonished by Francis: "You are the king's minister; I am his sister."[20]

Marguerite was a famous author. Most significantly, she stages the scene of multiple tale-telling in her *Heptaméron* as a replication of a game played by members of her immediate family—her mother, sister-in-law, and husband. The *Heptaméron* as a whole may thus be framed as, at least, a fictive family practice. Incest itself plays an important part in one tale of the collection. It is the last tale on the third day, narrated by Hircan, the character who supposedly represents Marguerite's husband. This tale was also selected to be among the fifteen tales that were anonymously translated into English in the *Queen of Navarre's Tales* (1597), so at least from an English printer's point of view, it was one of the important tales at the core of the collection.[21]

Thinking to chastise her fourteen-year-old son when he tries to make love to her serving woman, a mother substitutes herself for her servant, but instead of delivering the high-minded lecture she had planned on, she finds that "her anger turned to pleasure . . . so that she forgot she was a mother." Or, as the 1597 translation puts it, "she converted her choller into a most abhomiable pleasure, forgetting the name of mother" (K3r). She tells no one of this sin, hoping to expiate it by her silence and contrition, and she sends her son away. Further horrified to learn that she is pregnant by this encounter, she bears the child, a girl, and also sends her away to be reared by her own illegitimate brother. Much later, after her daughter is grown, her unknown father/half-brother meets her. "But no sooner had he caught sight of his daughter than he fell in love with her." He marries her and takes her home to his mother, who had warned him not to return until he was married. Upon realizing that her son's wife is their own daughter, the mother falls into despair. Consulting the papal legate at Avignon, she is told that she must not say anything to the children, for they had acted in ignorance, and consequently had not sinned.[22]

But she, their mother, was to do penance for the rest of her life without giving the slightest indication of it to them. The poor lady returned to her house, and not longer after that her son and her daughter-in-law arrived. They were very much in love. Never was there such love between husband and wife, never were a husband and wife so close, for she was his daughter, his sister, his wife, and he was her father, brother, husband. (321)

The story repeats the language of Marguerite's poem, which, as Elizabeth translated it, celebrates the same kind of union:

Kepe my harte then, my brother, and lett not thy enemy entre in it. O my father, brother, childe and spowse: with handes ioyned, humbly upon my knees, i yelde the thankes and praise. (300)

The older woman, who often moralizes the meaning of the tales (and who may represent Marguerite's mother, Oisille) acknowledges that the tale illustrates how, as a result of presuming to do good, much evil can come about. The moral that Marguerite's own mouthpiece draws, the aptly named Parlamente, is of a radical Protestant sort: "Be you assured, the first step man takes in trusting to himself alone is a step away from trust in God." While the story condemns the mother, the children are judged innocent, at least by the papal legate at Avignon (who serves a pope of uncertain authority); they are left alone and in ignorance, enjoying the intensity of their multiple familial relationships.

It is a curious story, and one which, in reanimating the incest metaphor, also revisits the question of the power of Church hierarchy versus that of the unaided human soul, although here the Church seems to have the last word, at least insofar as it protects the incest and allows it to continue. What is ultimately condemned is the mother's active—if inadvertent—desire for her son. The incestuous relationship between the children is, in contrast, strangely celebrated and authorized by their mother's continual penance for their blissful and oblivious happiness.

There is no reason to suggest that Francis I shared an actually incestuous relationship with his sister Marguerite, but the royal pair did have a very strong sibling tie that overrode other traditionally more weighted social, political, and religious connections. In contrast to the way the story seems to work itself out in the *Heptaméron*, family solidarity, crucially important to both Francis and Marguerite, was also fundamentally inimical to a centralized power in the Church. Until Francis felt personally affronted by the "affaire des placards" (one of the heretical posters appeared on the door to his own bedchamber), his bond with his sister overrode his need to control social unrest and to police orthodoxy, and he supported her in her fight with the Sorbonne. At least initially then, Francis placed family loyalty over support for religious orthodoxy; his valuing family over church was one more reenactment of a centuries long antagonism between two often competing forces in Western European culture—one, secular and familial, leading to monarchism and nationalism; the other, theocratic and pan-European, centered in Rome.

In this battle, one of the Church's strongest weapons against the growing power of aristocratic families had always been its ecclesiastical rules interdicting incestuous unions. The corresponding power to lift the ban and therefore to allow the intensification of aristocratic, in-marrying kinship ties is the power Marguerite recalls in her short story. A brief consideration of this centuries' long contestation will be a useful means for explaining the remarkably subversive power retained by Marguerite's metaphor of holy incest. Far from being merely scandalous or just a peculiar biblical trope, the metaphor speaks—however unintentionally—to great underlying changes taking place in European society at the moment of the Reformation, changes which subtend the more obvious revisions in the doctrine of communion.

Incest Rules and Church Property

The anthropologist Jack Goody has argued persuasively that the Church as an institution in western Europe quite specifically maneuvered social policy so as to reshape (and reduce) for its own benefit the power of the family. From the fourth to the ninth centuries, the Church became the largest single landowner in Europe, owning one-third of all property. According to Goody, one of the ways it managed the accumulation of so immense an amount of land was its power to restrict intermarriage in order to limit the circulation of property within a kinship. By this means, not only would the power of kinship be reduced, but also property would cease to flow down family lines of descent, and for lack of appropriate heirs, would more easily devolve upon the Church.

The Church effected this change by reshaping the incest rules, rewriting the Roman laws of prohibited degrees and expanding them, indeed, doubling them. By the time the laws were fully in place, as Goody explains, "one could no longer marry anyone from whom one could have formerly inherited; i.e. kinfolk."[23] Such maneuvering gave the Church a "powerful instrument" for reshaping society. Among many others, both Martin Luther and Henry VIII dealt with accusations of incest in their personal lives. Luther married a nun (his sister in Christ), which was forbidden by the incest laws. Both Luther and Henry (after the latter turned Protestant reformer) had argued against these strict and complicated incest rules,[24] protesting that they were in actuality a means for directly increasing Church revenues because the pope charged fees for granting dispensations.

Henry's argument suggests that he may indeed have intuited an underlying economic purpose to the Church's incest rules. But if so, his own "great problem," when the pope refused to dispense with the dispensation that had allowed Henry years earlier to marry his brother's wife Catherine of Aragon, only exposed a single (if royally important) example of how the Church profited from incest laws. Far more fundamental and valuable than money paid to the pope was the process by which the Church, making it impossible for even distant cousins to marry each other, made it more and more difficult for families to pass on property through successive generations; consequently much of the property passed to the Church instead. Even now, centuries after Henry VIII's dissolution of the monasteries, the Anglican Church remains the largest single property holder in England.[25]

This is not to suggest that the Church's early antipathy to aristocratic intermarriage and the extension of kinship among the elite was based primarily on a venal desire to accumulate property. From its earliest days, Christian teaching had offered freedom from the obligations of kinship and marital duty as a great spiritual opportunity, one commanded by Christ

in the Gospels when he said that one must leave father and mother to follow him. Elaine Pagels has argued how profoundly radical such a call would
have sounded at the time, spurring many early Christians to renounce the
worldly concerns of family in order to dedicate themselves to an entirely
new value system:

> Thus Jesus dismisses the family obligations considered most sacred . . . including
> those to one's parents, siblings, spouse, and children. By subordinating the oblig-
> ation to procreate, rejecting divorce, and implicitly sanctioning monogamous
> relationships, Jesus reverses traditional priorities, declaring in effect, that other
> obligations, including marital ones, are now more important than procreation.[26]

The later Church's attempts to control family practices grew in part
out of an authentically fundamental interest in ensuring spiritual opportunity at the expense of secular dynastic concerns. But such concern had
its self-interested side as well. In *The Knight, the Lady, and the Priest: The
Making of Modern Marriage in Medieval France*, Georges Duby traces,
with results similar to Goody's, the Church's gradual appropriation of the
aristocratic right to control marriage choices. Duby underscores how important it was for the Church to increase the rigor with which it enforced
incest taboos as a means for managing marriages. According to Duby, the
Carolingian church had some success in making aristocrats conform to a
newer, more rigorous morality of marriage, "except when it came to their
[the Church's] condemnation of what they called male adultery . . . and
of what they called incest. On these two points the two moralities—secular and ecclesiastical—could not be made to agree." The Church's interest
conflicted with the aristocratic demand that "the man should take his wife
from among his near relations."[27] Duby describes how the church finally
succeeded:

> gradually, wielding words and exclusions, the rigorist priests succeeded in dis-
> mantling that barrier. It took them a long time, though, to teach people to regard
> concubinage and illegitimacy as "unseemly." The battle to denigrate marriage to
> one's cousin met with even stronger resistance, for . . . such allegedly incestuous
> unions often [were able to] add to a family's prestige. (174–75)

In short, according to Duby, whether in the hands of dynastic aristocrats
or, increasingly, the churchmen, "Marriage was an instrument of control"
(283). As a means for regulating the flow of women and property, marriage was also a means by which the Church could wield power against
the laity, "in the hope of subjugating it." On the other side, "the head of

families used [marriage] as a means of keeping their power intact." Such programmatic usefulness for both Church and aristocracy in the control of marriage made it a battleground throughout the two centuries that Duby studies, the ninth to the eleventh, and the urgent need to wield that power remained, of course, long after the feudal period.

If Jack Goody and Georges Duby are right that the Church's complicated incest laws worked to increase ecclesiastical control and to expand its property, then a Protestant attack on the worldliness of the Church might usefully include a challenge to its right specifically to enforce such incest rules. That right, of course, is literally the basis of Henry VIII of England's challenge to the Church. And, at least metaphorically, Marguerite's central trope in the *Miroir* is designed to do the same thing. In this sense Marguerite's metaphoric incest is pointedly transgressive, and although it is highly unlikely that she was fully conscious of this effect, her central trope of incest becomes a profoundly reformist move. It functions as an attack on what scholars like Duby and Goody have revealed to be a constitutive Church practice of centuries' long duration.

Elizabeth's *Glass of the Sinful Soul*

The translation of Marguerite of Navarre's *Miroir de l'âme pécheresse* that Princess Elizabeth presented as a gift to her stepmother, the dowager queen Katherine Parr, had a handsome sleeve, or chemise, for which Elizabeth herself apparently had done the needlework (Figure 1).[28] Embroidered in bright turquoise blue and decorated with an interlaced design picked out in silver thread (which is still shiny today), the volume made an elaborate gift. Katherine's initials, "K.P.," are raised in cotton-batting-stuffed relief in the center of both back and front covers. At each of the four corners, raised-work embroidered silver flowers, representing pansies, indicate, as Lisa Klein has suggested, a nice pun on the French word for "thoughts," *pensées*.[29] The same batting is used to raise cord marks on the book's spine, as if the embroidered cover were part of the manuscript's actual binding, signaling another pun-like connection between the textile work as a cover for the lettered text within. Indeed, the contrast between the smooth, nearly professional perfection of the Gobelin-stitched embroidery with its elaborate interlaced design, and the rather awkward italic printing of the manuscript, reveals (if the cover does not betray the hand of a more mature sewing teacher) that even for the royally born Elizabeth the needle was a far more practiced instrument than the pen in an eleven-year-old girl's hand.

The text that Elizabeth translated was one that her mother Anne Boleyn had brought home from the court of Marguerite of Navarre, where she had been a lady-in-waiting. The fact that Anne's daughter dedicated the volume to the last of her many stepmothers may be no more than Elizabeth's attempt to please a queen of pronounced Protestant sympathies

Figure 1. *The Glass of the Sinful Soul*, Cherry MS 36, cover. Bodleian Library.

by translating the work of another such queen.[30] But it is very suggestive that the text of this translated poem, sent from one female family member to another, covered in a personally worked textile, results in a gesture that oddly resembles the symbolic nature of the trade in woven heirloom items that anthropologist Annette Weiner has found to be foundational for female communities in remote modern Oceania.

Reference is made to Weiner's theory of inalienable possessions in Lisa M. Klein's argument on the function of female gift-giving in Elizabethan society. The year Elizabeth gave Katherine Parr the translation, 1544, was the year she had been established in the succession by an act of Parliament, although she was still deemed illegitimate.[31] As a gift to a female member of her father's family—a family in which Elizabeth now had a slightly more secure place—the woven nature of the object calls attention to its inalienable status. While the actual content of Elizabeth's translation is not Klein's concern—her interests focus on the embroidery—the central trope of incest in the poem further insists upon the endogamous focus of this text.

In the protofeminist discourse of the Renaissance, pen and needle are usually opposed, of course, but here, in Elizabeth's first literary production, pen and needle go together to reinforce a gesture of intrafamilial authorship.[32] As Ann Jones and Peter Stallybrass have recently argued, far from confining women, embroidery and sewing, especially in an aristocratic setting, could well become a means for artistic display.

Whatever repressive and isolating effects sewing as a disciplinary apparatus might have been intended to produce, women used it both to connect to one another within domestic settings and to articulate public roles for themselves in the outer world.[33]

Nothing expresses more clearly the claims for female agency made by Renaissance embroidery and sewing than the cloth-draped interior of the Yorkshire Tudor manor Hardwick Hall. There, embroideries and other cloth hangings cover as much interior surface of the house as its famously expensive windows by Smythson glass do its exterior. (It is the windows for which the house received its famous jingle, "Hardwick Hall, more glass than wall.") The wall coverings were designed and produced by the home's owner, Elizabeth, Countess of Shrewsbury ("Bess of Hardwick"), in collaboration with her female household members and her professional male embroiderers. As Santina M. Levey explains, the typical subject matter of the hangings is the female virtues.[34] One set of very large appliqué hangings—made from recycled ecclesiastical cloth bought during the dissolution of the monasteries—celebrates a sort of city of ladies: illustrious historical women, along with their respective personified virtues: Zenobia (Magnanimity and Prudence), Penelope (Patience and Perseverance), Lucretia (Chastity and Liberality), Cleopatra (Fortitude and Justice), Artimesia (Constancy and Piety, which was Aeneas's heroic virtue). Other embroidered panels represent female allegorical virtues conquering various famous tyrants: Faith defeating Mahomet, Hope overthrowing Judas, Temperance conquering Sardanapalus. Such cloth work is both a collaboration among women and a gift between them: the Hardwick Hall records reveal that in 1591–92 Bess gave Queen Elizabeth's embroiderer a large sum of money to work pieces for a gown for the monarch; such payments are perhaps in lieu of actual cloth that may have been given at various other times.[35]

Elizabeth's hand-sewn gift to her stepmother is a small thing in comparison to these vast tapestries, but it participates in the same practice of female artistic expression, display, and exchange. It is clear from the dedicatory letter to her stepmother that Elizabeth expected Katherine to keep the volume private, at least (as she modestly says) until its faults have been corrected:

But I hope that after having been in Your Grace's hands there shall be nothing in it worthy of reprehension and that in the meanwhile no other (but your highness only) shall read it or see it, lest my faults be known of many. (112)

In essence Elizabeth is asking Katherine for her collaboration. She rightly expects that eventually others will read the volume. While not exactly assuming "publication," she reveals her concern for a performance that will doubtless be judged by Henry VIII. Her brief letter to Katherine is notable also for the emphasis it puts upon the incest trope in the text she has translated. The only thing she has to say about the content of Marguerite's poem insists upon the centrality of the metaphor of the incestuous female soul:

The which book is entitled, or named, *The Mirror or Glass of the Sinful Soul*, wherein is contained how she (beholding and contemplating what she is) doth perceive how of herself and of her own strength she can do nothing that good is, or prevaileth for her salvation, unless it be through the grace of God, whose mother, daughter, sister, and wife by the scriptures she proveth her self to be. (111)

The slipperiness of the familial positions is, in Elizabeth's interpretation, the central point of the poem. The tropic elision sacrifices no sense of concrete effect to the metaphorical nature of the multiple positions.

The authority for the metaphor, Elizabeth insists, is biblical. Marc Shell has argued powerfully that when as queen Elizabeth claimed to be both mother and spouse of the nation of England, she was using the kind of language she had found for the translation: the "mature Elizabeth . . . institutionalized that collapse [of familial relations] on a national plane at once secular and chaste," a synthesis which she had first essayed in her youthful translation (66).

It is indeed very probable that Elizabeth noticed the effectiveness of such multiple positions—so useful for preserving her autonomy—through her experience with such discourse while translating Marguerite's poem. But it is important to understand, when examining this earlier stage of Elizabeth's career, not only that these fluid positions were incestuous, but that they spoke to a contemporary ideological shift that had had the same usefulness for Marguerite of Navarre as for the younger Elizabeth: the metaphorical fluidity of the shifting family positions in the *Miroir* not only rested upon Marguerite's reading of scripture, but also cohered with the metaphorical flex made necessary by reformist doctrine about the decreasing materiality of the act of communion.

A "sacred" activity, which remained affectively saturated but no longer mediated by traditional forms of patriarchal power, the reformed view of communion also spoke to an intimacy that was no less real for being immaterial. To promulgate metaphorical incest as a correction of transubstantiation is to challenge the power of the same priestly group that was being challenged by radical Protestant notions of the memorial nature of the communion service. In both cases, the physical communion is seen as not physically and concretely actual; the "body" of the host is no longer the material corporeality of Christ. Nonetheless, the contact between believer and the Eucharist is theoretically now more, not less, "immediate," because no priest stands between believer and God in order to change the physical accidentals of the medium. Now the contact is made possible by direct intimacy between God and the (unworthy) self of the believer. In the same way, the intimacy of brother and sister, mother and child, father and child, is not concretely physical, but the metaphor layers the fullness of filial affection onto the potency of sexual desire, making a newer and more powerfully intimate contact out of the mix.

Susan Snyder has argued that Marguerite's use of the biblical story of Miriam, Moses' sister, lets the older female sibling vent her frustration at having been preempted as ruler by her younger brother Francis.[36] The poem is thus a subversive act whereby Marguerite's sister-soul plays Aaron-like rebel rather than loyal aide to the brother but nonetheless gains the inexplicable grace of forgiveness. Snyder points out that Elizabeth, at the time she translated Marguerite's text, was in the same situation vis-à-vis her younger brother King Edward. Thus the translation would have allowed Elizabeth to articulate a sense of disentitlement that she might have perceived as shared with her royal "sister," Marguerite. The Moses/Miriam story about sisterly betrayal speaks more directly to the actual historical facts, Snyder argues, than the trope of incest.

Snyder is right about the specifics of the parallel. But in weighing the relative heft of the two metaphors we must note that the Miriam section of the *Miroir* takes up fewer than a hundred lines out of Marguerite's original fourteen hundred. The major weight of the poem necessarily falls more heavily on the trope of incest itself than on the biblical story of the brother and sister couple, Miriam and Moses. That story reveals the biblical importance of the brother-sister connection; the incest trope expands that relationship to include all familial intimacies. And as the sacredly scandalous means to heal the soul's sinfulness, the trope makes incest speak to the same protestant doctrines at issue in Marot's equally transgressive psalms. Emphasizing the multiple family relations is how Elizabeth, an eleven-year-old reader, characterizes the *Miroir*, because that is what is most evident about the poem: it is a work fundamentally about oddly simultaneous familial relationships.

Bale's 1548 Imprint

When John Bale took Elizabeth's manuscript in hand (perhaps obtaining it from Katherine Parr herself) three years after she wrote it, his printer transformed Elizabeth's forward-looking italic secretary hand into a gothic-looking black letter type face, lending the text a traditional weightiness that underscored the devotional nature of the contents. Bale also included in the volume the translation of a psalm. He implies in the preface that it was written by Elizabeth, although, in fact, as David Kastan has argued, Bale himself was probably the author.[37] Bale had also included a psalm when he published Anne Askew's examination two years earlier with the same printer; the parallel suggests that he saw these female-authored texts in a similar polemical and devotional context, as essentially psalmic in the personal intimacy of their address to divine authority, an intimacy that discounts the need for priestly intermediary.[38]

A Godly Medytacy
on of the christen sowle, concer‐
ninge a loue towardes God and
hys Christe, compyled in frenche by lady
Margarete quene of Nauerre, and apte‐
ly translated into Englysh by the
ryght vertuouse lady Elyzabeth
doughter to our late souerayne
Kynge Henri the .viij.

Inclita filia, sereniſſimi olim Anglorum
Regis Henrici octaui Elizabeta, tam Græ
cæ quam latine fœliciter in Chriſto
erudita.

Figure 2. John Bale, ed., *A Godly Medytacyon of the christen sowle* (Wesel: Dirik Van der Straten, 1548), title page. Huntington Library.

The first examinaty=
on of Anne Askewe, latelye mar
tyred in Smythfelde, by the Ro=
myſh popes vpholders, with
the Elucydacyon of
Johan Bale.

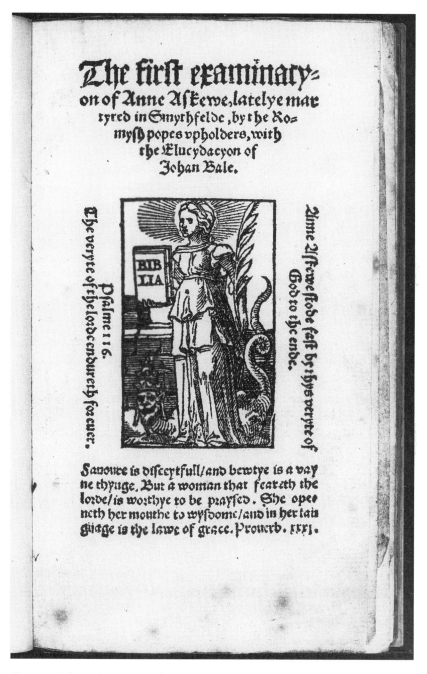

Anne Aſkewe ſtode faſt by thys veryte of God to the ende.

The veryte of the lorde endureth for euer. Pſalme 116.

Fauoure is diſceytfull/ and bewtye is a vay
ne thynge. But a woman that feareth the
lorde/ is worthye to be prayſed. She ope=
neth her mouthe to wyſdome/ and in her tan
guage is the lawe of grace. Prouerb. xxxi.

Figure 3. John Bale, ed., *The first examinatyon of Anne Askewe* (Wesel: Dirik Van der Straten, 1549), title page. Huntington Library.

That Bale chose to include psalms with both works may have been incidental, but with the *Glass* it may also derive from an attempt to replicate the inclusion in Marguerite's text of Marot's psalm. In any event, by keeping its psalmic association, the English version is placed in a penitential devotional context, which the black letter type would have emphasized.[39] Marguerite's original text had been printed in the humanist and more forward-looking roman typeface, a style that Elizabeth's handwriting had aimed to reproduce (down to the ornamental "hederas" or ivy-like decorations at the margins). But the more traditional black letter format remained consistent throughout the various reprintings of the text, and in part dictated the genres with which it would be reproduced and by which it would be read.

Although Bale retains Marguerite's preface, which humbly excuses itself as the "homely speech" of a "woman" (Bii), he cuts Elizabeth's private letter to Katherine, providing instead his own long dedicatory epistle and an elaborate woodcut (placed at both the beginning and end of the volume), which shows the kneeling princess Elizabeth, holding a book, before a much larger, nimbus-crowned Christ who is pointing upward (Figure 2). The Roman-looking pillars and walls behind the princess show cracks and stress marks, as if the triumphal, banner-hung pillar had sustained some damage and therefore was in need of reform—by means, perhaps, of the kind of immediacy of spiritual relationship presented in Elizabeth's poem. (Significantly, the woodcut illuminating Anne Askew's volume has a similarly cracked and ruined stone wall before which the nimbus crowned figure of Anne stands, holding an emblazoned Bible; see Figure 3). If we are to read the image of the damaged pillar as a representation of the crumbling Roman Church, it works to stage Bale's opening argument in his dedicatory epistle, which is, correspondingly, an attack on the illegitimacy of the "Romanish clergy," who have made themselves, falsely, into a "nobility digged out of the dunghill." In contrast to this debased nobility Bale praises not only the nobility of royal blood, represented by Elizabeth and her brother the reigning (Protestant) Edward IV, but even more singularly, the nobility of a kinship of believers attested to in scripture, the "heavenly kindred" of John. By joining this kindred, Bale stresses, the believer "becometh . . . the dear brother, sister, and mother of Christ" (Avii v).

Bale thus underscores the power of the intimate familial metaphor to attack the priestly structure of the Roman Church. He mocks the clergy for their foolish assumption that they can remake Christ in the Eucharist, contrasting the priests' "making" of the flesh with the gestational means by which Mary "made" the flesh of Christ, as if to reserve the term "making" for the language of familial relations alone:

Such power hath a priest (say they) as hath neither angel, nor yet man, be he of never so great authority, science, or virtue; for a priest by word may make Him and bear Him, whereas his mother Mary begat Him (bore Him they would say) but once . . . O blasphemous belly-beasts and most idle-witted sorcerers! (Aiv v)

The terms in which Bale authorizes the publication of Elizabeth's translation contrast humanist publication practices with monastic obscurantist elitism.

She haue not done herin, as ded the relygyous and anoynted hypocrytes in monasteryes cou-entes and coleges, in spearyng their lybraryes from men study-ouse, and in reseruynge the tresure contayned in their bokes, to most vyle dust and wormes. But as God hath graciously geue it, so do she agayne most frely distrybute it. (f. 40r)

Bale's presentation of this translation by the king's sister insists upon her humanist and reforming credentials. He singles out for praise her handwriting as well as her languages, and holds up her learning as a model after which other parents in the realm might educate their own children. Bale shows thereby his sense of the loss of the aura of Elizabeth's original manuscript—especially its Greek alphabet, no doubt—as the text was mass-produced for dissemination in his printed version. Because Bale could not reproduce the Greek letters, he had to transliterate Elizabeth's Greek. (This was rectified in subsequent editions when the printers had access to Greek type.)

In .iiii. noble languages, Latyn, Grek, Frenche, and Italyane, wrote she unto me these clauses folowynge. Which I haue added to thys boke, not only in commmendacyuon of her lerned youth, but also as an example to be folowed of other noble men and women, concernyng their chyldren. The written clauses are these, whych she wrote first with her owne hande, moch more fynely than I could with anye prentyne leter set the fourth. (f. 41r)

At the end of his epistle, Bale provides a roll call of illustrious queens and women warriors—Boadicea, Martia, Helena Salvia, mother of Constantine. He emphasizes that only a few of these women ruled alone, although the list includes "Cordilla the doughter of Kynge Leyer, and least of all her systers, as her father was deposed, & exiled out of hys

lande, she recyued, conforted, and restored hym agayne to hys princely
honoure, and reigned alone after hyse dethe, for the space of v. yeares" (f ii).
Marc Shell has argued that Bale's imperial Protestant vision here is a striking anticipation of Elizabeth's own rule. But it is also revelatory that, if
so, Bale does not necessarily imagine this least of the daughters ruling
without a husband. Cordelia is an exception to most of his examples from
history, who were women who married. The metaphor of the text itself
pushes Bale to imagine an Elizabeth who inhabits simultaneous familial
relations: he concludes by praying that she will be a "nourishing mother"
to God's "congregation."

Bale published his text when Elizabeth was fifteen. She would not
inherit the throne for another ten years. In the meantime, she would very
nearly suffer the fate of Anne Askew, burned at the stake at Smithfield.
When Mary Tudor came to the throne, she was not to be as tolerant of
Protestant leanings in her sister Elizabeth as Francis I had been of reformist
sympathies in Marguerite. That Elizabeth even survived to succeed Mary
seemed to many at the time, including herself, a God-ordained miracle.
On hearing of her sister's death, Elizabeth's spontaneous response was to
quote a psalm: "This is the Lord's doing and it is marvelous in our eyes."

Cancellar's Editions of the *Glass*

The text of Elizabeth's translation that in 1548 Bale had titled the "Godly
Meditation" was not published again until it appeared in 1568 by James
Cancellar, one time chaplain to Mary Tudor. In 1553 Cancellar had dedicated a volume titled *The Path of Obedience* to Queen Mary, in which
he instructed his readers in the prayers necessary for good subjects to use
in relationship to a prince who was head not merely of a secular government but of a spiritual one. (Mary had retained and redefined her father's
title, Defender of the Faith, but her second parliament had formally abrogated the title "Supreme Head.") In Cancellar's edition, Bale's Protestant
polemic gives way to a volume in which Elizabeth's book on holy incest
is made to serve the purposes of a resurgent Catholic Church. Cancellar
published the text twice in two different versions, once in 1568–69 (STC
supposition), and again in 1580, both times with the printer Henry Denham. The differences between these two versions are profoundly instructive of the difference a decade can make in the means for presenting the
soul's erotic address to a familiar (familial) God.

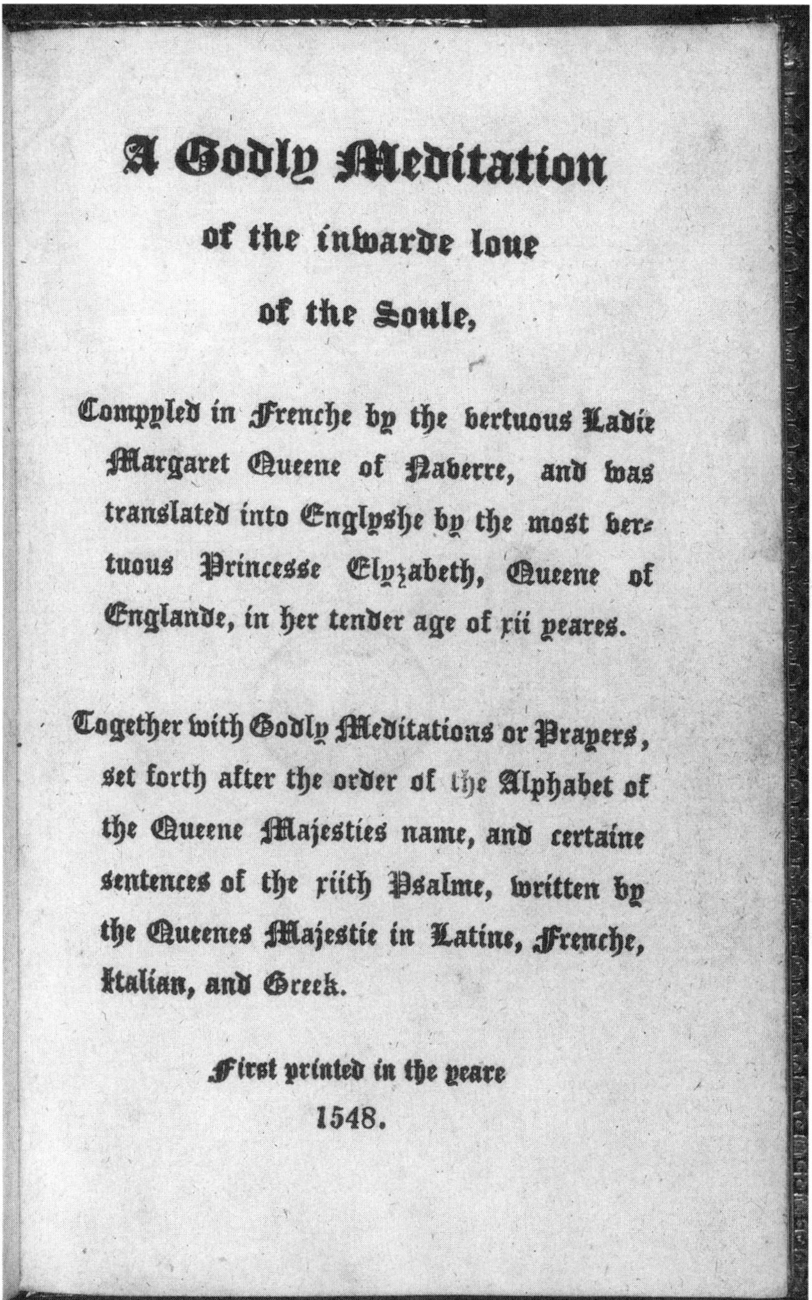

A Godly Meditation

of the inwarde loue

of the Soule,

Compyled in Frenche by the bertuous Ladie
Margaret Queene of Naberre, and was
translated into Englyshe by the most bertuous Princesse Elyzabeth, Queene of
Englande, in her tender age of xii yeares.

Together with Godly Meditations or Prayers,
set forth after the order of the Alphabet of
the Queene Majesties name, and certaine
sentences of the xiith Psalme, written by
the Queenes Majestie in Latine, Frenche,
Italian, and Greek.

First printed in the yeare
1548.

Figure 4. James Cancellar, *A Godly Meditation of the inwarde loue of the Soule* (London, Henry Denham, 1568–69), title page. British Library.

The 1568–69 version offers readers the translation with a new emphasis, retitling the *Glass* a meditation on the "inward loue of the Soule" (Figure 4). Cancellar drops Marguerite's preface, which Bale had included; the Frenchwoman's humility about offering the work of a "mere" woman may not have suited Elizabeth, a ruling queen. The title page nevertheless makes clear that the translation long precedes her reign, that it was done in "her tender age of xii yeares" and that it comes to the reader "Together with the Godly Meditations or Prayers . . . set forth after the order of the Alphabet of the Queene Majesties name." Separated from the text of the Meditation by an elaborate frontispiece (Figure 5), Cancellar's "Alphabet" is a virtual copy of one he had made for Robert Dudley in a volume printed in 1564 (Figure 6). These elaborate frontispieces display Dudley's and Elizabeth's arms, each circled by the belt of the "garter" with parallel mottos and boxed "Alphabets" of their names. The frontispiece makes clear Cancellar's underlying intended use of Elizabeth's poem. Although the two Alphabets were printed four to five years apart, the reuse of the similar format calls attention to a noticeable effort to pair them.

Figure 5. Cancellar, *Godly Meditation*, sig. D. British Library.

Dudley's Alphabet shows the Dudley bear and ragged staff with a motto (in black letter): "It is good for every estate, these few lines to imitate." There follows the acrostic on Robert Dudley's initials R.O.B. reading: "**R**emember thy Calling." "**O**bey thy Prince." "**B**eware of Ambition." This last enjoinder, of course, confronts directly Dudley's well-known designs on Elizabeth and the throne. It is announced on the book's title page that the text has been "Seene and allowed according to the order appointed in the Queens Maiuesties Iniunctions." In 1564 Dudley had been three years a widower and was making a concerted effort to become Elizabeth's consort (they were cousins—but, of course, even first-cousin marriage was legal in England, though considered incestuous by papal rules). A gift volume sent to Elizabeth by Catherine de Médicis in 1565 contains two elegias by Ronsard to Leicester and Elizabeth that make clear the French court's assumption that the two might well marry and beget children.[40]

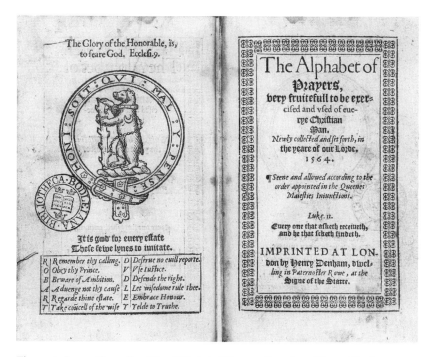

Figure 6. James Cancellar, *The Alphabet of Prayers* (London: Henry Denham, 1568–69), title page. British Library.

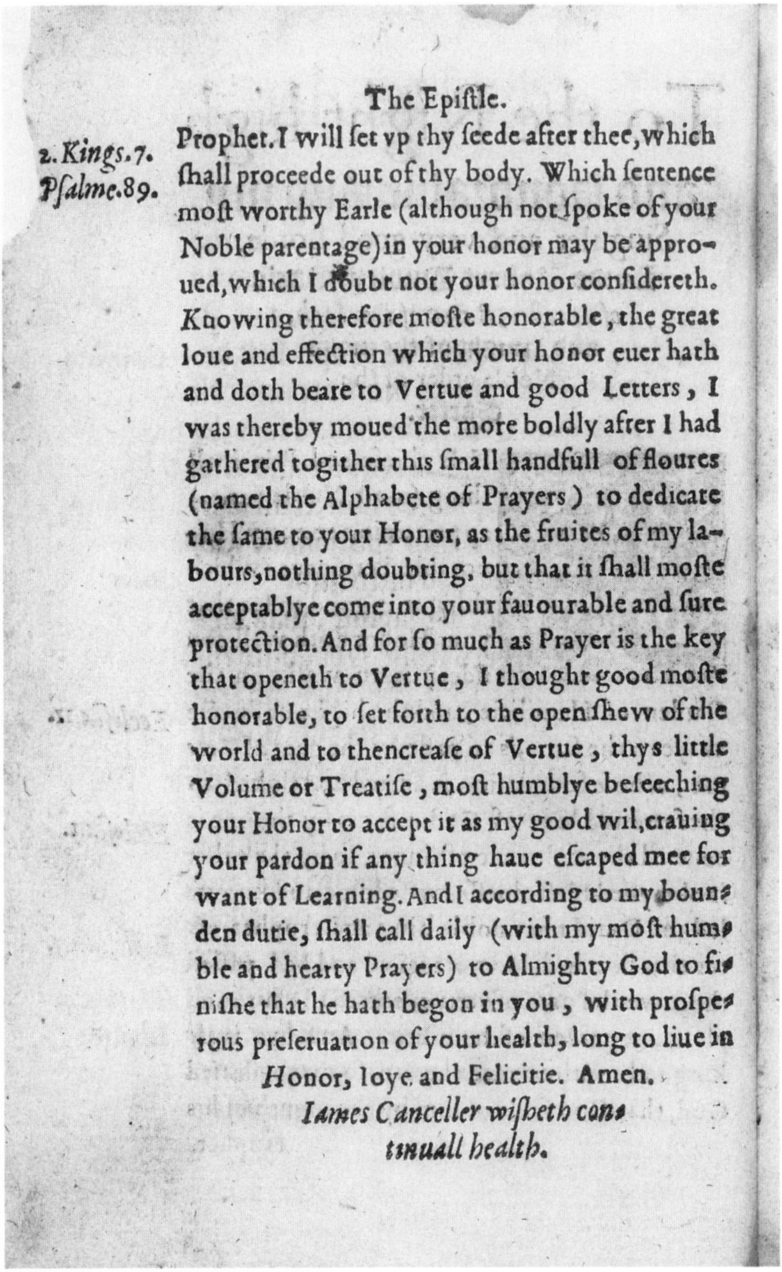

The Epistle.

Prophet. I will set vp thy seede after thee, which
shall proceede out of thy body. Which sentence
most worthy Earle (although not spoke of your
Noble parentage) in your honor may be approu-
ed, which I doubt not your honor considereth.
Knowing therefore moste honorable, the great
loue and effection which your honor euer hath
and doth beare to Vertue and good Letters, I
was thereby moued the more boldly after I had
gathered togither this small handfull of floures
(named the Alphabete of Prayers) to dedicate
the same to your Honor, as the fruites of my la-
bours, nothing doubting, but that it shall moste
acceptablye come into your fauourable and sure
protection. And for so much as Prayer is the key
that openeth to Vertue, I thought good moste
honorable, to set forth to the open shew of the
world and to thencrease of Vertue, thys little
Volume or Treatise, most humblye beseeching
your Honor to accept it as my good wil, crauing
your pardon if any thing haue escaped mee for
want of Learning. And I according to my boun-
den dutie, shall call daily (with my most humble and hearty Prayers) to Almighty God to fi-
nishe that he hath begon in you, with prospe-
rous preseruation of your health, long to liue in
Honor, ioye, and Felicitie. Amen.
Iames Canceller wisheth con-
tinuall health.

Figure 7. Cancellar, *Alphabet of Prayers*, sig. A2v. Bodleian Library.

Similarly in Cancellar's text, there is a dedicatory epistle to Dudley as the Earl of Leicester (a title he had been given only that year), which promises that, like the biblical David, the Earl "after that he had long trauailed and had passed thorowe the gate of vertue, [might enter] the fair and pleasant garden of humilitie." It was in this garden that God had made his dynastic promise to King David, "I will set up thy seede after thee, which shall proceede out of thy body." Thus Cancellar addresses Dudley, "Which sentence most worthy Earle (although not spoke of your Noble parentage) in your honor may be approved, which I doubt not your honor considereth" (Aii v) (Figure 7). And of course had Dudley actually succeeded in marrying Elizabeth, he might well have created such a royal dynasty. Thus, here, the prophecy given the biblical psalmist serves for Dudley a purely secular—and fleshly—notion of family designs.

Also included in the Dudley Alphabet is a "prayer for the Queene," plus a remarkable group of polemic prayers "against the Enimies of the Catholike Church":

Cruellye haue they (on euery syde) shead like water the bloud of thy faithfull and have despisd to bury them.
Deceitfullyne haue they crept into thine habitation: and with scorne and derision, haue they (O lorde) spoken against thee. (Ciiii)

Such a pro-Roman position may seem very strange in this setting, but the explanation is not far to seek. Apparently at this time, in an effort to gain a larger base of power, Dudley had negotiated secret deals with powerful foreign Catholics, in particular, forming a liaison with the Spanish ambassador Alvarez de Quadra. He had promised that, in return for Spanish and Catholic support for his bid to marry Elizabeth, he would support a move to send an English emissary to a proposed pan-European council aimed at reforming the church and ending the schism.[41]

Dudley had long been one of Elizabeth's truest familiars, a brother, as it were. Just how much their bond was a familial one is a point that needs some stressing. Dudley was the son of the duke of Northumberland, the man who had been regent for Elizabeth's brother when Edward was king; Northumberland had, therefore, acted as a substitute father for the family to which Elizabeth belonged, if she had any at all. (Prior to Northumberland's plot to marry Robert Dudley's brother Guilford to Lady Jane Grey, the granddaughter of Henry VII, and then to put Jane on the throne, he apparently had considered marrying Elizabeth himself.) It was for the Lady Jane plot that Dudley was imprisoned in the Tower at the same time that Mary sent Elizabeth there.

As the fifth son of Northumberland (too far down the line to be expected to inherit the title), Robert Dudley had been allowed to contract an early love match with Amy Robsart. It was this prior marriage which made it impossible for Elizabeth to marry him herself and which continued to make him an unsuitable choice for her (or for other high-born candidates, like Mary Queen of Scots) after his wife died in a suspicious fall. While later history has tended to exonerate Dudley of Amy's murder (cancer may have weakened her bones and made her deadly fall down a flight of stairs a likely accident), contemporary opinion, with some reason, held otherwise. In order to marry, Dudley and Elizabeth would have needed a very powerful source of outside support to move against the prevailing mistrust of the powerful earl.

Any (stillborn) program for the restoration of the Church is less obvious in the reproduced Alphabet Cancellar addressed to Elizabeth five years later, but the strategy of setting a symbolic son of David—possibly Dudley—upon the throne with the queen is clearly being repeated. Between the two editions of 1564 and 1568, Elizabeth had entertained marriage proposals from the Archduke Charles, but by 1568 Dudley had worked to undermine his rival's suit entirely. Meanwhile, Mary Stuart had become a prisoner in England and the cynosure of much plotting; the pressure to produce a successor to the English throne thereby gained new force. Significantly, in this context of a need for an heir, a prayer is attached to the letter T of Elizabeth's name, which repeats the prophecy given to Dudley in his earlier Alphabet:

Thou did promise unto Abraham, a Sonne when he was aged; thou fulfilledest thy promise in olde and barren Sara, bicouse thu louest truth. Thou madest promise unto David thy servant, saying of the fruit of thy body, will I set upon thy regall throne: and it came to passe, bicause thou lovest truth. (f. iiiv)

The still Roman Catholic Cancellar makes it very clear, however, that Elizabeth herself is not the spouse of Christ: the Church is that spouse, and the Church is an entirely separate and higher authority than the monarchy, one to which the queen herself must listen. Cancellar writes a prayer in her voice:

Giue me also (O holy father) a pure hearing, and not a corrupt hearing, but that I may throughe the teaching of the holye ghost hear thee, out of the Prophets, out of the Apostles, out of the penne of the Evangeliste, and out of the mouth of thy Spouse the Catholike Church: to whom thou sayest, I will send you as comforterer, even my spirite, which shall lead you into all truth. (Ci)

The boxed acrostic on the frontispiece of the Alphabet makes the eroticism implicit in the queen's prayer to God reasonably apparent. This erotic stance is now no longer spiritual: instead, it is made to serve a potentially secular dynastic purpose. Elizabeth is addressed in Latin as the daughter of her father Henry VIII, and she is told in the motto to "Embrace vertue." In the instruction attached to the L of her name, she is commanded to "Love perfectly."

But the love called for is not really that between the believer's soul and God. Instead, the terms of the soul's erotic address to the divinity are placed within a context that makes them speak to a sexual courtship program, as if Elizabeth's active statement of sexual desire for a spiritual bridegroom could be used as a platform to make her an earthly wife. Exhorted to "Love perfectly," she is told she is *not* the spouse of Christ, as she claims in the text of her translation, but that rather the Catholic Church is. She is reminded that she is not the daughter of Christ but of Henry VIII. Whom then should she love perfectly? Perfect love here would seem to lie not in being a bride of Christ (whose wedding ring was conferred on English nuns upon their solemn profession until the dissolution of the monasteries in 1536), but an earthly spouse in the person of Robert Dudley. For Elizabeth, the promised child (like that given the aged Sarah) would be an earthly offspring—a not impossible program for a woman who was after all only thirty-five years old in 1568. Clearly identifying himself with Dudley in 1564, Cancellar appropriates Elizabeth's early translation in 1568, publishes it, and puts it at the service of Dudley's program of dynastic ambition.[42] Cancellar's Dudley "Alphabet" for Leicester was reprinted a number of times throughout the 1570s.

By the time Cancellar reprinted the text again in 1580 in a small sedicesimo format, England was a different place, and officially Protestant. Elizabeth had been excommunicated by the pope for over ten years, since which time it had been treasonous to suggest reconciliation with Rome. Correspondingly, the reprint reflects these changes (Figure 8). Cancellar now prints a massive amount of entirely different front matter, which includes a new dedicatory epistle and a new preface, for which he mines Bale's "conclusion," thereby giving his text a properly Protestant tone. The frontispiece with its elaborate interlaced border is now similar to the "Physick of the Soul" and so is completely changed from the earlier presentation. In his new dedication, Cancellar praises the middle-aged Elizabeth's adolescent virginity, which he makes congruent with her education—both of which continue to empower her as a divinely protected ruler. (He had said nothing about either her virginity or her education in the earlier version.)

> O how greatlye maye wee all glorie in such a peerelesse floure of Virginitie, as is your grace, who in the middest of Courtly delices, and amiddest the intisement of worldlye vanities, haue by your owne choyse and election, so vertuousley and fruitfullye translated this vertuous weorke in your childhood and tender youth. O royall exercise in deed of a virginly education: O right precious fruite of Mayden-lye studies, worthie immortality of fame and renowne. (Aiii v)

Cancellar goes on to call attention to the failings of the earlier 1568 version of the meditation, and although he points out its corruptions, he never points out that *he* was the one who had published it:

> This precious Pearle of your trauayle (most gracious and Soueraigne Lady) long hath lyen hidden from the sight of your louing subiets: and now come to the hands of your faithfull obedient seruaunt, and daylye Orator, and the corruption & faultes of the olde print corrected and amended is now by him . . . dedicated to your Maiestie, as to the verie Patronesse and Author of the same. Whervnto most gracious Ladye, your humble Orator hath added certayne vertuous and godly Meditations, collected and gathered out of the holy Scriptures orderly set forth

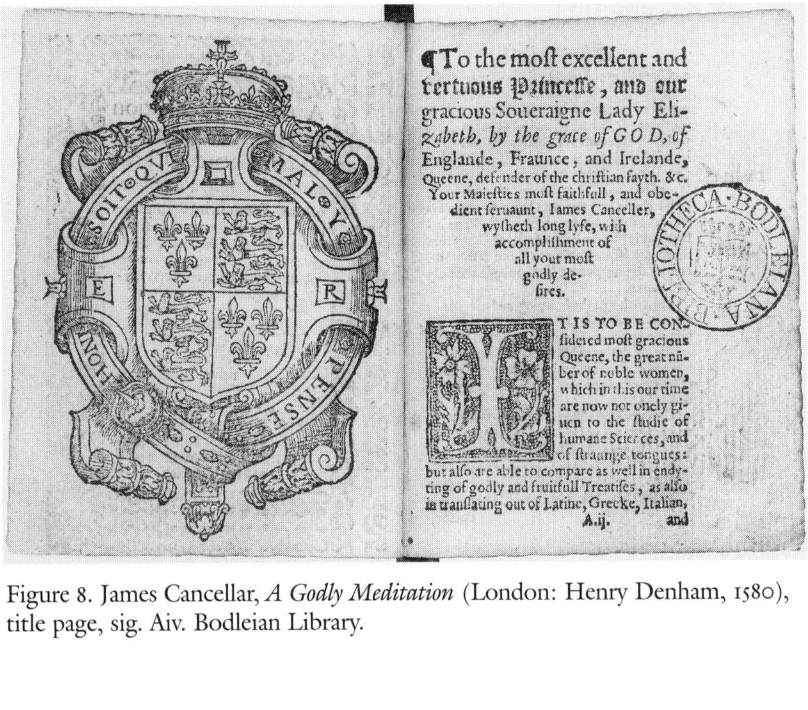

Figure 8. James Cancellar, *A Godly Meditation* (London: Henry Denham, 1580), title page, sig. Aiv. Bodleian Library.

after the Alphabet of your Maiesties name. Minding also most gracious Ladie, vnder your gracious favour, further to enlarge the same with godly Psalmes and prayers, to be the comfort of the godly Reader of the same: craving your gracious pardon, that so boldlye (being so vnworthy of myselfe) would take in hande to present to your Maiestie (so simple as I am) so precious a Iewell. (Aiv r)

Citing what at least appears to have been the queen's own desire to have the text of her translation republished (he claims that she had hoped "folks" would be made "familiar" with her treatise), Cancellar echoes language familiar from Elizabeth's speeches, in which the "folk" become her "family." It is, however, in his representation of the queen's relationship to Christ that the Catholic Cancellar makes his greatest alteration from his earlier version, a change that reflects the growing "cult" of Elizabeth.[43] His final prayer now makes use of the Protestant Bale's, in which the speaker requests that Elizabeth be given a special place in heaven after her death:

Wherefore, I beseeche Almightie G O D that it may (in the hartes of the readers therof) take no less place and effect, of godly knowledge, and innocent liuing, that by your Grace was ment in the translating of the same: whose act, most noble and gracious Princesse, hath deserued in this worlde, condign fame and renowne, with perpetuall memoire, & after this life a crown of imortall glorie and blesse in Heaven, eternally there to raigne with Christ our Lord, and sauior. Amen. Our Maiesties humble, seruaunt and dayly Orator, Iames Cancellar. (Av–Av r)

After praying that Elizabeth might rule with Christ eternally, Bale had added the short sentence, "So be it." Cancellar cuts this phrase, but even with the truncation, the address is clearly in the form of a prayer giving the queen a place in heaven as Christ's royal spouse. The main metaphor of the poem itself and the autonomous power that Elizabeth has attained by 1580 force even so reluctant a recusant as Cancellar to drop any dynastic plans for a married queen, dutifully subservient to the Church, and to acknowledge her remarkable status as Christ's spouse and England's virgin mother.

The 1582 Monument of Matrons

Henry Denham was Cancellar's printer for both versions of the text of *The Godly Meditation*; in 1582 Denham printed yet a third edition of the queen's translation, this time as the "Second Lampe of Virginitie" (Figure 9) The translation now served as the second of a five-part, multivolume,

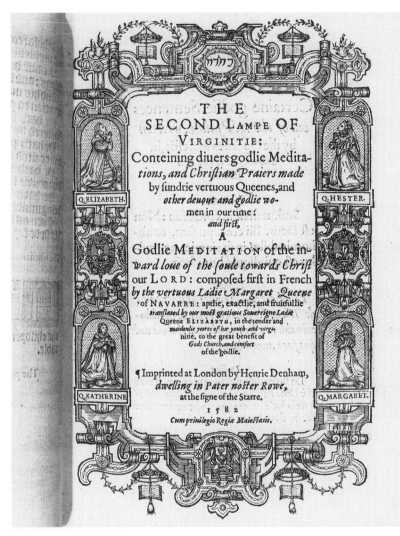

Figure 9. Thomas Bentley, ed., *The Second Lampe of Virginitie* (London: Henry Denham, 1582), Huntington Library.

elaborately produced book called *The Monument of Matrons*, which was assembled by Thomas Bentley. Bentley's dedicatory epistle places Elizabeth's work as an eleven-year-old within the context of other (literally) voluminous female authorities: whereas Bale had merely associated her with a list of famous women, Bentley collects and publishes a massive number of her fellow female authors, as if he were attempting to provide a thousand testimonies to match the thousand wise virgins of his biblical text. His list of famous women runs to two pages; he places asterisks by the names of those whose writings are represented in the volume.

Its placement amid this welter of female voices gives Elizabeth's translation a fundamentally different context from its earlier printings, which insisted upon Elizabeth's royal and unique status. We can look at this difference in setting in two ways. Either the Bentley anthology works to limit the potential power of Elizabeth's voice by submerging it among other women's prayers, or, as I shall argue, the presence of each voice collectively empowers female voices in the aggregate which thus becomes, as it were, a huge five-volume collection of homosocial female discourse. Jennifer Summit has argued suggestively that Bentley's compilation makes women's prayer "the defining genre of the Protestant commonwealth."[44]

In the "First Lamp," Bentley had printed numerous prayers by women recorded in the Bible. Elizabeth's translation appears in the "Second Lamp" (1–36), where it is followed by Katherine Parr's "Lamentations of a Sinner" (complete with a preface by William Cecil, 37–79), as well as some short prayers by Elizabeth herself on the occasions of her imprisonment and her coronation. The "Second Lamp" also includes prayers written by Jane Grey Dudley at the time of her imprisonment and impending execution, plus various prayers by other less famous women: Elizabeth Tyrwhit (103–38), Lady Frances Aburgavennie's deathbed prayers committed to her daughter May Fane (139–213), Mistress Dorcas Martin's prayers (221–46), including a catechism for children, and sundry other prayers made by an anonymous "Gentlewoman." The first four lamps run to 479 pages in the first volume. (Two more "lamps" were printed in subsequent years.)

While the frontispiece to *The Monument of Matrons* places Elizabeth in the company of three other queens—Katherine Parr, the biblical Hester, and Marguerite de Navarre—the prose context of the volume submerges her unique status among women in a massive demonstration of widespread articulate female piety and learning that reaches across classes and speaks from the multiple standpoints of the many different social roles women play, as mothers, daughters, queens, and housewives.

In the dedication to Elizabeth, Bentley explains his sense of his task, to "bring profit to the mysticall bodie, whereof I trust I am a member":

out of the admirable monuments of your own Honourable works and some other noble Queenes, famous ladies and vertuous Gentlewomen . . . to address and make readie these seven Lampes of your perpetuall virginitie, to remain unto women as one entire goodlie monument of praier, precepts, and examples meet for meditation, instruction and imitation to all posteritie. [As such he offers them to] your maiestie the most natural mother and noble nurse thereof; the cause of a virgin to a Virgine, the works of Queenes to a Queene, your owne praiers to yourself.

By turning Elizabeth herself into the church to which one prays, the church which is the "sweet spouse" of Jesus Christ, by transforming her as well into his own "deer mother," though a "virgin," Bentley appropriates the familial metaphor from Elizabeth's own text, reversing the careful distinction Cancellar had made between Elizabeth and the Church. Thus he prays that God

as your spiritual spouse to set your Maiesty (a most worthie and mightie gouernor of the same) ever as a seal upon his hart, to tie you as a bracelet upon his arm . . . to set his eie over you continuallie for your health, wealth, and prosperitie, to bend his desires alwaies towards you.

Louis Montrose has argued that a special quality of Elizabeth's cult was her unique license to inhabit the three different roles of an Elizabethan woman simultaneously—"Maiden, Matron, and Mother. . . . Because she was always uniquely herself, Elizabeth's rule was not intended to undermine the male hegemony of her culture. Indeed, the emphasis upon her *difference* from all other women may have helped to reinforce it."[45] But, as Bentley's collection displays them, we see these multiple roles replicated by many other women. Elizabeth's language in the poem on holy incest—which itself authorizes if not instigates her simultaneous inhabitation of the multiple roles of mother, spouse, daughter/maiden—leads off a truly impressive collection of female eloquence raised in praise and supplication. These prayers take place within the often daily round of women's activities—eating, speaking, working, teaching, at church and at home. In 1582 other (ordinary) women (and men) participate in the familial activities authorized by the queen's familiar relationship to God as set forth in the *Glass*. The Protestant female-embraced family takes to itself the authority of the Church to speak with God. Elizabeth's voice is only one among a welter of women speaking to God.

The "Third Lampe" prints a number of Elizabeth's Accession Day prayers, including one specifically written for the twenty-fourth year of her reign, that is, 1582. In this prayer, she has entirely and fully become the Spouse of Christ. In it she asks that God help her in

reigning blessedlie, ruling prudentlie, and like a louing mother, and tender nurse, giuing my fostermilke the good of thy word and Gospell aboundantlie to all, in all places of my dominion, and endeuouring my self faithfullie to discharge the great truth commited unto me: why thy sonne, to whome not onlie the sea and windes, but all creatures are subiect, shall come as King of kings to require an accompt of the counter charge committed unto me, I may be found faithfull, and not faile finallie in heauen, but in the pureness of my virginitie, and holinesse of mine innocencie, be presented to the lambe my soverign Lord and onlie God, my heauenlie Bridegroom and spirituall Spouse, my euerlasting king deer Christ and onlie sweet saviour Jesus, ther to see the Saints, and to be a Saint, and with all the holie Patriarches, Judges, Kings and Queenes, . . . to reigne with him over spirituall powers and principalities for euer, and sing the sugred songs of my wedding daie to my perpetual ioie. (272)

In the same section, Bentley also prints the Alphabet on Elizabeth's name that Cancellar had used in 1568 and in 1580, repeating for the "T"of her name the same prayers that had promised heirs to David and Sarah. Following the pattern, Frances Aburgavenie also has an acrostic on her name (Figure 10).

In the Third Lampe, sonship (and all family metaphors) are juxtaposed to a very peculiar text entitled the "King's hest," or "God's familiar speech" to the queen as "expounded by Theodore Beza out of David's psalms." The "King's Hest" is God's side of the dialogue with the incestuous female soul as that dialogue was imagined in Marguerite's poem and thereby in Elizabeth's translation. In the psalm paraphrase by Beza, we find the language of family relations writ large again, if also a bit more regularized, so that the queen marries only her brother and not her father.

In this dialogue, God addresses the queen as the "perfect virgin" chosen from the rest of the people:

And now then, deere daughter, consider diligentlie with thy selfe awhile, what maner of husband thou art coupled and conioined unto: learne of him alone (thy spouse Christ mine onlie Son I mean) to whom as this daie I married thee, what he requireth of thee: namelie that thou shouldest forget thine owne Nation, thy fathers house, and all other worldlie things, how that thou art come under his autoritie and into the family and spirituall societie of thy heauenlie Bridegroom. (308)

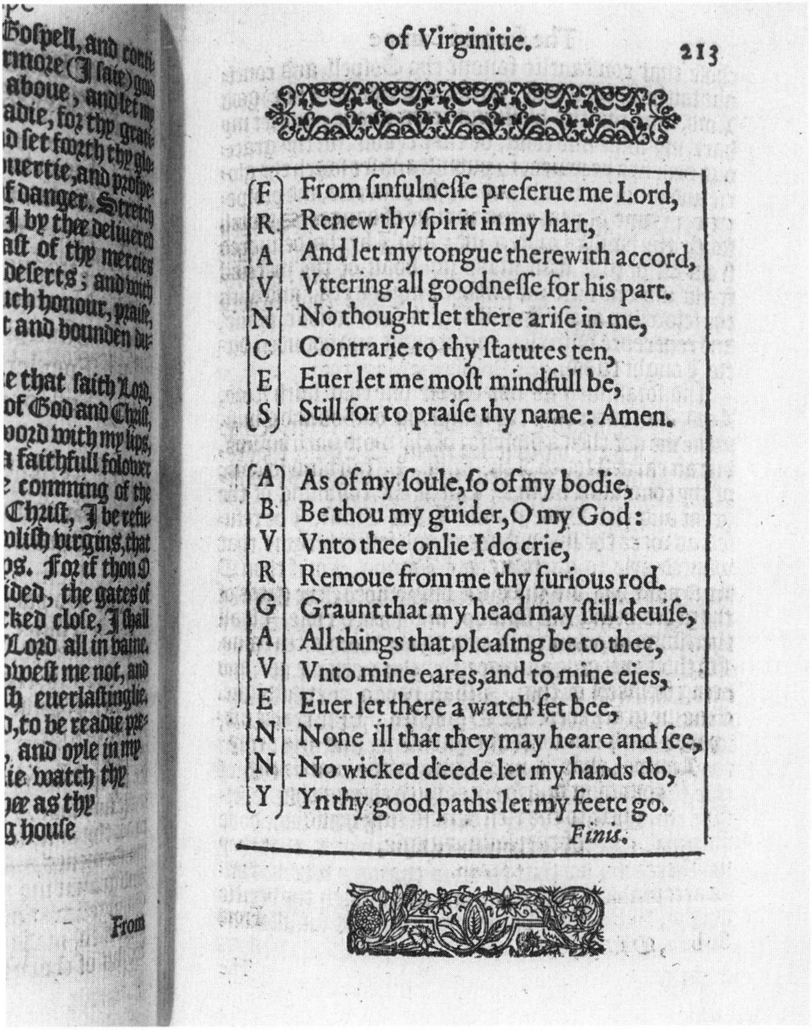

From finfulneffe preferue me Lord,
Renew thy fpirit in my hart,
And let my tongue therewith accord,
Vttering all goodneffe for his part.
No thought let there arife in me,
Contrarie to thy ftatutes ten,
Euer let me moft mindfull be,
Still for to praife thy name : Amen.

(bracketed acrostic: F R A V N C E S)

As of my foule, fo of my bodie,
Be thou my guider, O my God :
Vnto thee onlie I do crie,
Remoue from me thy furious rod.
Graunt that my head may ftill deuife,
All things that pleafing be to thee,
Vnto mine eares, and to mine eies,
Euer let there a watch fet bce,
None ill that they may heare and fee,
No wicked deede let my hands do,
Yn thy good paths let my feete go.

(bracketed acrostic: A B V R G A V E N N Y)

Finis.

Figure 10. Bentley, *The Second Lampe of Virginitie*, 213. Huntington Library.

The divine Father goes on to counsel his daughter to use an erotic propitiation with his Son, borrowed from the Song of Songs:

O kiss this my sonne Christ thy spouse betimes, least he be angrie, and then thou suddenly perish, when his wrath shall flame forth. Worship the lord I saie with due worship, and trust in him alone, as she that wholie dependeth upon his mercie, favour, and protection: so shalt thou be blessed, and thy throne shall neuer be shaken. (309)

This text continues by having Elizabeth respond in fervored baroque style, sounding a bit like Goneril or Regan vowing love for Lear:

Rabboni, my heart so boileth within me that I must needs burst forth that which it hath conceived; even a magnifical vow of a Queene consecrated to the king of heaven himself, and that with such zeale and fervencie, that no penne may seem to be able to attain unto the voice of the speaker. (321)

A broad range of scholars (E. C. Wilson, Peter McClure, Robin Headlam Wells, and Helen Hackett) have taken Bentley's text as simply a generic appropriation of Mariology for the growing cult of Elizabeth.[46] As I hope this context makes clear, it seems far more likely that Bentley was led specifically by Elizabeth's own familial incest trope in the *Glass* into constructing his dialogue between this loving father and erotically responsive daughter. The origin of the metaphor is the special relation the Virgin Mary has with her Son, but when Marguerite makes it the basis of her lament, she insists upon the sinful nature of this soul, a state that is less appropriate to the Virgin than it is to everywoman. And while it is also true that Elizabeth's virginity tended to usurp the power of Mary's as the Reformation and reign wore on, we must remember that the first articulation of Elizabeth's filial, maternal, and sororal spousalship of God was her own very young (and erotically charged) formulation. The terms of the *Glass* insist upon the sinner's abject foulness, a language which not only seems ill-fitting for the virtuous historical Mary, mother of God, but which can be placed, as we have seen, in a context of real erotic and earthly desire. Anyone who actually bothers to read Elizabeth's translation, along with the prayers of the other women that surround it in Bentley's volume, can find in the Beza-based prayer a simple enactment of the erotic relationship her text describes. If Elizabeth first learned this erotic language of incest from Marguerite de Navarre, then Bentley and the culture he represents found it authorized by the Princess Elizabeth herself, for whom, as a child of incestuous Protestant parents, it was decidedly not (merely) a Roman Catholic metaphor.

And as Elizabeth's own powerfully political Protestant formulation, it continued to circulate through the decades of her reign, first serving as a protection against Parliament's pressure to marry, and then becoming a language for consolidating the new English church. Elizabeth herself continued to make use of the language of the trope in a number of her key speeches. In 1559, for example, the first year of her reign, one of her earliest parliamentary addresses rebutted a House of Commons petition that she marry immediately; in it she suggested that the multiple familial relations she shared with her realm left no room for an actual husband:

"To conclude, I am already bound unto an husband, which is the kingdom of England, and that may suffice you. And this," quoth she, "makes me wonder that you forget yourselves, the pledge of this alliance which I have made with my kingdom." And therewithal, stretching out her hand, she showed them the ring with which she was given in marriage and inaugurated to her kingdom in express and solemn terms.[47]

More than simply being married to her kingdom, however, Elizabeth goes on to insist that she is also a mother to it, her subjects being her children and her kinfolk: "And reproach me no more . . . that I have no children; for every one of you, and as many as are English, are my children and kinsfolks, of whom, so long as I am not deprived and God shall preserve me, you cannot charge without offense, to be destitute."

What the unmarried queen brilliantly preserves in this reassignment of relations between the governor and the governed is the power to reserve to her own agency the erotic choice of a specific partner. In the same speech she takes care to commend the Commons for not "appointing" her a specific husband. If she does wed, she will choose whoever she thinks will best serve the realm: "I will promise you to do nothing to prejudice the commonwealth, but as far as possible I may, will marry such an husband as shall be no less careful for the common good, than myself" (59). She ends the speech, however, by reasserting that she hopes not to have children of her own body, and that she does not need to, already mother to a nation.

This familial trope of mothering appears over and over again in Elizabeth's speeches. She ends a speech in 1563, for example, with the famous admonition that "though after my death you may have many stepdames, yet shall you never have any a more [sic] mother than I mean to be unto you all" (72).

Many of her variations on the familial metaphor, indeed, are famous precisely because they are so strikingly gendered; they speak the quintessence of what we have come to think of as Elizabeth I's self-presentation. She incorporates into herself *all* the problematic family relationships of her own life—mother, stepmothers, father, brother, sister—and makes them all into the family of the nation she rules alone.

Such rhetoric by monarchs is of course not unique to her. In 1563 a set of prayers were published in which Elizabeth prays so "that I myself may rule over each one of them [her subjects] by Thy Word in care and diligence, infuse the spirit of Thy love, by which both they to me may be joined together very straightly, and among themselves also, as members of one body" (138). Here the metaphor borrows some of its corporate density from the very traditional political image of the body and body politic, as well as from the idea of the fleshly union of husband and wife, Christ and His Church. Elizabeth's sister Mary Tudor called England her spouse before her, and Jonathan Goldberg has rightly insisted on the malleable nature of Elizabeth's familial metaphor, which James I could wield as easily as his predecessor. Like Elizabeth, James I called himself a loving "nourish" father to his new realm of England.[48]

It was also part of her most intimate language. In a French prayer in her autograph manuscript prayer book (1579–87)—never printed during her lifetime—Elizabeth witnesses the metaphorical collapse between herself and the Church, Spouse of God, and understands herself, as in Bentley's *Monument*, to be the mother of her Father's children: "Therefore, my God and Father, I render Thee everlasting thanks that Thou hast given me the honor of being mother and nurse of Thy dear Children."[49]

Ward's 1590 Reprint of Bale's Text

The final edition of the *Glass* is Roger Ward's 1590 basic reprint of Bale's text. Ward reproduces Bale's Preface (in Roman type) and his Conclusion, but not the woodcut of the 1548 printing, which would have been inappropriate for a reigning queen, now just shy of sixty years of age. The title has also been de-eroticized for the middle-aged queen, as the love is for "God and His Church," not "and Christ," the bridegroom. In 1590, just two years after the Armada and with England still under the threat of Catholic Spain, Bale's language would have been a welcome articulation of an again crucial anti-Roman harangue.

Ward thus reprints Bale's excuse for the repetitiousness of the text:

"If the humble speech here do too much offend, consider it to be the work of a woman, as she in the beginning thereof hast most meekely desired" (E viii); he here repeats Bale's translation of Elizabeth's term "homely" as "humble." As to the tediousness of the repetition, he notes that St. John the Evangelist does the same, and he prints Bale's reminder to the reader that "a thing twise or thrise spoken entereth much more dayly into the remembrance then that is uttered but once" (E viii). Somewhat surprisingly, Ward does not update the text in any way. Thus Elizabeth is still referred to as the "king's sister" and not as a queen in her own right. Only on the title page is she named Elizabeth "our most gracious Soveraign."

Through these editions of the *Glass*, repeated four times throughout her long career, Elizabeth's familiar metaphor, borrowed from a sister queen, Marguerite, who like herself had been a sister to a brother monarch, entered deeply into the memory of the surrounding culture. The discourse she had first learned in her translation of the French poem had not only a long life but a complicated one. It was capable of serving the erotic program of an earthly suitor like Robert Dudley, as well as the political program of identifying Elizabeth with the Church and with the nation for which she could be both wife and mother. The poem was also able to authorize a vast array of prayerful eloquence written by an impressive number of high- and low-born women in the *Monument of Matrons*, and of exemplifying female learning through four decades of the sixteenth century (more, if we include Marguerite's original French texts). In sum, this "meditation," translated by an eleven-year-old princess, with its bizarre metaphor of holy incest, offered a remarkably supple and long-lived discourse for articulating female agency during the reign of an autonomous queen.

As we will see in our discussion of writing by Mary Sidney Herbert, Countess of Pembroke, one of the countess's poems may refer to Elizabeth's authorship of the *Glass*. When the countess dedicates to Elizabeth her own translation of the Psalms, which she coauthored with her brother Sir Philip Sidney, she seems to recall Elizabeth's poem on close familial relations. While Elizabeth's translation is a small example of the connection between trope of incest and female agency, it is a pointed one that had an influence, I suggest, far beyond even its circulation throughout Elizabeth's England.

It should come as no surprise that even before he came to the throne, James addressed Elizabeth in multiple family roles, just as Philip and

Mary had addressed each other. For example, James signs himself in a letter dated 1585, "your most loving and devoted brother and son."[50] Elizabeth, for her part, ascribes herself, "Your very assured, most loving sister and cousin" (262). She writes to James most consistently as "my dear brother," but he addresses her alternatively as "Madam and dearest sister," and "Madam and dearest mother." James was neither Elizabeth's son nor her brother. He was her second cousin, but insofar as he was attempting to consolidate his problematic position as her heir (however unnamed), he needed to make himself over into the metaphorical son who inherits the throne (as well as, perhaps, subtextually, the brother who by his male gender supersedes her in the claim to the throne).

But that James used the doubled terms of "brother and son" also suggests the continued potency of the discourse of simultaneous (literally incestuous) familial relations for addressing her agency. He was her "brother" in the conventional generic sense that they were both ruling monarchs, and so she was a sister queen. His position as her son is more strangely and purely symbolic: Elizabeth had executed his biological mother, but by letting the implication stand that he was to inherit her throne, turned him into her son. In another sense, Elizabeth's own children were all metaphorical and James had as much right as anyone did to claim himself to be one of hers.[51]

Many scholars have argued that Elizabeth I's brilliant foreign policy, which kept her realm at peace for the great part of her reign, relied on her continually unconsummated marriage negotiations. One way of looking at the agency she thereby exercised is to see it as the most spectacularly successful halt in the usual traffic in women of the period. Acting as her own patriarch, she could pretend to give herself to strategic person after person. Insofar as she never did so in fact, but withheld herself from the actual traffic, she maintained almost absolute agency. However, even Queen Elizabeth I did not have complete control over her fortunes as a woman in the marriage mart. As we shall see in the next chapter, at the moment when she apparently most seriously considered a truly exogamous marriage, she was forced to listen to the loud objections of the males of her adoptive "family."

3

Sir Philip Sidney's Queen

IN 1579—THE FATEFUL YEAR when Queen Elizabeth, aged forty-six, seemed seriously to be considering marriage to a royal Catholic, the Duke of Anjou, a man half her age—the young Sir Philip Sidney famously clashed with Edward de Vere, Earl of Oxford, on the tennis courts at Whitehall and wrote a letter advising the queen not to marry the Frenchman. By looking at the historical events of 1579 from the point of view of the traditional "traffic in women," we can better sense why Sidney took the risk he did in challenging a royal match both by quarreling with Oxford and by writing to the queen to oppose the alliance. As chosen spokesman for the Leicester-Sidney-Herbert family, Sidney was exercising the right of Elizabeth's extended kin to counsel her against exogamous marriage. Had she wed one of the Valois, not only might England have fallen into the greedy gaping gulf of foreign Catholicism that John Stubbs saw opening for the realm, but, more immediately, the Leicester faction would have lost its very real power at court (power that had just been grievously shaken by Elizabeth's discovery that Leicester had secretly married Lettice Knollys without asking his monarch's permission).

By counseling the queen not to enter the traffic herself, Sidney asserts the one authority left to men in her court for use against her sovereign agency: the cultural mandate whereby males, not females, choose the men women could marry. If we look again at the anthropological underpinnings of this most problematic moment in Anglo-French relations of the Renaissance, we will be better able to sense the resonance Sidney's letter had, not only for the queen but for the status of the Sidney family. If we then reread Sidney's authorship of the first sonnet sequence in the English language within the context of this letter to Elizabeth, we may be able to gain a new perspective on the particular symbolic capital that *Astrophil and Stella* was designed to create. For like the letter, and like the aborted duel with Oxford, the sonnet cycle works to revalue Sidney's social status in the face of the queen's displeasure. The tricky set of maneuverings during the crisis years of 1579–80 will also help us understand the peculiar kind of female agency which years later allowed Sidney's sister Mary Sidney Herbert, Countess of Pembroke, to arrange dual authorship for herself and her brother.

Sidney's use of a self-abasing emphasis on his socially inferior position paradoxically redounds to his greater honor in the challenge to the Earl of Oxford during the time of the marriage negotiations. Similarly, in *Astrophil and Stella* Sidney gains mastery by a strategy of self-abasement, taking control not merely of his text, but of his inferior social situation, and laying the groundwork for his sister's subsequent increase in the Sidney family's "cultural capital."

First, the tennis court quarrel: in Sir Fulke Greville's prose narration, Sidney is already at play on the tennis courts when

a Peer of this Realm, born great, greater by alliance, and superlative in the Princes favor, abruptly came into the Tennis-Court, and speaking out of these three paramount authorities, he forgot to entreat that, which he could not legally command. When by the encounter of such a steady object [as Sir Philip], finding unrespectiveness in himself (though a great Lord) not respected by this Princely spirit, he [Oxford] grew to expostulate more roughly. The returns to which stile comming still from an understanding heart that knew what was due to it self, and what it ought to others, seemed (through the mists of my Lords passions, swoln with the winde of his faction then reigning) to provoke in yeelding. Whereby, the less amazement, or confusion of thoughts he stirred up in Sir *Philip*, the more shadowes this great Lords own mind was possessed with: till at last with rage (which is ever ill-disciplin'd) he commands them to depart the Court. To this Sir Philip temperately answers; that if his Lordship had been pleased to express desire in milder Characters, perchance he should have led out those, that he should now find would not be driven out with an scourge of fury. This answer (like a Bellows) blowing up the sparks of excess already kindled, made my Lord scornfully call Sir Philip by the name of Puppy. In which progress of heat, as the tempest grew more and more vehement within, so did their hearts breath out their perturbations in more loud and shrill accents.[1]

Sidney's response puts Oxford "in his place"—specifically by insisting on his position *above* Sidney in the social scale, a superior position that requires a "natural" gentility, which Oxford's behavior contradicts. Sidney's request for "milder characters" depicts Oxford's behavior as out of character for his class, and hence finally *not* deserving of Sidney's due deference. Here, then, Sidney's humility—and specifically his sense of his own socially inferior position—is turned into a weapon against the very hierarchy that would limit the power of the inferior position.

Anthropologist Pierre Bourdieu may help us to understand the social dynamics of the nuanced moves in a process such as this challenge to masculine honor. Explicating the privileged notion of reciprocity subtending male-to-male exchanges outlined by Mauss, Bourdieu argues:

> A gift or a challenge is a provocation, a provocation to reply. . . . The receiver of a gift is caught in the toils of an exchange and has to choose a line of conduct which, whatever he does, will be a response (even if only by default) to the provocation of the initial act. . . . If, obedient to the point of honour, he opts for exchange, his choice is identical with his opponent's initial choice: he agrees to play the game, which can go on forever, for the riposte is in itself a new challenge.[2]

Most significantly, "only escalation, challenge answering challenge" signifies the continuation of the game. In Greville's account of the interchange between Sidney and Oxford one can count at least five separate challenges and ripostes (which are themselves further challenges). First is Oxford's illegal command to leave the court and Sidney's evidently very deferential refusal to do so. What the notion of legality supplies here is the possibility for an ideal equality in honor, such an equality being the presupposition on which the game of honor depends. Thus, as we see, if an earl unlawfully commands a gentleman, the nobleman may find himself confronting someone "princely"; yet, as Bourdieu notices, "the popular consciousness is nevertheless aware of actual inequalities" (13), and these inequalities provide infinite possibilities for strategies.

As Greville explains, Sidney most provoked Oxford by "yielding"—presumably by saying he would leave, but in such a way as to insult Oxford. Such "yielding," then, becomes a third riposte, itself a challenge. Then comes Oxford's direct command (presumably for a second time) to leave the court, followed by Sidney's temperate explanation that it is only the earl's bad manners that make him resist. In a sense, Sidney is doing here simply what is available to any social inferior when challenged by a social superior: according to Bourdieu, "in the case where the offender is clearly superior to the offended, only the fact of avoiding the challenge is held to be blameworthy, and the offended party is not required to triumph over the offender in order to be rehabilitated in the eyes of public opinion. . . . He has only to adopt an attitude of humility which, by emphasizing his weakness, highlights the arbitrary and immoderate character of the offense" (13).

Greville goes on to explain that there was an audience to the quarrel, as there is in all honor challenges. The audience for this interchange, however, was quite specific and significant: a group of French ambassadors who were at court for the Anjou marriage negotiations.

> The French Commissioners unfortunately had that day audience, in those private Galleries, whose windows looked into the Tennis-Court. They instantly drew all to this tumult: every sort of quarrels sorting well with their humours, especially this. Which Sir Philip perceiving, and rising with inward strength, by the prospect of a mighty faction against him; asked my Lord, with a loud voice, that which he had heard clearly enough before. Who (like an Echo, that still multiplies by reflexions) repeated this Epithet of Puppy the second time. Sir Philip resolving in one answer to conclude both the attentive hearers, and passionate actor, gave my Lord a Lie, impossible to be retorted, "in respect, all the world knows, Puppies are gotten by Dogs, and Children by men." (65–66)

This bizarre zoological riposte is not only "unanswerable," it makes clear the issue of class rank and family status at the heart of the conflict on the tennis court. The cross-species confusion corrected by Sidney's answer is weird and perplexing until we sense how it indicates the folly there is in misunderstanding (as the riposte implies) the most extreme exogamy, as if Oxford didn't know that only men beget children.

A too extreme exogamy was, of course, the very point of contention in objecting to Elizabeth's marriage with Anjou, a foreigner and a Catholic. English queens should only marry Englishmen, if they marry at all. In Greville's text the impasse exposes the Elizabethan hierarchy in its vulnerability to manipulation from below.

> Hereupon those glorious inequalities of Fortune in his Lordship were put to a kind of pause by a precious inequality of nature in this Gentleman. So that they both stood silent a while, like a dumb shew in Tragedy; till Sir Philip sensible of his own wrong, the forrain, and factious spirits that attended; and yet, even in this question between him, and his superior, tender to his Countries honour; with some words of sharp accent, led the way abruptly out of the Tennis-Court; as if so unexpected an accident were not fit to be decided any farther in that place. Whereof the great Lord making another sense, continues his play, without any advantage or reputation; as by the standard of humours in those times it was conceived. (66)

One might score the game so far: advantage Sir Philip. But at so politically charged a moment (and, indeed, following the rules for such interchanges), the fracas could not stop there. Greville reports that Sidney, hearing nothing from Oxford for a whole day, sent a gentleman to him to "awake him out of his trance," for the French would assuredly think any pause in response "if not a death, yet a lethargy of true honor in both." As Bourdieu points out, timing in such spontaneous exchanges is crucial to

how they are to be interpreted (8–9). The visit from the gentleman stirred
Oxford to think of sending Sidney a challenge to a duel. But while Oxford
debated his response, evidently the Privy Council got wind of the quarrel
and commanded a peace between the two participants. We have preserved
to us a letter from Sidney to Sir Christopher Hatton on the challenge:

> As for the matter dependinge betwene the Earle of Oxford and me, certainly, sir,
> howe soever I mighte have forgeven hym, I should never have forgeven myself, if
> I had layne under so proude an injurye as he would have laide uppon me, neither
> can any thinge under the sunn make me repente yt, nor any miserye make me goo
> one half worde back from yt: lett him therefore, as hee will, digest itt.[3]

Given this furious standoff, the Council decided to let the queen handle the matter. Her response was to make the issue of rank absolutely
explicit. According to Greville, she "like an excellent monarch" put before
Sidney "the difference in degree between Earls and Gentlemen, the respect inferiors owe to their superiors, and the necessity of Princes to
maintain their own creations, as degrees descending between the people's
licentiousness and the anointed sovereignty of crowns": "the Gentlemens
neglect of the Nobility taught the Peasant to insult both" (68). Sidney
responded by pointing out his legal rights as a member of the gentry; he
reminded her that she herself was content to cast her own actions into
the same molds her subjects did, and to govern all her rights by their laws.
He even went so far as to remind her that her father had passed an act
that allowed the gentry free appeal to him against the oppression of the
grandees (69). (What Elizabeth responded to this bold rejoinder, Greville
does not say, but the upshot was that Sidney withdrew from court for a
season.)

Greville's story is worth considering in such detail because, however
unreliable its idealizing treatment of Sidney, it aptly demonstrates the
strategies and subtle shades of power and ploy available to an Elizabethan
player within the complicated, interlinking codes which then organized
society. As Bourdieu argues, "the differences between the two parties [to
a challenge] are never clear cut, so that each can play on the ambiguities
and equivocations which this indeterminacy lends to their conduct. The
distance between failure to riposte owing to fear and non-reply bespeak-
ing contempt is often infinitesimal, with the result that disdain can always
serve as a mask for pusillanimity" (14).

It is clear from Greville's account that the queen's intervention was a
further and powerful step in Oxford's riposte to Sidney. Not only was she

of Oxford's pro-marriage party, she reinforced his point about social privilege. Her insistence on the absolute necessity for maintaining class and rank on the tennis court also pointed to what had been at the heart of the marriage question all along. Wallace MacCaffrey has persuasively argued that Elizabeth's uncharacteristic eagerness to get a husband, beyond any premenopausal desperation to produce an heir, had everything to do with her dwindling options in the war in the Netherlands. She could never embrace anti-Spanish action as an ally of a rebellion led by William of Orange (as was urged by the Sidney-Leicester faction) with the same enthusiasm that she could have used in support of such a policy on behalf of her own husband, a born royal.[4] She was understandably uncomfortable about committing herself to a war on behalf of a group of Protestants in revolt against their anointed sovereign—which is what Sidney had wanted her to do. An early and assiduous supporter of England's joining a Protestant League, Sidney was attempting to sway Elizabeth to forge alliances with German princelings and Dutch rebels.[5] The tennis court challenge was subtextually about Elizabeth's courtship of her royal French Catholic suitor, and was marked in its most "spontaneous" details by the realities of that larger court, and courtship, with its own central issue of rank. While of course no king would wish to ally himself with common rebels, Elizabeth's more precarious position as a *female* prince, unendowed with the gender natural to patriarchal authority, required her to insist on the privileges of birth above all else, for it was only by this instrument (literally by her father's will) that she held her throne.

If we avail ourselves of Bourdieu's view of the repertoire of strategies available to both sides in any series of exchanges, we can readily see how, in Elizabethan society, the shifting of the conflict from the tennis court to the Court itself, where Elizabeth held her corrective audience with Sidney, merely shifted the stage upon which the same game was played out. The real court of the game was, finally, the whole social organization of the Elizabethan polity, ranked into its appropriate hierarchical orders in support of the ultimate focus of power: royal prerogative. The honor code was closely associated with a feudal positioning of fealty to family above all else, an allegiance that monarchs like Henry VIII and his daughter Elizabeth had worked hard to replace with allegiance to the crown—just as the Church had worked hard to replace it by controlling marriages through the incest taboos. Elizabeth was never to be entirely successful in dispelling this threat, as the Essex Rebellion later revealed all too dramatically.

In Greville's text, Sidney has the last word even in authenticating Elizabeth's sovereignty: Sidney "obeyed not," and in his disobedience left "an authentical president to after ages, that howsoever tyrants allow of no scope, stamp, or standard, but their own will; yet with Princes there is a latitude for subjects to reserve native and legall freedom, by paying humble tribute in manner, though not in matter, to them" (69). Thus, because of Elizabeth's latitude, by humbling himself in manner, Sidney, according to Greville, reserves his freedom in matter. Sidney's allowed disobedience paradoxically affirms *Elizabeth's* princeliness. Tyrants (like her successor, James, under whom Greville wrote the *Life of Sidney*) allow no such latitude for play with strategies. Sidney's freedom to disobey the queen proves her a proper prince. And yet the truth is that Elizabeth's princely patience when attempting to settle the honor challenge between Sidney and Oxford was doubtless due to more than her regal forbearance. Her gender put real limits on her power, visible not only in her need to marry royally. If Henry VIII's laws granted Sidney certain statutory freedoms when appealing to his daughter Elizabeth, Sidney was also using a license with her that he held by the far older right of being male, just as years later Essex was to assume his right to chastise the queen for the wrong she had done both of them for breaking "all laws of affection . . . against the honor of your sex."[6]

As Greville tells the story of the tennis court fracas, its context is not only the Anjou match in general but Sidney's letter to Elizabeth about that affair, in which he directly attempted to dissuade her from marrying the French royal duke. The tennis match, at least as Greville saw it, was merely another version of the same conflict. The strategy of Sidney's letter to the queen was just as risky as his challenge to her favorite, Oxford, though unlike the challenge, the letter was not spontaneous. On November 2, 1579, the author John Stubbs and his printer Page had their right hands cut off for publishing a pamphlet against the same match, but by its private nature, Sidney's letter to the queen clearly transgressed far less than this public pamphlet had. (Nevertheless, the letter was widely distributed in manuscript; more than thirty copies are now extant.)[7] In defense of Sidney's conduct in writing to the queen, Greville argued that "this Gentlemans course was not by murmur among equals or inferiors, to detract from Princes; or by a mutinous kind of bemoaning error, to stir up ill affections in their minds, whose best thoughts could do him no good; but by due address of his humble reasons to the queen herself, to whom the appeal was proper" (61). Again, we see how a social inferior may triumph over his superior by stressing the humility of his position: how one may play the game of rank and so gain power from *any* position.

Sidney began the letter with a salutation to his "Most feared & beloved, most swete and gracious Soveraine . . . carying no other olive branches of intercession, but the lying myself at your feet, nor no other insinuacion . . . but the true vowed sacrifice of unfeined love, I will in simple & direct terms (as hoping they shall only come to your mercifull eyes) sett down . . . my minde in this most important matter."[8] Sidney's presence at the St. Bartholomew's Day Massacre, while in Paris in 1572, had profoundly affected him; now, a mere seven years later, a French match was being proposed for a second time. Sidney's personal motives in opposing the match had a great deal to do with his hatred of Catherine de Médicis, the Duke of Anjou's mother, who was thought to have arranged the massacre. He reminds Elizabeth that the "common people will know that [Anjou] is the sonne of that Jezabel of our age: that his brothers made oblacion of their owne sisters marriadge, the easier to make massacres of all sexes" (52). Sidney objects as much if not more to the kinship connection than to the man. The letter thus calls attention to the French lack of decorum in their own marriage-making. Rather than use their sister's marriage as a means to bond with another group of men, the Valois brothers murdered the groom's family members and coreligionists (although not the groom himself for Queen Catherine had managed to save him). So too, the queen mother, in Sidney's view, held far too much power in a transaction in which women were supposed to act as mere conduits of power. One does not, Sidney counsels, marry into a family whose marriage practices defy the rules for the creation of proper bonds between men. Sidney underscores the limitations Elizabeth should sense to her desire to marry into a high ranking, royal family by insisting that it is "the common people" who will know how inappropriate the match truly is.

Sidney's discourse in the letter is surprisingly blunt. For example, one of his reasons for opposing the match, while a clever move against the queen, is quite coarse: "Often have I heard you," he reminds her, "with protestacion say: No private pleasure nor self affection could lead you unto [marriage]. . . . Nothing can it adde unto you but the blisse of children, which I confess were an unspeakable comfort, but yet no more apparteining to him then to any other to whome that height of all good happes were allotted to be your husband. And therfore I think I may assuredly affirm that what good soever can follow mariage is no more his than any bodies" (55). In other words, any man who could impregnate Elizabeth would do as well as the French duke. Sidney utterly ignores the paramount qualification particular to Anjou—his royal rank, which included his direct connection to an anti-Spanish throne. Instead, Sidney reduces marriage to the bare business of biological reproduction, thereby implicitly reducing Elizabeth to that role.

Years earlier, in his first artistic effort, Sidney had written a masque advising the queen about marriage. In "The Lady of May," he offered Elizabeth a choice between a do-nothing shepherd and an overactive and—at least in Sidney's text, privileged—woodsman. At the performance of the masque, choosing against the advice offered her within Sidney's play, Elizabeth selected the sheepish shepherd. Interestingly, the note recording Elizabeth's refusal to follow Sidney's authorial intentions suppresses her reasons by means of a significant strategy: "it pleased her Majesty to judge that Epsilus [the shepherd] did better deserve her [the Lady of May]; but what words, what reasons she used for it, this paper which carieth so based names, is not worthy to containe."[9] Humility and a profound sense of social inferiority allow Sidney not merely to triumph over, but to obliterate, Elizabeth's challenge to his authority; such a move becomes a virtual Sidney signature.

Later, in the question of the real courtship of "Monsieur," Elizabeth ultimately did choose as Sidney had advised, against the marriage. Of course, it is possible that she never seriously intended marrying Anjou in the first place—although the anxiety of the Sidney-Leicester-Herbert faction suggests that the project was more probable than any other match proposed during her long reign, and that therefore opposition to it posed real hazards. Greville is aware of the risks Sidney took in his strategy of direct confrontation, but argues that his approach was itself his own best protection. "Although he found a sweet stream of Sovreign humours in that well-tempered Lady, to run against him, yet found he safety in her self, against the selfness which appeared to threaten him in her" (61). Greville's ostensible point here is that Elizabeth royally remained above faction, thus proving her proper princeliness—in implicit contrast to James's lack of it. But his language imposes on Elizabeth a schizoid character. Greville may owe this splitting of the "selfhood" of his prince to the traditional notion of the two bodies of the King (Sovereign and Lady); but he may be indicating as well the problematic fact that one of Elizabeth's bodies was female, a state of affairs which introduced constant static into the patriarchal politics of the period.

It is intriguing that Sidney was disposed to be so disobedient to his sovereign in these two particular, and parallel, episodes of duel-challenging and marriage-making. The two are not only linked in Greville's text, they are, anthropologically speaking, analogous. Bourdieu describes the challenge to honor as another version of the challenge implicit in the exchange of gifts. If the most precious gift that can be exchanged between men is a woman—given in marriage from one man or group of men to another—then to hand over a queen is tantamount to handing over a mother, especially as this forty-six-year old woman had been calling herself mother to a nation for Sidney's entire lifetime.[10] What links the two exchanges is not only the provocational nature of the two social interactions, but also the fact that the interaction takes place only between males. Honor challenges and marriage making are gender-specific activities, even in Elizabethan England. According to Bourdieu, honor

is very closely associated with virility . . . the point of honor is a permanent disposition, embedded in the agents' very bodies in the form of mental dispositions, schemes of perception and thought, extremely general in their application, such as those which divide up the world in accordance with the oppositions between the male and the female, east and west, future and past, top and bottom, right and left, etc., and also, at a deeper level, in the form of bodily postures and stances, ways of standing, sitting, looking, speaking, or walking.[11]

In refusing to heed her advice about his honor challenge, Sidney was exercising his right as male against her (female) interference. In writing to her about her choice of partners, he was exercising his male authority to restrict her freedom to bestow herself however she might wish. As a woman, Elizabeth continued to have less authority in these specific matters, even though she had fought for it throughout her reign. It seems she could exercise her right only to withhold herself from the traffic, not to trade herself out. Just as she herself did not belong on a jousting field.

That the mere commoner Sidney (at age twenty-two) had a right to advise a queen on whom she should or should not marry suggests how masculine privilege in this matter could trump both the authority of age and the power of rank. Just as he could confront the queen about Oxford's challenge to his virile honor, Sidney could assert his masculine rights against royal female prerogative. In both cases he won.[12] In both the matter of the challenge to honor and the marriage negotiations, when Elizabeth's real sex clashed with her figuratively male gender as patriarch, her royal authority was limited. Her royal prerogative to make an exogamous political bond was overcome by nationalist free-born gentry male birthright.

The pamphleteer Stubbs's attempt to speak for the country in a public arena had aroused her ire; Sidney's unprinted letter offended less not only because it was privately circulated but because Sidney's class, although still common, was distinctly "gentle" (whereas Stubbs, a lawyer, had no birth rank). And yet she was probably aware that both Stubbs and Sidney were likely to be speaking for the Leicester party in the Council.[13] Hubert Languet, Sidney's continental humanist friend, forgave Sidney the risk he had taken in writing the letter, because he assumed that Sidney had been asked to do so by the patriarchs of his group.[14] Otherwise Languet would have considered the act foolhardy: Sidney had been a most promising statesman, whom Elizabeth had entrusted as a very young man with an important embassy. From his vantage point outside of England, Languet worried that in the Anjou affairs, Sidney's affront had been so great he might have to leave the country. Significantly, however, Languet worried that Sidney had affronted the male in the case, not the female: he assumed that the threat to Sidney's welfare came not from the queen but from Anjou.[15] Such concern on Languet's part suggests further that it was Elizabeth's femaleness that allowed this most primitive resistance—a gender bias that may have been hinted at in Sidney's reminding her of her father's policies. It could not have been forgotten that Henry's policies were predicated on his fundamental and indeed violent desire to avoid female rule. And it was Elizabeth's repeated lament that this or that courtier or councilor would not have dared to treat her father as he was treating her. Thus, while the specifics of their encounter must remain speculative, there is certainly cultural authority for Sidney's otherwise most impolitic insistence that the queen not marry where she apparently wished. Her dynastic, royal (but female) privilege bows to his nationalist male principle, and to his representative role in her kinship. (Sidney's grandfather, the Duke of Northumberland, had in fact been regent when her brother Edward ruled and so had acted in the position of patriarchal authority to Elizabeth during this time.)

Greville reports that after the letter Sidney "kept his access to her Majesty as before," but in fact there was a period of forced—or self-imposed—rustication during which Sidney repaired to his sister's estate in Wilton. Scholars are undecided as to the motive for Sidney's withdrawal from court.[16] The ambiguity is one of the more intriguing aspects of his career—a point where we have lost the matter behind the opacity of a silent manner. Was he summarily sent down? Did Leicester advise him to leave? Or, as is now more commonly assumed, did he leave of his own choice, and if so why? His year's absence is the more interesting because scholars guess that it was during this time that Sidney began his accidental career, as he puts it in the *Apologie for Poetry*, of "paper blurrer," and wrote the first version of the *Arcadia* for his sister's amusement. Leonard Tennenhouse has argued that the political plot of the *Arcadia* pivots on a conflict between a "strictly patrilineal system of inheritance where power is always embodied in a male, and a bilateral system where power descends through the daughters of the first son." The central question then becomes "under what conditions could a female monarch marry without compromising the power inhering in the Crown."[17] Seen in this light, the *Arcadia* (written for his sister at his sister's home and narrating the love of two cousins for two sisters), in effect continues Sidney's consideration of the problematic Tudor traffic in women.[18]

When Sidney in his *Apologie for Poetry* laments how "idle England has grown so hard a stepmother" to poets that they are impoverished, we see again how Sidney uses poetry itself—the apologetic, defensive practice of it—as yet another strategy against the queen, best protected by its indirection. That he called England a "hard stepmother" suggests he had further resistance to Elizabeth's own maternal metaphors. One may in fact trace the progress of poesy in the *Apologie* from its derogated status at the opening to its ultimate reign as "monarch" over all the other arts. In *Young Philip Sidney*, John Osborne suggests a line of reasoning that gives this figurative usurpation at least a possible historical background. Briefly put, Sidney's preeminence at home among his uncle Leicester's radical-activist Protestant faction and his privileged treatment abroad, where he was nobly entertained, and indeed ennobled by continental defenders of the Protestant cause (such as Languet and his contacts), made him a very powerful opponent to the pacifist queen. With a political base in the Netherlands, Sidney could, Osborne argues, even "become the Dudley candidate for Elizabeth's throne."[19] However rash such a speculation seems, it does usefully remind us that Elizabeth's position was always far more precarious at the time than her huge historical success often allows us to realize. She may have had John Stubbs's hand cut off, but all she could do to Sidney was send him down from court (if indeed she even did that) and deny him lucrative appointments (as she definitely did do). But that by doing so she could also impoverish him was due in part to his dynastic misfortune, as well as to her royal disfavor.

Sidney's return to court, after his year's retirement following the debacle of the French marriage, occasioned the exchange of New Year's gifts: his present to Elizabeth was a "whip garnished with small diamonds,"[20] and that year he participated in a tournament in which he was a member of the Duke of Anjou's entourage. Greville suppresses the prior year's absence from court and other such conflictual features in his friend's and his sovereign's relationship, though he does constantly complain that Sidney had no proper stage on which to enact his heroic designs. Writing under James I, Greville needed to make both Sidney and his queen ideal exemplars of both courtship and sovereignty—of self-limiting power and expansive, imperial statesmanship. Therefore, the next episode Greville chooses to relate in the *Life*, after the tennis court challenges and Sidney's rebuff of the queen's chastisement, is Sidney's secret expedition with Sir Francis Drake to the West Indies, "wherein [Sidney] fashioned the whole body with purpose to become head of it himself" (70).

While Sidney's part in the Drake project was kept a secret from the queen, it was in due course found out, and just as he was on the verge of sailing from Plymouth, he was commanded to return to court by royal decree in the person of a peer of the realm "carrying . . . in the one hand grace, the other thunder" (76). The grace was, at long last, an appointment as governor of Flushing, in the Netherlands. Elizabeth had finally granted the appointment and done so in pursuit of the political line that Sidney's party had long been espousing. In his own pursuit perhaps of chivalric bravado as well as victory for the Dutch rebels, during a skirmish with Spanish troops, Sidney took off his thigh armor before charging the enemy, and received the bullet that, entering at the knee and shattering the thigh bone, left the festering wound from which he soon died at the age of thirty-one.[21]

But before narrating the story of Sidney's tragic end in 1586, two years before the defeat of the Armada, Greville outlines a map of his hero's imperial imagination in two chapters which encompass a remarkable analysis of the possible strategies open to England in what could and should have been, according to Greville's account of Sidney's plans, a concerted, strategic, and successful war with Spain. After canvassing all the political connections between such disparate territories as Poland and the Ottoman Empire (Sidney's imperial politics are global), the young strategist settled, so Greville records, on a scheme for taking the war with Spain to the New World. Sidney's intention was to plant England's empire on the mainland of America, thereby (1) draining England of the excess population that threatened its stability, while (2) increasing trade, and (3) hemming in Philip of Spain by cutting off his supply lines from the New World. On Greville's testimony, the foundations of the British Empire seem to have been laid in Sir Philip Sidney's prophetic imagination.

Specifically, Sidney intended to revive the hazardous enterprise of "Planting upon the Main of America" a "new intended Plantation, not like an Assylum for fugitives . . . but as an Emporium for the confluence of all Nations that love, or profess any kinde of vertue, or Commerce" (118–19). The word "plant" takes on a special character in Greville's text, serving as a link in his narrative, and contrasting the real politics of courtship (which Greville exposes in his analysis of his own, less heroically ideal life), with the heroic politics of his dead friend. Himself a much more successful courtier to Elizabeth than Sir Philip had ever been, Greville explains how such success came to be:

> I finding the specious fires of youth to prove far more scorching than glorious, called my second thoughts to counsell, and in that Map clearly discerning action and honor to fly with more wings than one; and that it was sufficient for the plant to grow where his Sovereigns hand had planted it; I found reason to contract my thoughts from those larger, but wandring horizons of the world abroad, and bound my prospect within the safe limits of duty, in such homes services, as were acceptable to my Sovereign. (149)

Greville would not plant America, but be a homegrown plant well-watered by his sovereign's hand. By his tragic death Sidney escaped such sad and resigned restrictions and sailed into history the most renowned member of his generation, as well as the most popular Elizabethan poet of the next century.[22] In this assessment of his own and his friend's lives, Greville reverses our usual sense of success and failure in court careers. Judged by the terms of the day, Greville was a far more successful courtier, because he had been chosen by Elizabeth, whereas, in Sidney's own admission, the queen was always "apt . . . to interpret everything to my disadvantage."[23] Greville, however, deprecates himself in relation to Sidney, the man who was not chosen and who therefore remained independent, glorious, and heroic. For his own strategic purposes at the court of James, Greville reverses the usual standard for evaluating a courtier's success: Sidney is to be judged not by what he accomplished, but by what he could have done, had his prince chosen him to do it.[24]

The same strategic purpose may have inspired Greville to suppress in the *Life* any mention of Sidney's sonnet sequence—the work through which the twentieth century has best known him.[25] Greville gives a full list of all of Sidney's other texts, stressing in particular the politically motivated translation of the Psalms and analyzing Sidney's didactic procedures in the revised *Arcadia*. Greville's unique suppression of one work, the influential sonnet sequence—which had spawned innumerable copies, and on which he himself had modeled his own sonnet cycle *Caelica*—may have been due to the genre's precipitous drop from fashion after the death of Elizabeth. If courtly compliment to a putative female reader had been fashionable at Elizabeth's court, it was distinctly not so under James, who had, not surprisingly, no taste for the form.[26] Accordingly, although *Astrophil* had been published in 1591, Greville neglects to include the sequence in the oeuvre, possibly because it no longer had a recognizable political function.[27] As we shall see in the next chapter, Sidney's sister made it a centerpiece of her very different edition of his works.

The brief and intense efflorescence of the sonnet sequence allows us, at least strategically, to speak about analogous political functions: on the one hand, a challenge on a tennis court and conflictual conversation between a sovereign and subject at court, and, on the other, the contextualizing negotiation for a marriage match, as well as a Petrarchan sonnet sequence that displays the maneuverings of an attempted erotic seduction—in other words, a "courtship."

Yet before going on to consider *Astrophil*'s peculiarly Elizabethan politics, we need to ask what does the reduplication of language in all these various kinds of "courtships" have to say about the relations between language and social practice in Elizabethan England? In another of his arguments, Bourdieu points to the defensive blindness of structural linguistics about the social context of the object it academically constructs. If language were as polysemous as linguistics would have it, "speech would be," according to Bourdieu, "an endless series of puns."[28] He objects to an artificial arena for language which specifically "breaks the organic relation between competence and the field"; such puns "are ungraspable in practice because production is always embedded in a field of reception. . . . One can only speak of the different meanings of a word so long as one bears in mind that their juxtaposition in the simultaneity of learned discourse (the page of the dictionary) is a scholarly artifact and that they never exist simultaneously in practice"—except, as Bourdieu allows, in actual puns (those produced for reception in the field).

This interesting quarrel with contemporary linguistic and semiotic theory indicates that the language of earlier eras, like the Elizabethan, was not so highly regulated as it is now and that, lacking dictionaries as we think of them, and obviously in love with wordplay (if we are to trust Shakespeare's representations of courtly chat and Spenser's practice in his dialogues) the Elizabethan era is a most interesting one for attending to the practical possibilities of wordplay in the social field. Not only were there no dictionaries at this time, save for books giving English equivalents of Latin words, other foreign languages, and technical (or "hard") words, there were also no rules by which to censure the pun as transgressive. Thus the simultaneity of meaning that marks a pun may not have been so odd and out of the ordinary.[29] What this means for our reading of sixteenth-century language is that not only must we attend to the polysemy of its texts—the punning potential of a word whose meaning would probably have been heard and seen by Elizabethan ears and eyes much more readily than by our far differently trained organs of perception—but that we must also attempt to hear the *social* resonance of wordplay. The simultaneity of meaning in a pun might provide a social as well as a verbal or poetic strategy. Read in these terms, the sonnet sequence Sidney wrote becomes a social practice that addresses relations of real power and does so through the most seemingly textual of verbal manipulations: his pun on the word "rich."

After reviewing the fascinating biographical and political context of the sonnet sequence in his edition of Sidney's poetry, William Ringler summarizes:

When we compare the known facts of Sidney's life during the years 1581–2 with the sonnets, we are immediately struck with how much of his biography he left out of his poems. He tells us nothing about the disappointment of his hopes in being superseded as the Earl of Leicester's heir, nothing about his trip to Antwerp, nothing about his dominating interest in politics and international affairs . . . and most significant, nothing about his activities in opposition to the proposed marriage of the Duke of Anjou and the Queen. The sonnets concern courtship, and yet they do not contain a single hint of the attempts being made at the time he was writing to marry him to Stella's sister, Dorothy Devereux, or of his own interest at the same time in Frances Walsingham.[30]

In a succession of relationships that were as close-knit as those of all the cousins and siblings populating *The Countess of Pembroke's Arcadia*, Sidney ultimately did marry Frances Walsingham rather than Stella's sister, and Frances, upon Sidney's death, married the Earl of Essex, Penelope Devereux's (that is, Stella's) brother. Prior to that, Sidney had been disinherited by the birth of a son to his uncle the Earl of Leicester and the earl's new wife, the Countess of Essex (that is, Penelope's/Stella's mother).[31] It was the birth of this child that in essence impoverished Sidney, for he had been expecting to inherit from his uncle Leicester should the man die childless. It had been in part the cachet of being Leicester's heir—that is, heir to Elizabeth's most powerful favorite—that had made Sidney so welcome on the continent, where Dutch and German princes were eager to marry him to a succession of their daughters. In a sense, the word "rich" refers to all the personal details he left out of the sequence—Penelope's sister, the Walsingham match, and especially the disinheritance by Stella's mother's giving birth.

Arthur Marotti has stressed the immediate historical context for Sidney's authorship of the *Astrophil* sequence: "when Sidney wrote the sonnets (or gathered them into a sequence), he was and *he was known as* a politically, economically and socially disappointed young man."[32] According to Marotti, love is not love in *Astrophil and Stella*, but rather Sidney's reorganization of his humiliating failure as a courtier: the whole sequence "wittily converts the language of ambition into the language of love" (402). But, as Marotti sees it, the problem for Sidney was that a private courtship finally provides "no compensation for sociopolitical defeat," especially because the sequence merely stages "a painful repetition of the experience in another mode" (405). Sidney is no more successful as a lover than he was as a courtier, and ultimately in the poems he is denied his lady's favor, just as he was denied his queen-lady's favors at court.

Yet what such an otherwise brilliant rereading of the sequence leaves out are the strategic possibilities opened to Sidney by his decision to write a Petrarchan sequence. A paradoxical strategy of sexual domination is one of the more intriguing interests of Petrarchan poetry. As Ann Jones and Peter Stallybrass summarize it: "although the lover depicts himself as humble suitor to a dominating lady, he actually performs an act of public mastery, demonstrating his virtuosity in the practice of a masculine convention."[33] Thus, while the language of love into which Sidney translates his political frustrations was perfect for the problem, such a discourse was not, as they point out, unpolitical to begin with: "the inequality of the servant . . . to his master . . . the inequality of the subordinated sex . . . to the dominant sex. . . . The blurring of these two discourses is the method by which Astrophil can continue to maneuver without too blunt a naming of unequal positions. He is concerned, indeed, not so much to alter the categories as to manipulate them so as to redistribute power" (60). The overt plot of the sequence, in which Stella denies Astrophil any final fulfillment, may repeat Sidney's public defeat in politics, but by the same token the author's total control over Stella as a (silent) character in his plot enacts his masculine, social mastery. Such a redistribution of power is at issue in any sonnet sequence (as in any honor challenge). What makes Sidney's sequence different is the remarkable historical specificity with which it attempts this reversal of fortune.

The signal point of interconnection between poetic text and cultural context is that Sidney distinctly identifies Stella as Penelope Devereux. He does so, moreover by her *husband*'s name, Rich. This is to identify Stella specifically in terms of the traffic in women, a procedure that may have carried for Sidney the complicated history of Penelope Devereux's involvement in a quite circumscribed traffic pattern, since she (as well as her sister) had once earlier been named as a possible bride for him. The certainty of this historical identification makes Sidney's sequence unique: while—pace A. L. Rowse—we will never know who Shakespeare's Dark Lady was, or resolve our doubts about Rosalind and Elizabeth Boyle in the *Amoretti*, or at this late date discover the identity of Petrarch's Laura, we do know, definitely, that Stella is Lady Rich.[34] She became Lady Rich in the same year that Elizabeth contemplated marrying the Duke of Anjou.

Having named himself Philisides (Philip Sidney) in the character of the Arcadian poet, Sidney continues that signal into the sonnets by a similar identification in the name Astrophil, properly spelled with the "i," for it takes a syllable from "Philip." But Stella is defined by her husband. What is, after all, in a name? If we pause for a moment to ask why the identification should come through Penelope Devereux's husband's name rather than her own, we see how the word "Rich" and the meanings it sustains in the sonnets not only name for Sidney his various sociopolitical failures, they offer a strategy for revaluing them. One could imagine a whole series of poems that might have identified her just as certainly—to take only one possibility—in terms of her mythically resonant name, Penelope. Is Stella Lady Rich not only because of her virtues and because her husband was wealthy and because he was enriched by winning her love, but because Penelope Devereux was the daughter of the woman who impoverished Sidney by giving a son to her husband Leicester, Sidney's mother's brother? Is she Lady Rich because her married name is the word for what Sidney has lost? Is it also that, by ironizing the name "Rich," Sidney avails himself of a poetic strategy that will allow him to claim his title as an autonomous author of his individual destiny, revaluing his career in his own terms?

Towards Aurora's Court a Nymph doth dwell,
Rich in all beauties which man's eye can see
. . .

Rich in the treasure of deserv'd renowne,
Rich in the riches of a royal hart,
Rich in those gifts which give th'eternall crowne;
Who though most rich in these and everie part,
Which make the patents of true worldly blisse,
Hath no misfortune, but that Rich she is. (sonnet 37)

    The notion of richness contained in Stella's real, historical name offers Sidney not merely the chance to identify her (and therefore allude to the dynastic disappointment her mother's marriage to his uncle had caused him), but also to query the issue of value, as Elizabethan society understood it to work in various social codes. Stella is "rich" in courtly reputation (achieved value), rich in her virtually royal nobility of character (class, or ascribed value), rich in spirituality (eternal crowns are better than earthly); she also has "patents," that is, monopolies, on the market in "true worldly bliss." Her only misfortune is that she is Rich, married to a dolt.[35] The dolt's name, however, allows Sidney to rename his own poverty: "now long needy Fame / Doth even grow rich, naming my Stellas name" (sonnet 35). How such a private revaluation of his sense of himself—no longer a defamed courtier, but a poet famously inspired by love—will affect that public career becomes an issue in the poems themselves.

"Art not asham'd to publish thy disease?"
Nay, that may breed my fame, it is so rare:
"But will not wise men thinke thy words fond ware?"
Then be they close, and so none shall displease,
"What idler thing, then speake and not be hard?"
What harder thing then smart, and not to speake? (sonnet 34)

    Sidney's worry about publication here not only alerts us to the problematic position that Petrarchan writing occupied at the time Sidney wrote (the poems would be thought fond ware), but also makes clear that the privileged audience for the sonnets consists of those "wise men" who would probably find them foolish. Not to be heard by them (the privileged readers) is, it appears, not to be heard at all. The sonnets were in fact closer than Sidney's other poetry, circulated to only the smallest coterie.[36] So it would appear that Sidney held to his decision not to publish; hence any argument that would claim that Sidney expected to make up for his dynastic disappointments, and answer the courts' murmuring specifically about his ambition (which he denies in sonnets 23, 27, and 30) by stunning them with his exquisitely displayed folly in love is certainly not a strategy that worked for Sidney in his lifetime. Indeed, he may never have intended to publish—that is to circulate in any way—*Astrophil and Stella*. (His brother Robert, for example, gave few clues as to the existence of his own poems, which were not published until 1984, and then from a single autograph manuscript.)[37] However, we need to remember, in evaluating how useful a strategy the sonnet sequence could have been in Sidney's overall career, that he did not live to implement it one way or the other. It is therefore a bit hasty to dismiss *Astrophil and Stella* as an actual social strategy by making the case that it made no difference in Sidney's life. For as an imaginary poetic (and potentially social) strategy it certainly does stage a recuperation of competitive authority among court wits and poetasters. It manages as well a nostalgic recapture of class rank.

Note, for example, Sidney's address in sonnet 37, in which he names Stella as Penelope Rich: "Listen Lordings with good eare to me / For of my life I must a riddle tell." Doubtless first an allusion to Chaucer's even then archaic oral stance, such an address asserts the high old aristocratic rank he ascribes to the poems by way of their imagined audience. Aurora's court, where Sidney enthrones Stella, is like the more valued courts of old than the Whitehall tennis courts. The Lordings are the audience, and the interpreters as well, who will figure the riddle of the name; they are distinguished from, presumably, the censorious auditors of a present-day court.

His other addresses are not necessarily to the high in birth rank, but to his fellow poets; as such Astrophil can lecture them on the value of their own poetic endeavors. If speaking and not being "hard" is less hard than not speaking, speaking to and being heard by an imaginary audience who will be daunted by the value of one's speech is, he claims, remarkably easy.

How falles it then, that with so smooth an ease
My thoughts I speak, and what I speak doth flow
In verse, and that my verse best wits doth please?
Guess we the cause: "What, is it thus?" Fie no:
"Or so?" Much less: "how then?" Sure thus it is:
My lips are sweet inspired, with Stella's kisse. (74)

In imagining the circulation of poems, Sidney imagines his own socially recognized mastery. As a textual battleground, the poems compete not only with his contemporaries Spenser, Greville, Dyer, Sidney's own brother Robert, and prior court poets in the English tradition such as Wyatt and Surrey, who had used Petrarch's mode for similar court-serving ends. His rivals include as well all the male continental practitioners of the sequence. That Oxford was known as a versifier might have some immediate significance. So, too, Elizabeth was known to be a poet.[38] Sidney throws his poetic gauntlet into this court, challenging even her admired Petrarch himself.

That Sidney's sequence specifically concerned an (identifiable) adulterous and unidealized passion (as Petrarch's did not) would have made it a commanding scandal in Elizabeth's court. That it was not addressed to the queen, at a time when the prevailing fashion was for courtly compliment of her in verse, may have been its most pointed aggression. He would not play politics by her rules, but would turn her Petrarchan forms to his own purposes.[39] So Sidney makes his bid for poetic fame by denying any such poetic aspiration, just as he denies any political ambition: "Stella thinke not that I by verse seeke fame, / Who seeke, who hope, who love, who live but thee." In this poem he eschews as well any specific Petrarchan prominence, traditionally based on the pun on Laura/laurel: "nor so ambitious am I, as to frame / A nest for my yong praise in Lawrell tree."

Sidney indeed claims to abjure the very name of poet: "In truth I sweare, I wish not there should be / Graved in mine Epitaph a Poet's name" (90). The name with which he consistently ends his poem is hers, Stella. But Stella, of course, is more than—so the historical identification says—a mere sign of his poetic fame, as Petrarch's pun on Laura/laurel implies that lady was. Unlike other mistresses of that tradition, Stella is real and identified, and thus Astrophil insists that his passion is no mere motive for verse-making.

Stella is the sign not merely of Sidney's poetic originality and authority, then, but also of his problematical historical situation. He turns his Petrarchan abasement into authority by manipulating a character, Stella, who allows him to woo her, conquer her, be rejected by her; in this way he discursively controls his own recent misfortunes in his career. His Petrarchan abasement changes his rank, from a vulgarity that the muses would never visit ("Muses scorne with vulgar braines to dwell"), to a private ease of nobility predicated on a kiss. A majesty of talent grants him, if only in his text, the power to make her say what he wants her to, as in the refrain to sonnet 4:

Take me to thee, and thee to me.
"No, no, no, no, my Deare, let be."
. . .
Wo to me, and do you sweare

Me to hate? But I forbeare,
Cursed be my destines all,
That brought me so high to fall:
Soone with my death I will please thee.
"No, no, no, no my Deare, let be."

Such a strategy turns traditional abasement into one kind of authority, in the process fulfilling the demands Sidney made on his countrymen in the *Apology*, to write as if they really were in love.

Sidney's actual marriage to Sir Francis Walsingham's daughter Frances (when Sidney was thirty and she sixteen) obeyed all the tenets of a patriarchal match, save for the fact that Elizabeth was not notified beforehand. When the queen objected that she had not been asked to give her approval to this signal traffic in women, Walsingham's excuse was that, the principals being of such low birth, he had not thought it necessary to ask her permission.[40] Again, we see how the hierarchy can be manipulated from below. The maneuver is so like the suppression of Elizabeth's remarks about her choice between the two suitors in Sidney's masque, *The Lady of May*, that one cannot help but wonder if the source was the same.

Paying tribute, in humble manner though not in matter, to the imperative of erotic desire, Sidney makes the sonnet sequence serve obliquely as a claim to his own political importance. Thus in sonnet 30 he lists all the thorny diplomatic problems facing the Elizabethan ruling elite: Would the Ottoman empire make another attack on Christian Europe? What of Polish-Russian relations? What would happen in the French wars of religion? How would the prince of Orange's rebellion fare in the Netherlands? How would the Irish rebels take the recent victories by his father? What would Scotland do?

These questions busie wits to me do frame;
I cumbred with good maners, answer do,
But know not how, for still I think of you. (30)

As Marotti acutely notes, it is at this (political) juncture that Stella is directly addressed for the first time in the sequence (401). The poem puts her (and privacy) directly in contrast to, and above in terms of value, the affairs of state that her important lover finds cumbering his public life. In opting for a different kind of courtship, private erotic suitorship, Sidney chooses a different kind of fame. He hereby rewrites his political frustrations as a courtier, defeats imposed from above by a queen jealous of the prerogatives he had insistently and persistently resisted, and claims that the choice not to be a famous statesman was his own. His strategy here, to make his lack of preferment look like his own choice by shifting the place of conflict away from the real court into his own psychic battles with honor and duty and desire, has certain costs. He is left enslaved not to a queen—like Greville, who let himself be planted where his sovereign's hand would place him—but to Stella, the nineteen-year-old wife of a courtly cipher, whose name punned upon the inheritance Sidney had in any case already lost.

What was Stella actually like? Greville consistently calls Sidney the "unattended Cassandra of his age," and we may note that Sidney's selection of Penelope Rich for his Stella was not only punningly appropriate to his predicament: it was in time to prove itself prophetically so, if we are to understand the underlying politics of the sonnet sequence as a subtle resistance to the queen. It proved to be a follow-up to the letter and quarrel on the tennis court. After Sidney's death, Penelope Devereux was evidently very instrumental in another move by the same powerful close-knit family of Elizabeth's symbolic kin (the Leicester-Sidney-Herbert faction) against her authority. Penelope apparently urged her brother the Earl of Essex's uprising against Elizabeth.

At his interrogation, Essex rather ungallantly blamed his sister for helping instigate his attack on the queen by making, in a sense, a challenge to his honor (i.e., masculinity): "my sister . . . did continually urge me on with telling me how all my friends and followers thought me a coward, & that I had lost all my valour . . . she must be looked to, for she had a proud spirit."[41] At the time of his uprising, Essex was married to Sidney's widow, Frances Walsingham. Essex, brother of the woman for whom Sidney had famously written that he had given up all ambition, husband to Sidney's widow after his heroic and very masculine death, could not have escaped the Sidney comparison, if not influence. Essex may not have rebelled because he had inherited Sidney's intransigence along with his wife and his sword (which Sidney had willed to him). But Essex clearly stood as an emblem of (as he emblemizes for us) male resistance to a female monarch, a resistance present in the dynastic faction for whom

Sidney had earlier been spokesman on the issue of the Anjou match. Penelope Devereux is without doubt Astrophil's Stella. She is also the only woman we know to have urged a rebellion against Queen Elizabeth.

Of course, at the time of Sidney's sonnets, aged eighteen, recently departed from a virtuous upbringing at her home with the Huntingtons, and just married to a rich heir, Sidney's Penelope Devereux Rich was doubtless not the rebel to all propriety and authority that she turned out to be. In contrast, at twenty-five, only six years after the sequence was written and three years after Sidney's death, she did begin an adulterous affair with a veteran of Zutphen, the battle in which Sidney was critically wounded. Lady Rich and her lover Sir Charles Blount had five illegitimate children during their long extramarital liaison. Interspersed between the first two children she bore Blount came the birth of her final child with Lord Rich (in all, she bore the two men ten children).[42] Ironically, she was socially accepted by the courts of both Elizabeth and James as Blount's official mistress until the two illicitly married, which they did after her divorce from Rich in 1605. It was only *after* they were husband and wife that Blount and she were ostracized. William Laud, who had performed the ceremony and who later became archbishop, kept their wedding anniversary, according to Ringler, as a day of penance.

Penelope Devereux also showed herself more loyal to Sidney's brother Robert than her own brother Essex was to be, and she risked censure to aid him.[43] She also proved more faithful to her brother than he to her. If it is true that at his trial Essex blamed her for instigating his revolt against the queen, it is the more surprising that she should risk her own safety by pleading with the queen—as she clearly did, for her letter survives—for clemency for the rebel. Her letter to Elizabeth is a strange text, perhaps not surprisingly filled with the language of the Petrarchan petitioner—as if Stella had made Astrophil's language her own. In Essex's sister's use of Petrarchisms to beg the queen to spare his life, we see how the metaphorics of courtship can be bizarrely literalized. Here is Sidney's Stella, speaking up for her brother Essex, the man who married Sidney's wife.

Penelope's letter makes clear that she had hoped to speak with the queen in person; she phrases her desire in a language of courtly compliment that seems strangely (erotically) Petrarchan, not merely because of the grim circumstances but for a woman-to-woman communication: "Earlie did I hope this morninge to have had mine eyes blest with your Maiesties beautie." Missing that opportunity, Penelope goes on to pen her letter, in which she worries that words—directed to your sacred wisdome should be out of season delyuered for my vnfortunate Brother, whom all men haue liberties to defame, as if his offences were Capitall, and he so base deiected a creature, that his love, his lyfe, his service to your Maiestie and the state, had deserved no absolution after so hard punishment.[44]

In a deftly extended conceit, Penelope paints her brother's enemies as gluttonous for revenge against him, stressing their appetites for this "feast," which after "digesting" their stratagems, will grow great like the giants, ready to threaten heaven. Only Elizabeth's beauty and mercy is strong enough to prove their "voyder"; her "excellent beautie and perfection will neuer suffer those fayre eyes to turn so farre from compassion, but that at the least, if he may not return to the happiness of his former service, to live at the feete of his admired mistress; yet he may sit down to a private life" (81).

By posing the choice as a chance for Essex to "live at her feet," the condemned man's sister radically changes her brother's language in his own plea to Elizabeth. In the letter Essex himself wrote to the queen, he repeated his stepfather Leicester's offer of long ago: vowing that he is "ever readie to be commaunded to dye at youre feete" (74). Instead, she asks that he might live at her feet, or at least live elsewhere. Otherwise, throughout, Stella's letter is far more Petrarchan in style than that of Essex, who, at the same time, wrote to Egerton that he wished to serve the queen only as far as his "dutie" required: "I owe her Maiestie the office: dutie: of an Earle Marshall of England; I have been content to doe her the service of a Clarke, but I can never serve her as a villain or a slave" (65).

For her part, Penelope employed a more supplicating style, the courtier's conventional self-abasing address, closing her letter with an elegant compliment:

But let your Maiesties devine power be no more eclypsed then youre Beautie, wch hath shyned through the worlde; and Imitate the highest in not distroyinge those that trust onlie in youre mercie; wth wch humble request I presume to kysse your sacred handes, vowinge the—obedience and endles love of. / Your Maiusties most duetifull and loyal Servant. (81)

It is, of course, dangerous to judge how well Sidney's sonnet sequence may have served his own ultimate political purposes—whatever those purposes would have been had he lived—by how well Penelope Rich mastered her lover's language and put it to political use. But as her letter demonstrates, she was highly skilled in putting that language at the service of Sidney's (as it were) successor, her brother, who stood condemned of treason against the queen. That her plea failed speaks to the paradox of any Petrarchan address in England at this time: that the ultimate earthly authority belonged to a woman who did retain a capital power, and who used it against the powerful who threatened her (England's only living duke, Norfolk, and a rival royal claimant to the throne, Mary Queen of Scots). It is not possible to claim that Essex's ultimate fate indicates just how powerfully the Sidney-Herbert-Devereux clan had long contested Elizabeth's authority. But it is undeniable that, bound together, through at least two generations, by interlocking marriages and erotic attachments among a complex assortment of brothers and sisters, brothers- and sisters-in-law, widowers and widows, this powerful family had often attempted to outmaneuver their female monarch by strategies that ranged from protective self-abasement to open rebellion. In the end, in a way literalizing the Petrarchan offer to die for her that he had inherited from his stepfather, the queen's last favorite Essex was commanded by her to do just that—on the scaffold.

We shall turn now to see how another sister addresses the queen on behalf of a brother, with far happier results, when Mary Herbert dedicates a presentation copy of Sir Philip Sidney's Psalms to Elizabeth I.

4

Mary Sidney Herbert
(with a Note on Elizabeth Cary)

ANNOUNCING AT THE CLOSE OF A POEM that she is the "Sister of that in-
comparable Sidney," Mary Sidney Herbert, Countess of Pembroke, chose
to identify herself as an author through a claim of kinship.[1] Of her few
extant original poems, three have her older brother as their subject matter. The translation of the Psalms, which scholars have agreed to call her
major literary achievement, she and Sidney coauthored: she completed the
work after his death, including the 107 Psalms he had left untranslated.
No other Renaissance woman writer is so identified with a brother—save,
perhaps, for Marguerite de Navarre. In fact, so close was the relationship
between the two Sidneys that, a generation later, the biographer John
Aubrey was to state baldly that their relationship was sexually incestuous:

Sir Philip Sidney was such here [at Wilton] and there was so great love between
him and his faire sister that I have heard old Gentlemen say that they lay together,
and it was thought the first Philip Earle of Pembroke was begot by him, but he
inherited not the witt of either brother or sister.[2]

Mary Sidney was only fifteen years old when she married a man in his
forties. At the time, her brother Philip was twenty-one; the siblings' close
proximity in age during their up-bringing makes the possibility of their
mutual erotic exploration possible, and critic Jonathan Crewe, who cites
Aubrey's gossip, takes the claim seriously. He argues that the passion
expressed in Sidney's sonnet sequence may well be about his love for his
sister: it was Mary for whom he named the prose romance he wrote at
approximately the same time as the sonnets. But in the end, Crewe rightly
dismisses Aubrey's gossip as just that. Whatever the status of any actual
erotic activity between brother and sister, what Crewe correctly emphasizes is the overall importance of endogamy (social, economic, psychological) to a gentry family like the Sidneys:

Radical endogamy (incest) is the real story of the aristocracy, whose loyalty to and affection for kin surpasses any national, centralizing, or counter-dynastic interest. There is a sense in which for Sidney to have succeeded at the Elizabethan court . . . would have been to fail, whereas his "failure" in that context enabled his return . . . to the family center of Wilton. From this base, another kind of power could be promoted and substantial, inalienable property could be accumulated. (83)

Crewe's formulation comes very close to the way anthropologist Annette Weiner described negotiations of rank in outlining the circulation of "inalienable possessions" among women in primitive societies (see Chapter 1). Crewe makes no reference to Weiner's work, and such an accidental convergence of terminology may be no more than that. But it is highly suggestive that, in entertaining for a moment the possibility of "incest" in Renaissance families, Crewe is able to articulate with such precision, in the language of Weiner's theory, the advantages that Sidney would have reaped from a return to his family when he rusticated at Wilton with his sister. By giving the *Arcadia* to her, Sidney makes it into an inalienable possession.

Scholars are quite divided over how to characterize the relationship between Sidney's literary productions and his complicated social circumstances. Formalists ask us to ignore the latter, still persuaded that in order to make the highest claims on our attention as readers, a man's literary productions must stand separately from any historical context.[3] Even if it were a desirable critical practice, however, it is hardly possible. In the particular case of Mary Sidney Herbert, Countess of Pembroke, biographical material is even more crucial than it is for judging her brother's work. The productions of the two Sidneys (connected as "coauthors" and as family members) must be studied together in order to see how their work enhanced the cultural capital of the Sidney family as a whole.[4]

No more than Crewe do I wish to argue whether or not the pair were in fact incestuous; what is significant to literary history is their cocreation of literary texts.[5] However, it is highly important for our understanding of female agency at this time that we understand the endogamous power by which each of these siblings ascribes to the other his or her ability to create. Sidney, in his dedication of the *Arcadia* to his sister, claims that she was the inspiration for his work. Mary Herbert, in her two poetic dedications of the Psalms, claims that she shared the authorship with her brother.

Sidney's dedication of the *Arcadia* is addressed to "MY DEAR LADY AND SISTER, THE COUNTESS OF PEMBROKE." He here calls attention to her doubled identity, one which she shares between two families:

her birth family of Sidneys, in which she is both "lady and sister," and her married family of Herberts (membership in which gives her the title countess). He closes the dedication by again indicating her natal family, praying that she "may long live to be a principal ornament to the family of the Sidneys," and he ends with the signature, "Your loving brother, Philip Sidney."

This dedication was printed in all the varying editions of the text of the romance and gave the work its title, *The Countess of Pembroke's Arcadia*. (So distinctive was this familial title that Mary Sidney Wroth, Mary Sidney Herbert's niece, mimicked it in the title of her mammoth prose romance, *The Countess of Mountgomerie's Urania*, which she dedicated to the wife of her cousin Philip Herbert, Earl of Montgomerie, the younger son of the Countess of Pembroke).

Sidney claims to be offering his sister a text no better than a spider's web, "fitter to be swept away than worn to any other purpose." In so doing he is subtly announcing a textile metaphor (domestic and female-centered) by which he ensures that his sister's aristocratic title will endure as the title of the *Arcadia*. Similarly, his use of a paternal metaphor (claiming that he has "fathered" a child he is loathe to acknowledge) speaks to her high station: he sends his "child" to her, hoping that she will protect it by allowing it to wear the "livery" of her name, trusting that its "chief saftey" will be that the "child" shall not "walk abroad." This means that the countess is to keep the text at home, to have it wear the Pembroke livery, presumably within the household. As a child/text that is not allowed to circulate abroad, Sidney's "trifle" will be kept safe. Such intrafamily exchange is by its nature illegitimate (and a language of bastardy informs the author's desire to cast his child out "in some desert of forgetfulness"). Sidney further appears to denigrate the text by feminizing its nature: it is "stuff" (or material) no better than what one would find in a haberdasher's shop, "glasses or feathers."

But viewed in light of Weiner's theory about the value placed on inalienable possessions never externally exchanged but circulated only within a network of female family members, Sidney's fascinating construction of his text actually speaks to the high worth he places on it. It is a possession he expects his sister to keep to herself and to share with a network of (family and mostly female) readers. Very possibly written while he was visiting Mary Herbert at Wilton, after leaving or being sent down from court (following the fracas about his letter concerning "Monsieur"), this offering of the trifle to his sister works to identify the text as a family gift at a time when the family was taking an aggressive and dangerous position in opposition to the queen. Written on and presented to Mary in "loose sheets," the gift (ostensibly to be treasured by her because it is such a gift) works, anthropologically speaking, to contradict Sidney's claim that the *Arcadia* is a trifle to be swept away.

Modern scholarship has tended to take Sidney at his word and to see the text of this original version as the less important of the *Arcadia*s. And in fact the Pembroke family did choose not to publish what scholars came to call the "Old Arcadia"; it was not printed until the twentieth century.[6] That the hero of the text is a cross-dressed male, incestuously (and homo-erotically) desired by three separate members of the same family (mother, father, and daughter), makes the plot a comic counterpart to the potential for familial intimacy that the dedication emphasizes.[7] By marking the Countess of Pembroke and her female associates the privileged readers of his text, Sidney was free to play with gender codes in creating his five-act comedy. The narrative stages itself as a romance circulating among a specifically female readership. For example, in the manuscript version, when the narrator first comments on Pyrocles, explaining that henceforth he will now use the Amazon name (and female pronoun) to refer to the hero, he directly addresses the ladies reading the work.

Such was this Amazon's attire: and thus did Pyrocles become Cleophila—which name for a time hereafter I will use, for I myself feel such compassion of his passion that I find even part of his fear lest his name should be uttered before fit time were for it; which you, fair ladies that vouchesafe to read this, I doubt not but will account excusable.[8]

One of the most marked changes in the incomplete revised versions of the text published by Fulke Greville was the excision of addresses to this female readership, as the later epic version was intended for a wider and more masculine readership.[9] Even with these changes, however, Greville chose to include the dedication to the countess in his edition, appending a note on his editorial practice.[10] By adding Sidney's preface to his sister the countess, Greville allows his own published version to present itself as an endogamously circulating shared gift.

As Wendy Wall has acutely observed, the insistent familial privacy of the dedication to the Countess of Pembroke works so that the prose itself, "his textual 'child' . . . emerges as part of the glorious Sidney family."[11] The countess of course owed much of her own power not to the Sidneys but to the wealth she commanded as her husband's wife and as mistress of the estate at Wilton, a center for a coterie of poets (including Samuel Daniel and Abraham Fraunce, as well as Spenser). But she continually used that power to glorify her brother—and thereby her own natal family.

Only two years after his famous nephew's death at Zutphen, Robert Dudley, the Earl of Leicester, also died. The massive number of memorials to Sir Philip Sidney dropped off precipitously immediately thereafter, for there was then no patron to reward poets for further eulogies. Eleanor Rosenberg and Margaret Hannay separately note that it was not until the Countess of Pembroke began her own patronage of poets that the tributes to her brother again began to flow (including the collection by Spenser). As Hannay puts it, "the Countess herself instigated this movement to revive the memory of the Dudley/Sidney alliance." The countess inherited her position as patroness of Protestant poets—just as she also inherited Spenser—from her uncle Robert Dudley, Earl of Leicester, via her brother Philip Sidney; such an inheritance underscores the familial nature of the agency for building cultural capital. Samuel Daniel articulates the specifically dynastic nature of her role by addressing her as "patronesse of the Muses (a glory hereditary to your house. . .) ."[12]

Nothing could demonstrate more vividly the distinctly heritable nature of this "glory" than that her son also wore the mantle of literary patron: William Herbert and his brother Philip were the dedicatees of William Shakespeare's first folio. Alone, William Herbert was so honored by Ben Jonson's *Works*, and a hundred titles besides, more than any other peer of the realm. And, as we shall consider at greater length below, this patron of the arts, something of a poet himself, had an affair with his first cousin, Mary Sidney Wroth. Wroth was the daughter of his mother's (and Sir Philip's) younger brother, Robert Sidney, who, as we shall see, was himself a writer. It may well have been this later first-cousin incest which instigated Aubrey's scandalous gossip about Wroth's uncle and aunt, Philip and Mary Sidney. At the very least such gossip demonstrates how female agency comes to be associated with trangressions of the incest taboo.

When Crewe speaks of "inalienable property" created by Sidney, he means the literary texts Sidney produced; in Crewe's argument, it is through his writing that Sidney ultimately (and knowingly) recoups any failures he may have experienced in his political career.[13] Yet it is not necessary to appeal to such an anachronistic sense of intellectual property to make the claim that the poetic investments Sidney undertook did, in fact, "pay off." While there is no reason to think Sidney held any modern sense of his ownership of texts (in a time when there was no copyright, no authorial control over texts, and when publication posed real problems in perceived loss of status), the practice of poetry within the family and, beyond that, within an aristocratic coterie could secure not only for a man but also for a woman a reputation for possessing great cultural capital. Indeed, such possessions, if marked by a close association with a female family member, are less likely to circulate and therefore may in part circumvent the loss of prestige associated with the stigma of print.

It was in great part due to the efforts of the Countess of Pembroke herself that Sidney's achievements were immortalized after his death; she thereby aggrandized not only herself but also the whole Dudley-Sidney-Pembroke alliance which had been cemented with her marriage. Fulke Greville was the first to print the revised, heroic *Arcadia*; he clearly preferred to suppress all memory of *Astrophil and Stella* in his much later *Life*. It was left to the countess to publish the full sequence in the 1598 collection of Sidney's works. By also including the poem that punned on "Rich," the countess's edition made completely public the identification of Stella as Penelope Devereux. Penelope was stepdaughter to the Earl of Leicester and was therefore part of the Sidney-Dudley kinship network. By publishing the hybrid form of the romance, joining the heroic first three chapters to the final two chapters from the earlier, comic manuscript, the countess gave the literary world the text it continued to know as *The Countess of Pembroke's Arcadia*.

Importantly, the 1598 collection of her brother's works that she published included not only the edition of the *Arcadia*, the sonnet cycle, some further sonnets, and the *Apologie for Poetry*, it also put into print his early masque "The Lady of May" as if this occasional piece—counseling Elizabeth to marry the Earl of Leicester—had the same weight as the other texts in Sidney's oeuvre. Hannay suggests that the countess's 1598 edition was "virtually a Collected Works of Philip Sidney," and that, moreover, the publication "did much to legitimize print" (48). If so, the text may well have achieved this early, revolutionary feat because all the work was so resolutely embedded in the familial space of the culturally pivotal Sidney family.

The Preface to the published compendium of Sidney's writings makes overt the countess's collaboration with her brother in reconstructing his text. As Wendy Wall astutely points out, the monstrous, illegitimate child, which is at the center of Sidney's conception of poetic fatherhood in his self-deprecating dedication to his sister, is turned into a creature of noble blood by the printer Hugh Sanford's Preface to the Reader:

To the Reader: the noble, the wise, the virtuous, the courteous, as many as have had any acquaintance with true learning and knowledge, will with all love and dearness entertain it, as well for affinity with themselves, as being child to such a father.[14]

Wall notes the paradoxical class relations between the two prefaces and how Sanford's version makes the metaphor of paternity speak no longer to the illegitimacy of the text but to its safe public acceptance. The procedure seems also to work against what ought to be the perceived stigma of print; "Sidney's dedication of his trivial amateur labors to his sister is thus recast as her dedication to him of the published monumental folio" (156). I would like to argue that what allows the claim to work is the immense prestige displayed by the family in their exchanges with each other. They are not purveying goods to the public; they are instead offering noble gifts to each other. The child is legitimized by the father's prestige, which is guaranteed by the aristocratic sister's interest in it. The text continues to wear her livery even more so when it does travel abroad than when it was in more restricted circulation. Sanford makes the case that because the countess has emended the text, "it is now by more than one interest The Countess of Pembroke's Arcadia; done, as it was, for her; as it is, by her" (60). She now shares in the authorship of the text.

Sanford also insists upon the memorial nature of her activity: "Neither shall these pains be the last . . . which the everlasting love of her excellent brother will make her consecrate to his memory" (lxii). Many scholars have noted the complicated way in which the Countess of Pembroke's memorialization of her brother simultaneously creates both their authorities. What needs to be stressed here is that the tactic undertaken by her, a textual endogamy of the most intense and intimate kind, fundamentally increases the prestige not only of brother but also of sister, as members of the same family. Hence Philip Sidney's illegitimate fathering is turned into the greatest possible gentility by his sister's memorial act. His text becomes part of her authorial agency. While many have noticed this paradox, anthropological theory allows us to see how the paradox works; the private transaction may be published, but that fact does not therefore derogate the authors' status, because their sibling connection insists upon the gift as a noncirculating, inalienable, and therefore highly valued possession.

Just how important this cultural posture could be to the reception of a literary work can be glimpsed in the difference between the prestige enjoyed by Sidney's *Arcadia* and Robert Greene's *Pandosto*, first published simultaneously. The two texts ought to have been considered in the same generic class (romance), but they were not. As Lori Humphrey Newcombe has argued, the "co-producers" of Sidney's text "employed strategies of social distinction" so that Sidney's prestige in print was protected just "as he had protected it in manuscript."[15] Newcombe goes on: "The events that led these two writers' reputations to converge and then diverge suggest how collectively authorial reputations were made and how contingent was the divide between literary and popular print." The letter addressed by Sir Philip to the countess is an important item in this "strategy of social distinction." Newcombe understands the importance of Sidney's aristocratic sister to the process: "Coding his position through his disposition as pet brother of a countess" (39), Sidney's letter, which is found in none of the manuscript versions of either the New or the Old *Arcadia*, transported the coterie prestige to the print book. Newcombe's dismissal of the intimacy she senses between the brother and the sister— Sidney is the countess's "pet brother"—reveals I think not only how disturbingly intimate the connection was in this context, but also how entirely strange it is to us. If we add to this the fact that the letter belonged to the countess, who supplied it to Greville for the first print version, we can sense even further how it was her agency that forged the link.

The same tension between professional publication and private circulation surrounds the countess's own first printed elegiac poem on her brother. "The Doleful Lay of Clorinda" was published as a part of Edmund Spenser's *Astrophel: A Pastorall Elegie upon the deth of the most Noble and valorous Knight, Sir Philip Sidney* (1595). Forming as it does one of Spenser's pastoral volumes, *Astrophel* participated in Spenser's formidable authorial professionalism via print. As Louis Montrose has persuasively argued, Spenser's first entry into the public eye was with a printed (if anonymously authored) book, *The Shepheardes Calender* (1579).[16] It was a remarkable publishing event, heralding the advent of a new author, bristling with preface, footnotes, and woodcuts, all of which worked to substitute the text itself for the class status Spenser lacked as an artisan's son. The all-important coterie circulation is fictionalized by the group of shepherd poets and represents the endogamous aristocracy to which Spenser as a commoner could only aspire. Although Montrose does not distinguish between print and coterie circulation, he usefully emphasizes how Spenser's praise of Elizabeth is also an advertisement for himself: when Colin's song about Elizabeth in the April eclogue "is sung by another Shepherd for a rapt audience of his peers . . . Spenser/Colin's royal encomium is already in circulation, being reproduced and doing its work in society, which is to advertise the author as much as it is to celebrate the monarch" (321). In a similar vein Richard Helgerson has shown how Spenser constructed his poetic persona into the literary role of the Laureate.[17] Montrose specifies that this role included particular reference to the construction of the monarch herself, specifically to the poet's ability to contest the monarch's supremacy in terms of gender.

The specifically Spenserian pastoral context may thus be said to carry within it one set of negotiations between private coterie circulation and publication, the very set of terms that had already been played upon to great effect by the operation of Sidney's and his sister's shared agency. Scholars now appear ready to take Spenser at his word when he tells his reader that the song he "rehearses" is by Astrophel's sister; she is rightly the first (after the poet himself) allowed to lament Sidney: she takes precedence over all the professional poets because of her family connection:

But first his sister that Clorinda hight,
The gentlest shepheardesse that lives this day:
And most resembling both in shape and spright
Her brother deare, began this dolefull lay.
Which lest I marre the sweetnesse of the vearse,
In sort as she it sung, I will rehearse.[18]

Much like the rehearsal of Colin's song in the April Eclogue, this rehearsal of the Countess of Pembroke's song brings into print what had been a coterie performance. If the poem is not indeed solely authored by the Countess of Pembroke, at the very least, it is a collaboration between her and Spenser. The eclogue is in the countess's voice, a voice that uses all of her own favorite poetic techniques as well as Spenser's. For example, the verse contains the echoing internal slant rhymes of "losse" and "lasse," used by the countess elsewhere, and her favored word "reft" to describe what has happened to her brother: "o death that has us of such riches reft." The very figure of an echo itself becomes central to the positioning of the speaking "self" within the poem:

Then to my selfe will I my sorrow mourne,
Sith none alive like sorowfull remaines:
And to my selfe my plaints shall back retourne,
To pay their usury with doubled pains.
The woods, the hills, the rivers shall resound
The mournfull accent of my sorrowes ground. (19–24)

As we shall see, this echo figure will become equally important to the countess's niece Mary Wroth, in the first poem in her *Urania*, but what is more important here is the construction of the speaker as someone in lonely desolation, someone who speaks to no audience and whose voice is only echoed to herself. The circulation of this song is thus only within the "selfe," or at the furtherest extension, to the coterie of women whom Astrophel had entertained with "lovely layes, riddles and maery glee"; punningly, the countess tells these "lasses," "Your mery maker now alasse is dead" (48).

Again the poem expresses not only an appropriately familial and female-circulating grief, it stages expression of that grief as a preeminently private act; Clorinda bewails a "private" lack, which, while primarily focused on her brother's death, also insists upon the intimate and withdrawn nature of the lament. Through such a "private" imaging do Pembroke — and Spenser—evade the stigma of print. He claims to print her poem as he heard it privately from her, and she thereby lends him the powerful status of the sincerity of her intimate, aristocratic lament for her dead brother. This is a collaboration in authority as well as authoring, as if Spenser had borrowed the strategy from Astrophel himself.

Two further unpublished poems that the countess wrote in dedication of the Psalms to Elizabeth work in a similar way, by a similar set of strategies. In a sense their unpublished status, and their address to the countess's twin authorizing agents—her brother and Queen Elizabeth—demonstrate that in some sense the *Arcadia* did not need to be printed in order to accomplish its feat of authorizing the Sidneys. Indeed, the published version merely accomplished a widening of the arena in which, paradoxically, this particular text remained within the family.[19] So too, the countess's "private" pastoral elegy, although printed in Spenser's collection, remains within the family arena. The countess chose not to circulate the collected translations of the Psalms in print but rather to distribute them in manuscript, where they had an immense influence on subsequent religious lyric. Samuel Daniel clearly did not expect their failure to be published to have a deleterious effect on the fame of the Countess of Pembroke's Psalms; in fact, he prophesies that her name will be known to history by this work.

So long as Sions god remained honored;
And till confusion hath all zeale bereaven,
And murderd Faith . . .
Here thou surviv'st thy selfe, heere thou art found

For late suceeding ages, fresh in fame:
This monument cannot be overthrowne,
Where in eternall Brasse remains thy Name.[20]

The two dedicatory poems exist in a single manuscript, with an earlier version of one of them appearing in Daniel's papers. When the poems are read together they provide a remarkable sense of the countess's own sense of her poetic vocation. In her poem to Elizabeth, the countess makes her presentation of the translation of the Psalms a gift that is remarkably similar to the translation Elizabeth had long ago offered to Katherine Parr—a translation to which the countess may be referring at the close of her poem. More crucially, the importance of the brother-sister tie in both poems resonates closely with the family metaphor of holy incest in Elizabeth's translation of Marguerite of Navarre's *Miroir*.

Although addressed to Elizabeth, the lyric that begins, "Even now that Care which on thy Crowne attends" is as much about Sir Philip Sidney as it is about the queen. The incomplete nature of his part in the project of translation, due to his tragic early death (hence the countess's need to complete the translation of the Psalms for him), speaks indirectly to Elizabeth's notorious neglect of Philip during his lifetime.

Then these the Postes of Dutie and Goodwill
Shall presse to offer what their Senders owe;
Which once in two, now in one Subject goe,
The poorer left, the richer reft awaye:
Who better might (O might ah word of woe.)
Have giv'n for me what I for him defraye.

How can I name whom sighing sighes extend
And not unstopp my teares eternall spring?[21]

That Sidney was the "richer" sender is clearly metaphorical, for he was in fact quite poor. The word may also recall the richness of *Astrophil and Stella* with the identifying pun the countess was very careful to include. As Hannay points out, the poem is an admonition to the queen to continue the activist Protestant agenda for which Philip had sacrificed his life and for which he had undertaken the translation of the Psalms.[22] His sister's prodding of the queen takes the form of an apologetic acknowledgment that Elizabeth will have little time to read the humble verse she sends:

One instant will, or willing can she lose
I say not reading, but receiving Rimes,
On whom in chiefe dependeth to dispose
What Europe acts in these most active times? (4–7)

But the countess is willing to risk offense because, while deploying the traditional contrast between *otium* and *negotium*, she implies that Elizabeth's special election by God to be queen has also graced her with a special ability to make rhyme-receiving a part of her normal "exercise."

What heav'nly powers thee highest throne assign'de,
Assign'd thee goodnes suting that Degree:
And by thy strength thy burthen so defin'de,
To others toile, is Exercise to thee. (13–16)

The chiastic contrast between "toile" and "Exercise" highlights the earlier alliterative zeugma on "rimes": Elizabeth has little time to read, or even to receive, rhymes. But in insisting on the queen's reception of the poems, the countess emphasizes the status of the Psalms as her gift. Reading the Psalms, as opposed to merely receiving them as a gift, of course, in metrical translation à la Clément Marot, was a very activist Protestant thing to do. It was the reason, no doubt, that John Bale had claimed for the princess Elizabeth authorship of the translation of the psalm which he had included with her translation of Marguerite's *Miroir*.

One of the most influential aspects of the Sidneian Psalms, recognized by contemporaries and by scholars alike, is the remarkably various experimentation with verse forms within it. In the process of mimicking Marot's metrical variety, the Sidneys managed to assemble a vast compendium of English metrical forms. In view of this metrical emphasis in the translations, it is strange to see that the countess writes her poem to Elizabeth in ottava rima, while composing the poem to her brother in a modified seven-line rhyme-royal stanza. It is also significant that Spenser had used the rhyme-royal stanza for his elegy on Sidney in the volume he had dedicated to Mary, Countess of Pembroke in 1591, *The Ruines of Time*. Therefore it seems likely that the countess chose the form for its elegiac nature rather than as a pointed contrast to her poem to Elizabeth. Still, she makes a very interesting choice: she privileges her brother with the more august metric form and silently derogates the queen.

Especially when we compare this dedicatory poem with a letter she sent to Elizabeth a year later thanking her in advance for taking care of her son William at court, the poem's tone of address to the queen is remarkably double-edged. As Hannay points out, her stress on Elizabeth's royal duties in the service of Protestantism insists upon Elizabeth's earlier neglect of Philip's cause. Perhaps even more pointedly, her very offering of the translation as feudal "rent" calls attention to how little financial support Elizabeth had offered to the Sidneys in the past. Elizabeth should think of the poems, she says, as:

. . . small parcell of that undischarged rent,
From which nor paines, nor paiments can us free.
And yet enough to cause our neighbours see
We will our best, though scanted in our will:
And those nighe feelds where sown'n thy favors be
Unwalthy do, not elce unworthie till. (35–40)

Good tillers of the field, the Sidneys work hard to repay their sovereign's bounty; their neighbors know how hard they labor to make this rent. The family only seem to fail in that one particular field where the queen's favors are sown; however hard they work, this field remains unwealthy, even though their tillage elsewhere proves not at all unworthy. It is hard to imagine a more left-handed tribute.

The Countess of Pembroke's main metaphor for the text she is sending Elizabeth is cloth; not only is the text a *textus*, a woven thing, the English translation of the Psalms provides a different "dress" for the Hebrew King David. In presenting the translation as woven material, or "stuff," the countess includes her brother in the process of weaving (although she differentiates between the two), just as he had included her in the *Arcadia* by giving her the "stuff," the haberdasher's glasses and feathers:

. . . but hee did warpe, I weav'd this web to end;
The stuffe not ours, our worke no curious thing,
Wherin yet well see though the Psalmist King
Now English denizend, though Hebrue borne,
Woold to thy musicke undispleased sing,
Oft having worse, without repining worne; (27–32)

She rings a quite particular change on the metaphor, however, when she specifies that the text is to be made into a "liverie robe" (just as Sidney had asked her to protect the *Arcadia* in her livery): "And I the Cloth in both our names present, / A liverie robe to bee bestowed by thee." If the two translators, brother and sister, pay their feudal "rent" by giving

their overlord the raw cloth, they expect her to make it into a livery robe
to be given to her other servants.

The cloth then transforms again; it becomes "holy garments," which
"each good soule assaies, / Some sorting all, all sort to none but thee."
Individual psalms will apply to all readers, but the entire set of poems
applies only to Elizabeth, for only she, like their author David, is royal.

A king should onely to a Queene bee sent.
Gods loved choice unto his chosen love:
Devotion to Devotions President:
What all applaud, to her whom none reprove. (53–56)

This text, like Elizabeth's own embroidered gift of a translation to her stepmother Katherine Parr, works like the woven textiles circulating among
women, articulating in the exchange the closely interlocked social hierar-
chies among interlocking families.

The complicated language of rent and repayment, debt and bestowal,
defrayal and discharge mark a densely hierarchical relationship that is gendered explicitly female only at the end of the poem, when the countess
names herself the single, female giver of the gift, just as Elizabeth is the single, female ruler who receives it. Her final compliment to Elizabeth is to
say that she outstrips even King David: first, she is ruler over two hemispheres (rather than only one); second, God protected her directly when
"the very windes did on thy partie blowe"—a reference to the Armada. But
more specifically, in contrast to David, who was visited by the Queen of
Sheba, it is kings who wait upon Queen Elizabeth, and the countess notes
that this is a paradoxical state as strange as mainlands doing obeisance to
an island:

Kings on a Queene enforst their states to lay;
Main-lands for Empire waiting on an Ile;
Men drawne by worth a woman to obay;
One moving all, herselfe unmov'd the while: (81–84)

A strange conflation of terms makes it difficult to see just what task is
finally the actual subject of the poem, as the countess collapses the work
of her translating the Psalms with Elizabeth's own activities as ruler and
poet. Speaking to her muse (which has been enjoined not to fly as high as
eagles), Sidney's sister cautions, "But softe my muse":

Thy utmost can but offer to hir sight
Her handmaides taske, which most her will endeeres; (89–90)

"Her handmaides taske" may be the countess's own offering of the poems, a gift to a mistress from her handmaid. But she may also be saying that her muse can only outline what the queen must do as a handmaid to God. Both will sing like David, if only Elizabeth can achieve (and the poem prays for her longer life) what men will praise after her death. In that longer life, Queen Elizabeth may be more triumphant in rule and in her own praise of God, outstripping even David:

And pray unto thy pains life from that light
Which lively lightsome Court, and kingdome cheers,
What wish she may (farre past hir living Peeres
And Rivall still to Judas Faithfull King)
In more then hee and more triumphant yeares,
Sing what God doth, and doo what men may sing. (91–96)

Hannay suggests that the last line of reference to Elizabeth's own "singing" of what "God doth" may refer to her translation of Marguerite, *The Glass of the Sinful Soul*, which had been included, as we have noted, in the *Monument of Matrons*, the compendium of Psalm-inspired meditations dedicated to Elizabeth.

But the prayer that Elizabeth might *do* more than David ("doo what men may sing") is, of course, yet another Sidney plea for the activist intervention in the Protestant cause for which her brother had died. Thus the poem to Elizabeth is constantly circling about the old family project, although, as Hannay notes, the plea is also interesting for what it leaves out of its petition. There is no praise of Elizabeth's beauty, her chastity, no compliment by way of mythological reference; instead the poem insists upon duty, upon the time-consuming and arduous task of ruling over a Protestant realm, as if this were a poem above all about work: "Truthes restitution, vanitie exile, / Wealth sprung of want, warr held without annoye" (8–9). The economics of dutiful achievement are presented as the same for both Elizabeth and the Sidneys. The latter group has managed to till their fields and pay their rent as best they might, just as Elizabeth has managed to make restitution of truth and created wealth out of want. Indeed Elizabeth is so capable that she transforms "toile" into "exercise." The language of shared work again insists upon the shared political project, one which outstrips even King David's honors. The project is not merely Protestant but global (two whole hemispheres honor Elizabeth), just as, according to Greville, Sidney's plan had been to take a global war against Catholic Spain into the western hemisphere.

The economics of debt also mark the countess's other dedicatory poem to her brother; but the metaphor here is one of fluids flowing, not the exchange of livery cloth.

As little streames with all their all doe flowe
to their great sea, due tributes fatefull fee:
So press my thoughts my burthened thoughtes in mee
To pay the debt of Infinits I owe
To thy great worth; (32–36)

This "flowe" is due, doubtless, to the blood the poet shares with Sir Philip Sidney, which makes its appearance in the poem in the guise of a reference to the famously festered wound that caused his death, the memory of which has caused her heart's tears to fall.

Deepe wounds enlarg'd, long festered in their gall
Fresh bleeding smart; not eie but hart teares fall.
Ah memorie what needs this new arrest? (19–20)

In the poem to Elizabeth the countess had feared the mention of her brother's work in translating the Psalms would "unstopp" her "teares eter- nall spring." The "arrest" of memory in this poem works to unstop the flow:

Oh! when to this Acompt, this cast upp Summe,
This Reckoning made, this Audit of my woe,
I call my thoughts, whence so strange passions flowe;
How workes my hart, my sences striken dumbe?
That would thee more, then ever hart could showe,
And all too short who knew thee best doth knowe
There lives no witt that may thy praise become. (43–49)

The language of debt here clearly echoes the lament that Astrophil made in the Sidney sonnet about how much his love for Stella has cost him in terms of his career at court.

With what sharpe checkes I in my selfe am shent,
When into Reason's audit I do go:
And by just counts my self a banckrout know
Of all those goods, which heav'n to me hath lent:
Unable quite to pay even Nature's rent,
Which unto it by birthright I do ow:
And which is worse, no good excuse can show,
But that my wealth I have most idly spent. (sonnet 18)[23]

Unlike her brother's audit, however, the countess's passion fulfills rather than betrays a birthright; the translation of the Psalms pays, as we have seen, the rent owed to the sovereign; her brother's worth, far from being unable to pay Nature's debt, is of a quality "exceeding Natures store" (l. 36).

The countess's insistence on the strangeness of the passions set flowing (by her casting of accounts of what she owes her brother) is in itself strange. To say that her senses are "stricken dumb" insists on her inability to articulate the nature of this strangeness, when the poem is her articulation. A "stranger" is the opposite of an intimate, of course; by the term the poet suggests that the issue in question is a problematic tension between propinquity and distance. If she does not here refer to some out-of-the-ordinary passion for her brother, she certainly associates the flowing outburst of her passionate feelings for him with her own practice of poetry. Sidney himself had used such a metaphor to talk about his verse writing in the first sonnet of the sequence, seeking "if thence would flow/Some fresh and fruitfull showers upon my sunne-burn'd braine" (7–8). His sister's baroque-sounding twist on the metaphor, however, owes much to the wound she has remembered earlier in her poem:

To which these dearest offrings of my hart
Dissolv'd to Inke, while penns impressions move
The bleeding veines of never dying love. (78–70)

The countess shares the poetic comparison of writing ink to heart's blood with a number of contemporary poets, most notably Spenser, who referred in his first sonnet to lines "written with teares in hart's close bleeding book." And as we shall see, the trope will be impressively reused in the *Urania* by her niece, Mary Wroth.[24] But in the case of the Countess of Pembroke, the metaphor is far more personal: she owes her art to her brother more literally than any sonneteer owes his mistress/muse: First of all, they have co-authored (both given birth to) the poems in the text that is being dedicated. Moreover, the metaphor speaks to shared family blood as well, a blood Philip Sidney has already shed in dying for a cause, and that she sheds again in writing about her loss of him. In these ways, the Countess of Pembroke's claim to write is prominently predicated on her being "coupled" with her brother:

To the pure sprite, to thee alone's addres't
This coupled worke, by double int'rest thine:
First rais'de by thy blest hand, and what is mine
Inspired by thee, thy secrett power imprest.

So dar'd my Muse with thine itselfe combine,
As mortall stuff with that which is divine,
Thy lightning beames give lustre to the rest (1–7)

Although she protests that she has only "peec't" together what Sidney left undone (in a further use of the cloth-making metaphor she employed in the poem to Elizabeth), she is also making a greater claim for her love of him, which is never done "nor can enough in world of words unfold." Her love has produced poetry. And although she suggests that her hope is that the Psalms will be known only by Sidney's name, the fact is the countess herself wrote by far the greater part of the text.

Receive theise Hymnes, theise obsequies receive;
If any marke of thy sweet sprite appeare,
Well are they borne, no title else shall beare. (85–87)

Such a gallant granting of the major authorship to her brother may well be a reference to the fact that his heroic prose romance carried her title as its title; she is returning the compliment by which he gave to her his own strange birth. If his text is always titled *The Countess of Pembroke's Arcadia*, so it may be fitting that their *Psalms* be known by the Sidney name only.

Mary Ellen Lamb takes exception to the way the second poem ends in a death wish; she finds this move fundamentally characteristic of the countess's self-limiting ambitions in her poetry.

I can no more; Deare Soule I take my leave;
Sorrowe still strives, would mount thy highest sphere
Presuming so just cause might meet thee there,
Oh Happie change! could I so take my leave.
    By the Sister of that Incomparable Sidney

Lamb writes that "The countess's concluding desire for death implies her absolute detachment from any desire to influence the affairs of this world through her writing."[25] Lamb goes on to argue that because the countess completely contradicts this desire not by taking her leave, but by writing elaborately experimental poems to be copied for circulation to the queen and publishing other works, this stated desire for death must be a cover for her writerly ambitions. "The *ars moriendi* tracts offered a model of heroism that women might emulate without violating the dominant sexual ideology," hence the countess's many texts about death and dying: "the countess's translations embody a female literary strategy through which women could be represented as heroic without challenging the patriarchal culture of Elizabethan England" (119). Lamb is concerned to articulate the strategies by which women authors circumvented the "system which contained them" (3); she sees Mary Herbert's apparent lack of ambition as one way of managing such circumvention.

However, if we see that the countess's literary conversation with her brother is in fact an affirming result of that very system of containment—that an intra-familial dialogue is the place from which an aristocratic woman may most conveniently speak, because there she not only articulates her own "desire," she also aggrandizes her family—we are in a better position, I think, to see how this conversation functions, and how it shares its power to construct both the authorities of the Countess of Pembroke and of Sir Philip Sidney. Lamb is of course right; the countess can do what she does because she has tapped into the arena of women's activity which a revised feminist anthropology has taught us is a place of great power for them—the passing on of inalienable possessions within a family at death.

The power lies at the site where the traffic in women allows certain females to take full possession of the space of endogamous halt. Allying herself with a male family member, insisting on her sibling status, the female can speak. (The rather similar sibling attachments of, for example, Dorothy Wordsworth, Christina Rossetti, and the Brontë sisters suggest that the structure may well have resonance even beyond the Renaissance.) If the woman does not speak an endogamous erotic desire, she speaks the desire to speak and to be heard, to write and to be read, and to participate in a family project (even one as large politically, at least by Greville's account in the *Life of Philip Sidney*, as the founding of the trans-Atlantic Protestant New World). Expecting her impact on the world to come through the cultural capital of her natal family does not mean that the countess fails to exercise a real agency of her own.

Lamb's objections to Mary Herbert's thanotological pacifism are understandable, for on the surface it reads so little like the kind of agency we associate with modern women's liberation and seems so assiduously to court the kind of limits the present-day feminist project seeks to overgo, specifically a containment within what we think of as the private space of the family. But as I hope is clear, the function of family and kinship in the traditional society of England during the Renaissance was very unlike nuclear family functions in the twenty-first century, and we will misread the strategies used by women of this period to capitalize on the agency their social structures did allow them if we do not take into account the extremely different kinds of social conditions at work during the time in which they wrote. Far from being a way for the countess to disguise her agency, her identification with her brother was a means to create it, just as, for Sidney, his heading his romance with his sister's title—a far grander social name than his own—helped aggrandize his text.

Not all women writers of the Renaissance fit this pattern. I do not mean to claim that the endogamous turn to consolidating power within an aristocratic kinship network was the *only* means for gaining access to public utterance. The countess's contemporary Aemelia Lanyer was a low-born woman of the artisan class who gained no position by her own family name. She found voice, however, by becoming a member of and celebrating an all-female aristocratic coterie. In *Salve Deus Rex Judaeorum*, a volume of poetry she published in 1611, Lanyer pays tribute to the Countess of Pemboke. She celebrates the countess's identification of her authority with her brother Sidney, clearly demonstrating that this attachment was no reason for another woman not to praise her. Lanyer's "Description of Cookham" in the same volume anticipates by a number of years Jonson's country-house tribute to the Sidneys, so in essence her poetic practice found a site similar to the Sidneys; her tribute to the countess reveals an acute understanding of the familial site for female homosociality, and for female literary agency.

This nymph, quoth he, great Penbrooke hight by name,
Sister to valiant *Sidney*, whoose cleere light
Gives light to all that tread true paths of Fame,
Who in the globe of heav'n doth shine so bright . . .
. . .
So that a Sister well shee may be deemd,
To him that liv'd and di'd so nobly;
And farre before him is to be esteemd
For virtue, wisdom, learning, dignity.[26]

Pamela Benson has brilliantly suggested that in her tribute, Lanyer is copying the countess's own translation of Petrarch's *Triumph of Death*.[27] The image of the chair in the poem is thus a reference to the triumphal car translated from Petrarch by the countess; as such it carries not only the image of Laura (and the lamented hero Philip Sidney), but also the book of Lanyer's own making. Lanyer's triumph is enhanced by her homosocial female connection to the countess, whose mourning for her brother Lanyer understands and appropriates.

Of course, not all early modern women writers hobnobbed with aristocrats, and even those who did were not engaged in a project of familial aggrandizement. Isabella Whitney and Elizabeth Cary are two more writers of the period for whom low birth and problematic endogamous relations provided little support for their agency. But even with Whitney and Cary, an anthropological understanding of the empowerment offered by close filial ties helps contextualize some important aspects of their work. When Whitney, for example, chooses a last will and testament form for a long poem, her choice evinces an important understanding of the traffic in women and posits the crucial intensity of the brother-sister tie as one of the firmest foundations of female agency. In the collection of poetry she published in 1567, Whitney includes two poems addressed to her brother "Brooke." In the section entitled "Certain familiar Epistels and friendly letters by the auctor: With Replies" (f. Cvii), there are also poems to her younger sisters.[28] Her poem to her brother specifically characterizes him as her mainstay in life:

But styll to friends I must appeale
(and next our Parentes deare.)
You are, and must be chiefest staffe
That I shal stay on heare. (Cvi–r)

He is not only one of her readers and but also one of the heirs to her "estate." Whitney, of course, has nothing. As a penniless laborer, she has nothing to bequeath; such a paradox provides the central conceit of her "Last Will and Testament." What she wills, then, is her poetry itself, which in terms of the trope of the dispersal of an inheritance, becomes something like an inalienable possession—a poetry she also shares with her sisters as addressees of the text. It is as if she were putting herself in the one class position in which a woman could write, bequeathing a legacy not to her close family members, but to the metropolis which, in this case, becomes kin. The city of London becomes personified as an executrix of her estate, for example; each article she bequeathes becomes an inalienable object that, in Weiner's terms, is to be kept by Whitney's heirs, not used for commerce. By such means does the "luckless" Whitney take possession of the city and her own poetic agency. So even in the case of low-born Whitney, the fiction of passing on the inalienable possessions of a proper inheritance, structures her longest poem.

Elizabeth Cary is another special case in point. She was treated with great harshness by both her own birth family and the kinship into which she married, and while it is to one of her daughters that we owe the history of her embattled life, she stands quite outside any empowering vision of the familial site. Indeed, one might say that her work aims fundamentally at exposing the horrors of an aristocratic family network. Yet, in *The Tragedy of Mariam*, a closet drama she published in 1611, we see how a woman who in both her writing and her life positively eschews her natal family still focuses on the fundamental brother-sister relationship as a most pivotal one in the text.

Like Lanyer, Cary's work in the genre of closet drama owes a great deal to the Countess of Pembroke's earlier example. Another of the countess's important works was her translation of Robert Garnier's *Marc-Antoine*, a closet drama first published in France in 1578. Often dismissed from serious critical consideration because it is a translation, the play is now recognized as part of a genre of French-inspired Senecan plays, a form that allowed writers to comment on risky political topics.[29] Barbara Lewalski lists as other examples of the genre Samuel Daniel's *Cleopatra* and *Philotas*, which was a companion piece to the countess's *Antonie*, and Fulke Greville's *Mustapha*.[30] The countess's play is the first in this line, so she may in fact be said to have introduced (like her brother) at least one continental genre. Before we go on to consider Cary's original script, it may be helpful to glance briefly at the example the countess's translation offered another female writer.

Garnier's *Marc-Antoine* is set at the historical moment immediately after Antony has fled from Actium; the countess's translation uses the blank verse style of the public stage; thus Anthony laments that Cleopatra has ruined his life:

> I honor have despised,
> Disdained my friends, and of the stately Rome
> Despoiled an empire of her best attire,
> Contemned that power that made me so much feared;
> A slave become unto her feeble face. (I.11–16) [31]

Cleopatra, for her part, takes the blame for the defeat, yet insists upon her own constancy to her lover. She also refuses to make peace with Caesar in order to protect her children. The final act V is given over to her long speeches, whose most poignant moments are her farewell remembrances of her children, just prior to her death.

> Antonie by our true loves I thee beseech—
> And by our hearts' sweet sparks have set on fire

Our holy marriage and the tender ruth
Of our dear babes, knot of our amity—
My dolefull voice thy ear let entertain
And take me with thee to the hellish plain,
Thy wife, thy friend. (V.153–59)

In this version, Cleopatra uses no asps to kill herself. She simply dies, no
Roman suicide but rather a loyal and loving wife.

Following the countess, Elizabeth Cary lodges her *Tragedy of Mariam*
at the same conjuncture of ancient history when Antony and Cleopatra
were defeated by Rome. The tragedy of Mariam is the tragedy of the
Judaean Herod's wife, the Herod Antony had befriended. When Antony is
overthrown, everyone in Judaea assumes that Caesar must have put Herod
to death, and many take the opportunity to make arrangements that they
know Herod would have opposed. When, however, Herod proves to be
still alive, he is forced upon his return, by his sister Salome's lies and by
Mariam's own resistance, to put his wife to death.

The play makes much of a comparison between Mariam and Cleopatra, in which Mariam's beauty is far superior. In some sense, Cary's insistence that Mariam was far more beautiful than Cleopatra is as remarkable
a challenge to a male-authored tradition that holds Cleopatra to be the
most alluring woman of antiquity, as was Christine de Pizan's justification
of the incestuous Semiramis in the *City of Ladies*. With ringing anaphora,
Cary rewrites Marlowe's famous praise of Helen's beauty, gives it to
Cleopatra, and then demeans it in comparison with the attractions of her
own heroine:

That face that did captive great Julius' fate,
The very face that was Anthonius' bane,
That face that to be Egypt's pride was born,
That face that all the world esteem'd so rare:
Did Herod hate, despise, neglect, and scorn,
When with the same, he Mariam's did compare. (IV.viii.546–52)

But Mariam's greatest difference from Cleopatra is her moral supe-
riority: she is chaste. And, unlike Cleopatra, her greatest mistake is to
assume that by being chaste she has fulfilled her entire duty as a wife.[32]
Her fault, attested to by everyone including Mariam herself, is that she is
(and here she is very much like Shakespeare's Cleopatra), too outspoken.[33]
In the actual plot of Cary's play, however, the cause of Mariam's vulnerability is not that she is too blunt but that she no longer shares Herod's

bed. Her ultimate revulsion against her husband is certainly understandable: not only has he twice commanded her own death (if he should
chance to be murdered in Rome), he has executed both her brother and
her grandfather. This wrong done to her natal family motivates Mariam's
refusal to continue a sexual relationship with Herod. She withholds herself from the already trafficked-in relationship, because her spouse has
broken the alliance that was presumably formed when the two families
became connected through marriage.

Thus the play opens with Mariam castigating herself for feeling any
pity at the news that Herod is dead.[34] He killed her brother, therefore any
mourning for him is unreasonable:

When Herod liv'd, that now is done to death,
Oft have I wish'd that I from him were free.
Oft have I wish'd that he might lose his breath,
Of have I wish'd his carcass dead to see.
. . .
Then why grieves Mariam Herod's death to hear?
Why joy I not the tongue no more shall speak,
That yielded forth my brother's latest doom: (I.i.15–18)[35]

With the arrival onstage of Mariam's mother in the next scene, this
theme is hammered home: Alexandra rails at her daughter's tears; she
should show no sorrow at the death of her brother's murderer, the tyrant
who has also murdered Mariam's grandfather, Alexandra's own father:

What mean these tears? My Mariam doth mistake,
The news we heard did tell the tyrant's end:
What weepst thou for thy brother's murd'rer's sake?
. . .
Did not the murder of my boy suffice,
To stop the cruel mouth that gaping stood,
But must thou dim the mild Hircanus' eyes?
My gracious father, whose too ready hand
Did lift this Idumean from the dust:
And he, ungratefull caitiff, did withstand
The man that did in him most friendly trust. (I.ii.78–96)

When Mariam finally does rebel against her husband, she cancels a duty
which the chorus and Mariam herself have seemed to accept as fully
appropriate to the function of a wife, that is, to obey and to accept her
husband's word as her primary authority.[36] She tells him directly that he
has abrogated his rights as her husband:

Your offers to my heart no ease can grant,
Except they could my brother's life restore.
No, had you wish'd the wretched Mariam glad,
Or had your love to her been truly tied:
Nay, had you not desir'd to make her sad,
My brother nor my grandsire had not died. (IV.iii.111–16)

And she sarcastically refuses to accept Herod's repentance for these acts:

Herod: Did I not show to him my earnest love,
When I to him the priesthood did restore,
And did for him a living priest remove,
Which never had been done but once before?
Mariam. I know that, mov'd by importunity,
You made him priest, and shortly after die. (IV.iii.133–38)

Herod's response to this is a fundamental statement of the husband's right (the very right Petruchio, for example, insists upon in *Taming of the Shrew*)[37]: "I will not speak, unless to be believ'd."

Miriam spends a great deal of time worrying about her own indecorous speech; she has apparently been too public in her condemnation of Antony, a fact that she laments in the very first line of the play:

How oft have I with public voice run on
To censure Rome's last hero for deceit: (I.i.1–2)

The Chorus agrees with Mariam that her major problem is an excessive publicity in her speech and behavior:

That wife her hand against her fame doth rear,
That more than to her lord alone will give
A private word to any second ear. (III.iii.227–29)

Here we see an extreme version of the tenet that chastity, silence, and obedience are inextricably linked wifely virtues, but this stricture by the Chorus still does not account for Herod's rage against Mariam. Her deepest fault is not her public speech, but that she tells him, privately, that she cannot forgive him for murdering her brother. She does not fail in chastity (in which she has, indeed, put too much faith), or in the proper observation of privacy in her speech, but in disobedience. In the Chorus's extremely conservative opinion, a wife has no right to privacy, even in her thoughts, apart from her obedience to her husband:

When to their husbands they do themselves do bind,
Do they not wholly give themselves away?
Or give they but their body, not their mind,
Reserving that, though best, for others' prey?
No sure, their thoughts no more can be their own,
And therefore should to none but one be known. (III.iii.233–38)

Herod insists upon obedience from Mariam specifically by asking her to believe that he loved her brother, even though he murdered him. It is by just such a rhetorical tour de force that Shakespeare's Richard III seduces Anne of Warwick. ("What though I killed her husband and her father? / The readiest way to make the wench amends / Is to become her husband and her father"; I.i.153–55). Mariam is not so gullible or tractable.

The play thus poses the demands on a woman to be chaste, silent, and obedient in terms of a wife's willingness to forget her loyalty to her natal family. Yet Mariam insists that this bond has its own rights. Caesar, after all, is in part motivated in his attack by Antony's neglect of Caesar's sister Octavia, the woman who was to have been the bond between them. When the bond is ill-treated, it may become a legitimate cause for war, just as Lepidus fears in Shakespeare's *Antony and Cleopatra*.[38] In the same way, if a husband murders his wife's brother, she is absolved from her vows of obedience.

Mariam's resistance to Herod because of the sibling tie she feels to her murdered kin is contrasted with Salome's claim to have felt the same. In Salome's case, however, the claim that she hates her husband because he threatened her brother Herod is mere sham. Thus Salome persuades another brother Pheroas to tell Herod the lie that she divorced her husband Constabarus because he had plotted against the king by refusing to fulfill Herod's order to execute the sons of Babas.

But tell the King that Constabarus hid
The sons of Babas, done to death before:
And 'tis no more than Constabarus did.
And tell him more that [we] for Herod's sake,
Not able to endure [our] brother's foe,
Did with a bill our separation make,
Though loath from Constabarus else to go. (III.xii.70–76)

By covering her transgression with this lie, Salome reveals in her hypocrisy the legitimacy of Mariam's own reasons for withholding her sexual favors from Herod. Presumably if Salome assumes that Herod would forgive her for arrogating to herself the freedom of a Jewish male to divorce (as long as she did it for love of her brother), then in the world of the play this familial tie deserves great fealty.

In return for her brother's lie, Salome promises to help Pheroas with his own problem with Herod, who has commanded him to marry their niece. Pheroas wishes instead to contract a marriage of the most exogamous kind: he wants to marry a slave with the very strange name of "Graphina." Margaret Ferguson and Barry Weller point out in their edition of the play that this name is original to Cary's version of the story (18), and suggest in their notes that the odd sobriquet speaks directly to the feature by which Graphina is most compellingly characterized: her silence. They argue that her name, taken together with the attribute of silence, is "intended to evoke writing (*graphesis* in Greek) as a "silent" form of speech (160 n.18). The suggestion seems to hint that to write and to publish anonymously (as Cary did) may be an acceptable way around the strictures of wifely silence and obedience. Graphina describes for Pheroas her own character-istic attitude toward female speech and obedience, which is the polar opposite of Mariam's (and Salome's). What worries Graphina is the trans-gression against his own class position which Pheroas would undertake in his exogamous marriage to her.

In my respect a princess you disdain;
Then need not all these favours study crave,
To be requited by a simple maid?
And study still you know, must silence have,
Then be my cause for silence justly weighed,
But study cannot boot nor I requite,
Except your lowly handmaid's steadfast love
And fast obedience may your mind delight,
I will not promise more than I can prove. (II.i.64–72)

Here the marriage partner who stands at an exogamous extreme (a slave) offers silence as the best means for obeying her husband. Ironically, the endogamous choice (Herod's niece) is also unable to speak, according to Pheroas, but that is because she is an "infant," a baby, literally pre-verbal: "Scarce can her infant tongue with easy voice / Her name distinguish to another's ear" (II.ii.17). She is unable to use her speech to show her obe-dience and so Pheroas abjures her, "What though she be my niece, a princess born?" Instead, he asks Graphina to speak ("Move thy tongue"), for wifely silence itself—when her husband has bid her speak—"is a sign of discontent" and disobedience. Graphina behaves the way the Chorus and Herod would have all wives behave, that is, she obeys by speaking only privately, on command of their husbands. And even here, she speaks (Cordelia-like) merely to explain why it is best to be silent.

The intermarriage Herod commands his brother to make, and which Pheroas enlists Salome's aid to avoid, is not presented as incestuous. But clearly Herod's program of consolidation of kinship and family solidarity, the reason behind his murder of Mariam's brother, requires such close-knit alliances. This part of the story is not in Lodge's translation of Josephus's *History of the Jews* (1602); the inclusion of Graphina in the drama helps to emphasize the exogamous nature of proper wifely silence, and to contrast with the endogamous foundation of legitimately transgressive wifely behavior.

In Cary's drama, Salome of course contradicts this pattern by her vehement and transgressive claims to take on the male prerogative to contract a marriage, which is excessively exogamous, to one Silleus, an Arabian prince. A foil to Mariam, as Ferguson and Weller point out, Salome is the villain of the play, an inheritor of the agency of the Vice,[39] and as such, a figure who virtually personifies Evil Female Desire. Compelling in her energy as all vices are, Salome announces her freedom to act on her own desire now that her brother is dead:

But he is dead: and though he were my brother,
His death such store of cinders cannot cast
My coals of love to quench: for though they smother
The flames a while, yet will they out at last. (I.iv.265–68)

What she proposes to do is to divorce her second husband, Constabarus, and take a new one, the Arabian prince Silleus. She well understands the revolutionary nature of the project: she will simply take upon herself the freedom that Old Testament law granted men to divorce their wives, thereby winning greater freedom for women.

If he to me did bear as earnest hate,
As I to him, for him there were an ease:
A separating bill might free his fate
From such a yoke that did so much displease.
Why should such privilege to man be given?
Or given to them, why barr'd from women then?
. . .
I'll be the custom breaker; and begin
To show my sex the way to freedom's door. (I.iv.301–10)

Anticipating Milton's arguments for divorce by thirty years, Salome
here makes an argument Mariam never even begins to imagine. (This is
not to say, of course, that the author of the drama cannot imagine it.)
Indeed, it is clear that Cary's willingness to air the possibility of justifiable
divorce is part and parcel of her meditation on just how marriage ought
to be constituted. Salome is not as revolutionary, however, as this reasoning seems; she only thinks of taking on to herself such authority because
her brother the king is dead: were he to live, she could betray her husband
Constabarus to him, and Herod would presumably have the problematic
spouse executed.

If Herod had liv'd, I might to him accuse
My present lord. But for the future's sake
Then would I tell the king he did refuse
The sons of Barabas in his power to take.
But now I must divoce him from my bed,
That my Silleus may possess his room. (I.iv.313–18)

Salome only concocts her revolutionary legal plan because her brother is
not there to execute her will. In some fundamental sense, then, the remarkable agency she arrogates to herself is a substitute for her brother's
patriarchal power. Cary places a distinct limit on this power, however, when
she has Salome reason that the law she will use is very easily manipulated:

And with an offring will I purge my sin:
The law was made for none but who are poor. (I.iv.311–12)

In so characterizing Old Testament law, Salome uncovers the fundamental nature of its limitations. The Old Law, in working by a legalistic liter-
alism, can be adjusted through various accounting practices. The New
Law instituted by Christianity, of course, makes sacrifice and the payment
of debt a different thing entirely, and Salome's reasoning here bespeaks
the need for the kind of sacrifice that Mariam will be forced to make.

Elaine Beilin usefully points out the Christological parallel in struc-
turing the details of the messenger's description of Mariam's death:

At the climax of the play is the transfiguration of Mariam: her death is an allegory
of the Crucifixion, for she foreshadows the redemption from the old law, typified
by Herod's kingdom. By transcending his earthly authority, she points to a higher
and final authority.[40]

Cary had ultimately converted to Catholicism in a spectacular revolt against
her Protestant husband, the Viscount Falkland, who virtually tortured her

with penury and with the deprivation of her children.[41] Disinherited as well by her father, Cary ended up an impoverished woman, living alone, attended by only a single loyal servant. At the time when she published *Mariam*, however, she was still a nominal Protestant and her conversion lay twelve years in the future. It is debatable then, just how the religious terms by which she corrects Salome's sedition (and therefore limits the implications of Mariam's revolt) are functioning in the play. Clearly, religion was the efficient cause of Cary's break with her own husband, but whether in *Mariam* conversion covers for female autonomy or female autonomy covers for it, is hard to judge.

As reported by the Nuncio, Mariam's death scene suggests that the freedom the heroine experiences at her execution has to do with the elusive power of speech itself. Herod asks him what Mariam said in her last moments:

O say, what said she more? Each word she said
Shall be the food whereon my heart is fed.
Nuntio. "Tell thou my lord thou saw'st me loose my breath."
Herod: Oh, that I could that sentence now control. (V.i.71–74)

Mariam's ambiguous remark makes the claim that her death, her loss of breath, is at the same time a means of freeing her speech, such as one might "loose" an arrow or a hawk to fly freely. This implication is emphasized as Herod with another pun wishes he could recall his own sentence of judgment against her, and at the same time laments that he is unable to "control" her speech—unable thus to impose a restricted meaning on her last words in which she has finally evaded her husband's control. He cannot control her speech even by killing her.[42]

The Christological parallels once again saturate the passage. Herod's wish to be fed with Mariam's words recall the very (contested) terms of the Mass whereby one feeds on the "Word" of God, either literally (in Catholic doctrine) or commemoratively and spiritually (in Protestant teaching). The resonance, however one interprets it, insists upon Herod's lack of understanding of what such words are going to mean in the future, because of the miraculous birth that will take place during his governorship (and which he will try to avoid by slaughtering the innocents).

The strangest aspect of Mariam's sacrifice is the treacherous behavior of her mother Alexandra at her execution. Having railed against her daughter for lamenting Herod's supposed death rather than vaunting over the destruction of an enemy of her family, Alexandra quickly proved a turncoat. Upon Herod's return, she counsels Mariam to make peace with him. When Mariam walks to her death, the unnatural Alexandra, to save herself, even taunts her own daughter. According to the Nuntio:

She told her that her death was too good
And that already she had liv'd too long:
She said, she sham'd to have a part in blood
Of her that did the princely Herod wrong. (V.i.41–44)

This remarkable betrayal, so convincingly contrary to any sentimental view of mothering, makes Mariam's self-sacrifice an action completely disconnected from the "blood" of her natal family. Making no answer to her mother, but merely smiling a "dutiful, though scornful smile," she apparently dismisses her own family with the same finality with which she announces to Herod with her last words that he has no ultimate control over her. Exiting the traffic in women altogether by dying, Mariam fulfills a saintly sacrifice; in this way, her story ceases to be a secular piece of history about marriage relations and becomes a sacred prophecy. The Chorus, "a company of Jews," unknowingly prophecies what the day has accomplished:

This day's events were certainly ordain'd,
To be the warning to posterity:
So many changes are therin contain'd,
So admirably strange variety. (V.i.289–92)

Ultimately disconnected from any sustained identification with either brother or mother, Mariam's sacrifice is not finally made for her family, but for what her death will mean in the future. "This day alone, our sagest Hebrews shall/In after times the school of wisdom call" (V.i.93–94). Very different from the Countess of Pembroke's family-enhancing authorial stance, Cary lodges female agency in her play within a non-familial religious discourse. It is perhaps suggestive, given this direction for the expression of female agency within the play, that three of Cary's daughters and one of her sons entered Catholic monasteries on the Continent.[43] The disavowal of family for faith that the mother writes about, her children enact in their lives.

Yet, even though Elizabeth Cary can in no way be said to lodge her sense of agency within the continuing power of her natal family, either in life or in art, her play does dramatize the importance of this connection both in instigating Mariam's rebellion and in understanding Salome's claims for such revolutionary empowerment. To ask, then, the same questions of Cary as we do of Elizabeth I and Marguerite de Navarre, the Countess of Pembroke and Mary Wroth, is to discover alternative answers to interesting cruxes in her work. That Cary ultimately goes beyond the language of endogamous halt suggests the power that religious discourse has to counter the power of the family as a means for assisting female authority. Just as, in *The Tragedy of Mariam*, the Jewish heroine may be said to be transformed into an agent of Christian prophecy, leaving both her families behind, so one of the author's daughters will write her mother's life from the confines of a convent in Cambray, safe, in that very traditional haven, from the silencing powers of the traffic in women.

5

Spenser's Britomart

LIKE MANY OF SHAKESPEARE'S comic heroines, Spenser's Britomart exercises immense agency while dressed as a man. She travels without being traded; she goes into battle, rescuing both women and men; she is neither silent nor obedient. And she is doing everything in her considerable power to locate the man who will put a proper end to her chastity. So full and "modern" does her agency seem that for neophyte readers of Spenser it is often difficult to read "allegorically." She seems to inhabit an ontological space very different from the Redcrosse Knight or Guyon, whose existence as characters fades before her greater substantiality. Even Spenser's narrator seems to be blinded by her presence and notoriously confuses the male knights, forgetting for a moment that it is the Redcrosse Knight and not Guyon who accompanies Britomart in Book III on her first adventure in the Castle Joyeous.[1]

But Britomart's character, far from realistic, is a remarkable amalgam of traditional literary figures and historical negotiations; she takes her nature most immediately from Ariosto's and Tasso's woman warriors, who of course are descendants of Virgil's Camilla and the post-Homeric Penthesilea.[2] And as we have recently come to recognize, Britomart also owes a great deal to Spenser's problematic shadowing of his first reader, Queen Elizabeth, whom he invites in the proem to Book III to see herself reflected in "mirrors more than one."[3] Britomart is unlike the virgin Elizabeth, however, whose "two bodies" are represented in Spenser's epic by two entirely different characters: Belphoebe, who represents the queen's private chastity, and Gloriana, who figures forth her public rule. Britomart is motivated by an overriding erotic desire of the most active and pointedly dynastic sort. Indeed, her love quest is exogamous to such an extreme that it almost comes full circle and precipitates itself back into endogamy: she falls in love with an image she sees in the magic mirror that Merlin made for her father, King Ryence. The heroine's father nowhere figures in the poem. Britomart keeps her love a secret from him and the narrator specifically tells us that Britomart sneaks away to seek her lover without King Ryence's knowledge. However, the fact that Britomart first develops her passion by looking in a mirror magically constructed to enable her father to view threats to his kingdom suggests that her sight of her lover there (while contained within the parameters of a specifically patriarchal power) is being coded as just such a threat.

I have argued elsewhere that the comedy attached to Britomart is a way of limiting the menace her power as a warrior would otherwise pose: although a knight on a quest, she is a fundamentally comic heroine who, like Viola and Rosalind after her, gives us occasions for laughter, as when, for example, she is lustily pursued by Malecasta, or when she pines away for love of a man she has never seen in the flesh. In this approach, Spenser follows most closely the risible delights of his precursor, Ariosto.[4] But buried within the comedy of Britomart's excessively Petrarchan infection by the disease of love is a remarkable signal to the incestuous substratum which underlies all such engagements of active female agency in this period. As we shall see, when Spenser borrows language from Ariosto's Fiordespina, who laments a monstrous same sex-passion for Bradamante, he is recasting Ariosto's materials and unintentionally demonstrating the close connections between incest and same sex desire, as parallel evasions of the proper traffic in women.

That Spenser doubles the virginal Belphoebe (the praiseworthy exemplary of Elizabeth's chastity) with Britomart, whose agenda is actively and aggressively sexual, suggests his critique and containment of the power of the queen's virginity. Spenser, of course, had had his part to play in the fracas over the Anjou match. Working as Leicester's secretary at the time, Spenser had dedicated the *Shepheardes Calender* to Philip Sidney; he also published an episode in his Chaucerian *Mother Hubbard's Tale* that clearly registered criticism of the match. As we have seen, he collaborated with the Countess of Pembroke on the publication of the collection of elegies for Sir Philip Sidney, and may even have acted as coauthor with her of the "Lay of Clorinda." He is, at the very least, its presenter in that volume. He was distinctly a client of the Sidney-Leicester-Essex group; indeed the Earl of Essex paid the expenses of Spenser's funeral only three years before he himself was executed. This is not to say that Spenser's critique of Elizabeth's power was solely motivated by his loyalty to his patrons; he was most closely allied to Sir Walter Raleigh, who stood apart from that faction. But his closeness to this family grouping does suggest not only that they had a true eye for poetic talent, but also that Spenser

shared with them a cultural concern for the problematic status of Eliza-
beth's anomalous female agency within Elizabethan society. Named for
Elizabeth, the epic could not escape concern with the disruption of the
Tudor traffic in women which her female sovereignty posed her culture.

Britomart

Unlike the heroes of the other books of *The Faerie Queene*, in Britomart
in Book III does not appear to visit the Templar center of her particular
"virtue," and therefore receives no direct vision of that which empowers
her. In this (as in her sex) she is anomalous. The Redcrosse Knight is
treated to a vision of the New Jerusalem in the House of Holiness in
Book I. Guyon and Arthur both spend time at the House of Alma and
there read their respective histories in Book II. In Book V, Britomart does
have a vision in Isis Church, which articulates the appropriate dynamics
of the virtue of Justice, but the vision makes clear how her power limits
Justice, and for that virtue Artegall and not Britomart is the central warrior. Even Calidore is allowed a brief glimpse of the power of poetic form
in Book VI before he inadvertently destroys it. The anomalous form of
Book III makes it most like the hero-less, more "Ariostan" interlace of
Book IV, where the marriage of the Medway and the Thames might be
considered the allegorical "core," but it is a site that no individual character visits.

The Garden of Adonis, in Book III has a "Templar" experience at its
center, but Britomart does not go to the Garden. Indeed, it is difficult to
specify the relationship of this allegorical essence to the virtue of chastity
the heroine represents. Of course, Britomart is elsewhere in the presence
of the myth of Venus and Adonis, for it is represented on the tapestries
she views at Castle Joyeous, so it is clear that the story of Adonis—both
in malo and *in bono*—has a great deal to do with whatever we are to understand the chastity of Book III to be about.

It is possible to draw many filiations between the titular character
and the Garden of Adonis; among them, the garden points to the fact that
Britomart's chastity is not to remain virginal but to embody a married
chasteness that includes within it the full force of sexual desire: the garden
is a setting for the eroticism that powers the eternally fecundating cycles
of sexuality. But the most direct textual link between Britomart and the
myth of Adonis is far more problematic than any shared sense of the

philosophical centrality, if not the virtual sacredness, of sexual activity. This link bears directly on the problem of incest that haunts active female desire, a monstrous overblown desire emblemized by the incestuous giantess Argante. That the text chooses to contain the threat with comedy only heightens the fact of its presence at the origin of Britomart's erotic arousal.

In canto ii, the narrator gives us a flashback to the origin of Britomart's quest in faerieland to find Artegall; in this backstory we are treated to a comic view of the heroine's falling in love with an image in a looking glass. The comic tone of this fairy tale moment is made obvious by the bathos of the language used to figure forth what ought to be a magical and mysterious enchantment:

> The damzell well did vew his personage
> And liked well, ne further fastned not,
> But went her way; ne her vnguilty age
> Diud weene, vnwares, that her vnlucky lot
> Lay hidden in the bottom of the pot;
> Of hurt vnwisht most daunger doth redound:
> But the false Archer, which that arrow shot,
> So slyly, that she did not fele the wound,
> Did smyle full smoothly at her weetless wofull stound. (III.ii.26)

In essence, Britomart, having seen the desired figure in the mirror, takes contagion from the fact that "the faire visage" is now "written in her heart." This process of writing on or in a heart later becomes more tragically literalized in the baroque conceit of Amoret's torture, which Britomart must overcome in the final moment of her quest in Book III. So this earlier comic moment may be seen as the origin of that knightly challenge. But while the plight of Amoret is delivered with all high seriousness, this one is funny: "lot" and "pot" is too bathetic a rhyme for rendering Merlin's world of glass to leave its high Arthurian solemnity undeflated.

Linda Gregerson has analyzed Britomart's gaze into the specular surface in her father's closet as an originary moment for the "Reformation" subject; that is, she takes this incident (as well as Eve's gazing into Narcissus's pool in Book V of *Paradise Lost*) to be the inaugurating moment for a "Protestant" subject. Making reference to Jacques Lacan's theory of the mirror phase to underscore the way that these moments are originary for early modern subject formation, Gregerson identifies the desire revealed to Britomart as the tricky negotiation of relations between a fantasized whole self and the equally idealized other.[5]

While Gregerson's main concern is Protestant theories of images and therefore of representation, she points out the fact of monstrosity that underpins the origins of Britomart's desire, and suggests how extremes of endogamy and exogamy may be akin. In so doing she usefully pinpoints the theoretical parallels between the endogamies of incest and "unnatural" same sex relations as alternatives to the proper dynastic traffic in women.[6]

Chastity's exemplary pathway moves between excessive likeness (the incestuous primary family, the narcissistic gaze) and excessive difference (the outlandish margins of exogamy). Time and again . . . Spenser makes the case that love's two versions of monstrous trespass are structurally implicit in one another. (70)

Gregerson reads Britomart's saga as an antitype of Malbecco and Hellenore's, a narrative that outlines the "traffic" in women, or, more properly put, the way women function in the imaginations of men. Even if it is true that *The Faerie Queene* cannot offer (as Gregerson complains) any real insight about the "psychic, social, or erotic behaviors and imaginations of women," as "Spenser is no feminist" (52), nonetheless, Britomart's saga has much to tell us about the culture in which his contemporaneous female authors lived—especially those who, like Mary Wroth, read his poem quite carefully, and sympathetically. As we shall see, Wroth will rewrite the scene of Amoret's torture and rescue in *The Countess of Mountgomerie's Urania*.[7] Indeed, so compelling to this female reader and writer was this moment in Spenser, that she rewrote it two separate times[8] In order to understand what Wroth does with the scene, it will be useful to consider Spenser's preparation for it in some detail.

Again, Britomart's own articulation of the process of falling in love is expressed with comic bathos, and Spenser continues to insist that we look at our heroine's emotions humorously. For example, he creates an unusual scene when staging Britomart's conversation with her nurse about love, in which the two women discuss the effects of Petrarchan conceits. Despite its humor, what they have to say to each other is fundamental to Spenser's agenda in Book III. Britomart refuses to be cheered by Glauce's optimistic counsel (the nurse has argued that the heroine's wound, because it has no real cause—but came merely from a mirror—can be cured):

Nor man it is, nor outher liuing wight:
    For then some hope I might vnto me draw,
    But only th'shade and semblant of a knight,
    Whose shape or person yet I neuer saw,
    Hath me subiected to loue's cruell law:

The same one day, as me misfortune led,
I in my father's wondrous mirrhour saw,
And pleased with that seeming goodly-hed,
Vnwares the hidden hooke with baite I swallowed.

Sithens it hath infixd faster hold
    Within my bleeding bowels, and so sore
    Now ranckleth in this same fraile fleshly mould,
    That all mine entrailes flow with poysnous gore.
    And th'vlcer groweth daily more and more:
    Ne can my running sore find remedie. (III.ii.38–39)

Glauce's response to Britomart's lament addresses the excessiveness of
her Petrarchan metaphor: "why make ye such a Monster of your mind?"
Her response is not really monstrous; it is perfectly natural, according to
Glauce, that she should fall in love with "the semblant pleasing most your
mind"; what would be truly monstrous would be to do as certain women
have done. Glauce's list is instructive.

Not so th'Arabian Myrrhe did set her mind;
    Nor so did Biblis spend her pining hart,
    But lou'd her natiue flesh against all kind,
    And to their purpose vsed wicked art: (III.ii.40–41)

Britomart's love is to be distinguished from Myrrha's incestuous love
for her father Cinyras, or Biblis's for her brother, or Pasiphaë's for a bull.
Britomart's progeny will be Britain's kings. In contrast, Pasiphaë's coupling with a bull produced a monster, the Minotaur. And the offspring of
Myrrha's incestuous intercourse with her father was none other than the
boy Adonis. A product of incest, Adonis inspires in the far more mature
Venus an engulfing love that is like that of a mother for her child, and
so itself seems like incestuous desire. The Venus-Adonis story is narrated
twice in Book III, and is connected with the story of Venus's search for her
son Cupid. Indeed, the interchangeability of Adonis and Cupid throughout the narrative of Book III insists upon the haunting mother-son incest
that answers the father-daughter incest out of which Adonis was created.

    C. S. Lewis long ago remarked upon the crucially problematic "skep-
tophilia" that marks the tapestries of Venus and Adonis—a lust of the eyes
that represents Malecasta's unchastity as well as the very procedure by
which the viewer looks at the tapestries.[9] The ekphrastic analysis of the
tapestries forces the reader to enact, in slow motion as it were, the problematic "skeptophilic" gaze that is powerfully erotic in its parcelization of

body parts. Just as Malecasta attempts to bed the sleeping Britomart, Venus entices the boy to sleep. Once he ceases to move, he becomes a static image; then she bathes him, and cradles him in her arms.

And while he slept, she ouer him would spread
    Her mantle, colour'd like the starry skyes
    And with ambrosiall kisses bathe his eyes;
    And whilest he bath'd, with her two crafty spyes,
    She secretly would search each daintie lim, (III i.336)

Like the "gaze" of classical cinema theorized by Laura Mulvey, this remarkable visual scrutiny by Venus anatomizes Adonis, dissecting his body into separate parts like a series of close-ups to be gazed upon one by one.[10] Usually only the purview of a male spectator, Spenser grants this objectifying vision to the dominant female, Venus, as she peruses an adolescent male body. In a fundamental sense, the tragedy woven on the tapestries works itself out in terms of mother-son relations. Venus sees Adonis's desire to hunt the boar as a mere game, "cruell play"—as if Adonis were a child—and she warns him against it, to no avail. He is gored by the boar and dies. In the stanza in which he languishes from what is, essentially, an emasculating wound, the reader inherits the position of the gazing Venus, the seeing agent, directly addressed by the narrator:

Lo, where beyond he lyeth languishing,
    Deadly engored of a great wild Bore,
    And makes him endlesse mone, and euermore
    With her soft garments wipes away the gore,
    Which stanes his snowy skin with hatefull hew:
    But when she saw no helpe might him restore,
    He to a dainty flowre she did transmew,
Which in that cloth was wrought, as if it liuely grew. (III. i. 38)

Gazing on the transformed Adonis, the reader assents to the powerful capacity of art to represent nature, even to supersede it, so that by Venus's magic weaving the dying Adonis is turned into a work of art, one which appears to live. By the metamorphosis of her art, Venus is able to arrest the process of death and to turn Adonis into a flower—which, when represented on the tapestry, looks alive.

Sight, as opposed to vision, is a fundamental problem from the opening cantos of Book III—it is "Gardante" who wounds Britomart in the Castle Joyeous—and the incertitude of sight is being interpreted for us from the moment we see the heroine gazing into Merlin's globe. Is the mirror a "pot" or is it a globe? Is it a comical fairy tale bromide, or is it a carrier, like Aeneas's shield, of a heroic destiny? The object itself, the magic mirror, is spelled by Spenser "mirrhour," and this word tantalizingly recalls Myrrha, the daughter who, by committing incest with her father, created Adonis. The problem of the threatening agency of female desire continues to haunt the story of the origins of Britomart's pursuit of her erotic destiny throughout the book.

It is Glauce, a comic character (on whom Shakespeare may have predicated Juliet's laughable nurse) who contains the threat posed by this haunting speculum. Concerned about Britomart's lovesickness, Glauce undertakes to "cure" it with a witch-like spell, which is comic not only because it is ineffectual, but also because it is so absurdly ritualistic. In her old woman's magic, the lowly "pot" makes its amusing return.

> But th'aged nurse her calling to her bowre,
> Had gathered Rew, and Sauine, and the flowre
> Of Camphora, and Calamint, and dill,
> All which she in an earthen Pot did poure,
> And to the brim with Colt wood did it fill,
> And many drops of milke and bloud through it did spill.

> Then taking thise three hairs from off her head,
> Them trebly braded in a threfold lace,
> Around about the pots mouth, bound the thread,
> And after having whispered a space
> Certaine sad words, with hollow voice and base,
> She to the virgin said, thrise sais she it;
> Come daughter come, come: spit vpon my face,
> Spit thrise vpon me, thrise vpon me spit:
> Th'unenven number for this business is most fit. (III ii.49–50)

The Variorum long ago noted that Glauce's herbal recipe is one for barrenness and, had the spell worked, Spenser's dynastic plans for Britomart (and his imitation of Ariosto) would have been precipitated into disaster. It does not work, of course, for such "idle charmes" cannot remove a love properly rooted in a noble breast—or in a proper womb like Britomart's. Merlin's laughter dismisses Glauce's weak witchery.

> The wisard could not lenger beare her bord,
> But brusting forth in laughter, to her sayd;
> Glauce, what needs this colourable word,
> To cloke the cause, that hath it selfe bewrayd? (III.iii.19)

Merlin redefines Britomart's looking in the glass as a vision of providence:

It was not, Britomart, thy wandring eye,
　　Glauncing vnwares in charmed looking glas,
　　But the streight course of heauenly destiny,
　　Led with etnerall prouidence, that has
　　Guided thy glaunce, to bring his will to pass. (III.iii.24)

Her gaze, in other words, was not "skeptofilia"—not the gaze of erotic
dismemberment and mastery—but a true vision of the whole unfolding
future in which dynastic generations will end in the imperial rule of Elizabeth I. Elizabeth's own barrenness, of course, poses Merlin (and Spenser)
a terrific narrative headache, and with her the wizard necessarily ends his
prophecy:

But yet the end is not. There *Merlin* stayed,
As ouercomen of the spirites power,
Or other ghastly spectacle dismayed,
That secretly he saw, yet note discoure.
Which sudden fit, and halfe extatick stoure
When the two fearefull women saw, they grew
Greatly confused in behauioure; (III.iii.50)

　　As is typical of allegory, the subsequent narrative of the Garden of
Adonis provides a gloss on the genealogy Merlin has given, explaining how
generation occurs, and how generations can succeed each other down
through the ages, so that they may culminate in the virgin Elizabeth (who
will end the series with her problematic chastity). The return appearance of
this generational narrative now takes a different perspective on Venus's
power to halt time, first expressed in her transformation of Adonis into a
flower within Malecasta's tapestries. The garden is a fecund and a logical
place for a portrayal of the cycles of sexual generation, very different from
the ekphrastic stasis of the tapestry at Castle Joyeous. In Spenser's garden,
a medievalized Neoplatonic theory makes substance or matter eternal while
the forms themselves die.[11] This constructs the feminine substratum as the
indestructible, permanent element, while Adonis, the masculine Father of
Forms, becomes the element that dies and is reborn. In the earlier ekphrastic episode of the tapestry, Venus stops the natural process of Adonis' dying
and transmutes him into a static objet d'art. In the Garden of Adonis, another kind of temporal stasis allows for the "happy" ending, as if the metamorphosis of Adonis can be achieved simply by rewriting the myth.

This second version of Venus and Adonis's love is predicated on a huge subjunctive: "But were it not that time their troubler is." Spenser here creates the stasis achieved by ekphrasis through a very different means: by obliterating the image of a personified Time beating down the flowers with his "flaggy" wings, and offering in its place a strangely subjunctive narrative, for with "were it not that Time their troubler is" Spenser is able to contradict the fact of Adonis's mortality. The scene that follows Spenser's remarkable statement imagines in sexual terms what an undying materiality would be like. Read out in terms of the myth of Adonis, this subjunctive fantasy can take place because of Venus's restraint of the boar within the cave that is hewn underneath the Mount of Venus in the Garden. As Lauren Silberman slyly remarks, one has to be impressed by the stamina of Venus's lover here, for the eternality of the never fading flower of the tapestry now resides in a continuous copulation, the phallic (and death-dealing) boar penned in continuous contact with Venus's fecundating powers, housed in the cave beneath the Mount of Venus.[12]

I have elsewhere argued that, seen from the point of view of the collectivity of female readers whom Spenser signals so overtly at the outset of the canto, the Garden of Adonis may appear a place of delightful pleasure where sexual intercourse takes place eternally with a never failing lover. In contrast, when seen from the point of view of a male reader, the landscape appears profoundly threatening: the symbolic detachment of the boar from Adonis's body can be read only as another version of the boar's wounding him, that is, a castration.[13]

What is interesting about the placement of this canto in a book about Chastity, in which Britomart is the protagonist (in which she wounds Marinell and is herself wounded), is the central place it gives to female sexuality. The subject is one that is usually, in this period, repressed off the surface of a text, or at least delivered *in malo*. But unlike the cave of Night, for instance, or the cave of Error, here is a cave that is presumably good. What is the relationship of this vision of female generative power to the agency of Britomart?

We may find a key to what Spenser is doing here in the fact that the Garden is the place where Amoret was raised. We putatively arrive at the Garden in answer to the question of how Belphoebe could be the way she is. But instead of telling us about Belphoebe's nurture by Diana, the narrator shows us instead the place where Venus raised Belphoebe's twin sister Amoret. By switching his focus to Belphoebe's sister, Spenser prepares for the remarkable scene in which Britomart rescues Amoret from her torture by Busyrane. And it is in this sense that Britomart does "visit" the Templar center of her book: her visit to the chamber is where she undoes the spell through which Amoret, a character nurtured by the Garden, is held captive in the most perverse kind of sexual torture.

The scene of Amoret's torture is a central one for understanding what it is that Britomart accomplishes and how that achievement connects to Spenser's allegory. Gordon Teskey, one of the most recent critics to grapple with the problem that the scene poses, elevates it beyond a mere quirk of Spenser's into a fundamental fact about allegory itself. His argument is so suggestive that it bears rehearsal in some detail. Teskey's analysis goes a long way toward illuminating the peculiar kind of female agency that haunts any allegory (with its female personifications of vices and virtues). While Teskey does not address Spenser's earlier meditation on the problem of female sexuality in the Garden, his discussion of Amoret may help us to understand what is at issue in Book III as a whole.

In Teskey's terms, the scene of Amoret's torture is one of "capture," where allegory makes clear the epistemological "violence" that is at the heart of the trope of personification. Because personification is a trope by which abstractions, figured as masculine in Western philosophy, take on the narrative agency of material bodies, and is often imagined as feminine, the mode of prosopopreia (or personification) requires a violent appropriation of female materiality by male abstraction. The trace of this violent capture lies in the characteristic predication of the feminine gender to refer to personifications of abstractions. Thus the personification Justice, who engages in just actions, is a woman; Boethius's Philosophy is a woman who carries books; in *Roman de la Rose*, Lady Reason is a woman who offers reasonable arguments. But what happens, according to Teskey, in the scene of Amoret's torture—and in Dante's confrontation of Francesca da Rimini in the fifth canto of the *Commedia*—is that we see this process of capture caught halfway.

In the more powerful allegorical works this prevenient violence is unexpectedly revealed at moments that are so shocking in their honesty that they are consistently misread as departures from allegorical expression. Such moments literalize a metaphor from Neoplatonism, the moment of raptio, or "seizing," in which Matter perversely resisting the desire of the male, must be ravished by Form before being converted and returned to the Father. We are confronted with a struggle in which the rift between heterogeneous others is forced into view. The woman continues forever to resist being converted into an embodiment of the meaning that is imprinted on her.[14]

Paul Alpers long ago noted that the stanza of Amoret's torture was a central moment for Spenser's poetic:

And her before the vile Enchaunter sate,
Figuring straunge characters of his arte,
With liuing bloud he those characters wrate,
Dreadfully dropping from her dying hart,
Seeming transfixed with a cruell dart,
And all perforce to make her him to loue,
Ah who can loue the worker of her smart?
A thousand charmes he formerly did proue;
Yet thousand charmes could not her stedfast heart remoue. (III.xii.31)

Teskey agrees that the moment is pivotal, and summarizes: "In a literary genre concerned more than any other with the metaphysical implications of gender, such moments are infrequent. It is more broadly characteristic of allegory—though by no means more true of it—for violence such as this to be concealed so that the female will appear to embody, with her whole body, the meaning that is imprinted on her. When this occurs, we have personification" (19).

Such an argument not only makes a more powerful case than the gender of Latin nouns for the otherwise odd reliance on so many female agents in allegorical narratives, it also points to what it is that Amoret *cannot* be made to represent, and, therefore what Britomart achieves by freeing her from this capture. If Teskey is right, it makes sense that readers have found it difficult to locate the exact motivation of the scene of Amoret's torture. While Amoret cannot be guilty herself of the transgressions for which we see her being punished, it is equally difficult to see how Spenser can escape the guilt that Busyrane exhibits in this writerly torture.[15] As Harry Berger has succinctly put it: the "busy-reign of the male imagination becomes busier and more frenzied as the feminine will recoils in greater disdain or panic."[16] Teskey's point about the gender question here is that by envisioning Amoret's torture Spenser is only being honest about the machinery of his genre. Busyrane is not at fault in this scene; allegory is. Allegory—at least here—is held responsible for its necessary (and violent) appropriation of a female-gendered materiality. In Teskey's formulation, "material in allegory [is] that which gives meaning a place to occur but which does not become meaning itself" (19). For women to be the material site of meaning when they can have no access to that meaning situates allegorical processes within the same problematic for female agency that Lévi-Strauss exposed by saying that men use woman as signs in the semiotic system of kinship but women cannot speak for themselves in that system.

Such a congruence between modern anthropological theory and Renaissance philosophy should alert us to the density of significance in Spenser's scene. It also makes more significant what Teskey necessarily neglects to consider (he is not writing a commentary on Spenser's poem). Amoret is not the only female agent in Spenser's scene. Britomart's presence makes all the difference. Because she is there, Amoret's situation is different from that of Dante's Francesca, where instead of a female in full battle dress, there is a doubled male poetic tradition in the persons of Virgil and Dante. Teskey also tends to slide by a problematic part of the issue he uncovers in his discussion of the parallel scene in Dante. He notes that, like Spenser with Amoret, Dante lays bare the workings of allegory in the Paolo and Francesca scene: "In reading the episode it is of some importance not to mistake which sin is reaching out to Francesca to make her its mask. Given the authority with which the word *lust* has been applied to her, it should be noted that the word *lussuria* is used in the canto only to characterize Semiramis, a rather special case" (26).

But what Teskey does not explore is that Dante has chosen Francesca's company very carefully; what she and Semiramis—the quintessential exemplar of mother-son incest—have in common is a female sexual desire that is fully enacted. *Any* fully active female desire is thus portrayed as being as frightening as Semiramis's trammeling of the law against mother-son incest; Semiramis "libito fé licito in sua legge"; she made lust licit in her laws. As we have seen in her appearance at the opening of Christine de Pizan's *Book of the City of Ladies*, Semiramis is a "special" case only in that she names what is horrifying about active female desire itself. All the laws of exchange require a quiescent female desire that will passively follow the traffic path chosen by males. When Francesa resists capture, thereby insisting on her own residual agency, Dante warns us against that agency by associating her with Semiramis' transgression of the incest taboo. Spenser likewise confronts the power of maternal female sexuality in the scene in which Britomart makes Busyrane reverse his verses and so heal Amoret's wound. If I am correct in the following suggestion, Spenser's choice here is a unique moment in early modern literature and makes his "honesty" of a sort that defies categorization; it is of a far more scandalous quality than Teskey would probably want to claim. In this scene, Amoret's heart is withdrawn from her chest cavity and placed in a bowl of blood:

At that wide orifice her trembling hart
Was drawne forth, and in siluer basin layd,
Quite through transfixed with a deadly dart,
And in her bloud yet steeming fresh embayd. (III.xii.21)

It is this "wound" that Britomart makes disappear:

The creull steele, which thrild her dying hart,
Fell softly forth, as of his owne accord,
And the wide wound, which lately did dispart
Her bleeding brest, and riuen bowels gor'd,
Was closed vp, as it had not been bor'd,
And euery part to safety full sound,
As she were neuer hurt, was soone restor'd:
Tho when she felt her selfe to be unbound
And perfect hole, prostrate she fell vnto the ground. (III.xii.38)

Many readers have assumed that the softly falling dart recalls the postcoital detumescence of the human male penis. And many readers have also noticed that being rendered perfectly "hole" does not mean that Amoret is no longer penetrable; though virginal, she is still capable of intercourse, that womanly potential being indeed her characteristic quality. But what no readers appear to have remarked is that the horrifyingly large and gaping wound that closes up to a normal "hole," from which formerly protruded a large and detached bloody object, very accurately mimes the gory actualities of childbirth. In childbirth, an internal body part does seem to be torturously extruded from the female vagina, which, rather startlingly, then returns to its former state and without a death-dealing amount of pain. (We should remember that the stanza does not describe the heart's reinsertion into the body, but simply the closure of the opening, as if the point is not to reinsert the pulsing organ but simply to close the "wide wound.")

To suggest this new understanding of one aspect of Amoret's "torture" is not seriously to revise our traditional interpretation of what Busyrane is attempting to do to her, or why. It may serve instead as one more way of seeing his attempt to textualize Amoret's experience; that is, to turn Amoret's physical, material experience into a poetic text by borrowing her fecund, bodily-based creativity in order to make poetry of his own. To see the healing that Britomart helps to achieve as imaging what happens to the female body at the moment of giving birth is, however, to see in a new and useful way what Britomart learns from attending on

Amoret. This moment of magically self-healing physical protrusion (this bloody creativity) is precisely where Britomart's own heroically erotic energies are leading her. (We are given a briefest glimpse of this moment of parturition in Book V, when Britomart dreams of giving birth to a lion in Isis Church.)

What is shocking about Spenser's "honesty" is that, in this interpretation, he is giving us an unusually close look at the details of childbirth, as they might be observed by a witness, as he may well have himself observed them (or, possibly, only bowls of blood being taken out of the birthing room). For example, during the earlier Cupid's pageant that Britomart watches, we see Amoret walked between the figures of Cruelty and Despight; the action is not far from a midwife's usual treatment of a laboring woman, who would be walked during some of her early contractions. When the narrator asks, "Ah who can love the worker of her smart?" the text contains an awareness that there is a kind of pain (caused by an infant's birth), in which a woman can love the one who causes her that pain.

Amoret patiently resists Busyrane's textualization in this least textual of all moments in human experience. (One might well imagine that the multiform metamorphoses of Busyrane's tapestries, representing a male god's repeated transformation, mimic the all too visible but seldom represented changes in the female human body both before and after birth.) This is not to suggest that Spenser's concerns are purely focused on the materiality of the female body to the neglect of the nature of poetic language. As many have noted, what is at issue in Busyrane's torture is the nature of Petrarchan discourse. But as his name suggests, Busyrane is dealing not only with physical pain but, in Spenser's usually punning manner, with the very question of the trope of "abuse" in language, that is, in George Puttenham's discussion of overly strained metaphor, catachresis.

But if for lacke of natural and proper term or worde we take another, neither natural nor proper and do untruly applie it to the thing which we would seeme to express, and without an iust convenience, it is not then spoke by this figure *Metaphore* or of *inversion* as that before, but by plaine abuse, as he that bad his man go into his library and get him his bowe and arrows.[17]

As Lisa Freinkel explains, those critics actually misunderstand the term when they take Puttenham's discussion of "abuse" to mean an extreme torture of language away from its proper meanings. Puttenham's definition implies that "abuse" is a figure for *all* uses of language that twist words away from their literal meanings (160). The proper rhetorical term for this, as Freinkel points out, is "catechresis," but like Teskey's argument about "personification" in allegory, what is illuminated in Busyrane's torture is the cost to the literal that such a procedure entails. The elision of childbirth into an image of the bleeding heart would be such a catachrestic procedure. If one thinks of the opening sonnets of Sidney's *Astrophil and Stella* and of Spenser's own *Amoretti*, we see this procedure in play: superimposed on the metaphor of male poetic parturition (the creation of a literary work being often referred to as "giving birth") is a vision of inscriptions on the heart. Thus Sidney tells us he is "great with child to speak and helpless" in his "throes" until his muse tells him to "look in thy heart and write." So too, Spenser tropes his opening poem by having his own words "written with tears in heart's close bleeding book."

Spenser, however, may also be signaling us in Book III to be aware of such problematic issues as actual material impregnation and the pains of parturition within a narrative about chaste female agency. He prepares us for this by the oddity of Amoret's mother's impregnation by the Sun and then her painless birthing in the Garden of Adonis. Having slept through both, Chyrsogonee conceives without pleasure, and thus without pain gives birth. She unconsciously produces the twins Amoret and Belphoebe in a trance; the physical details of the delivery are skimmed over, as if the only details that might be given would necessarily include the pains of childbirth itself.[18]

The sunne-beames bright vpon her body playd,
Being through former bathing mollifed,
And pierst into her wombe, where they embayd
With so sweet sence and secret power vnspide,
That in her pregnant flesh they shortly fructified. (III vi.7)
Faire Crysogone in slombry traunce whilere:
Who in her sleepe (a wondrous thing to say)
Vnwares had borne two babes as faire as springing day.
Vnwares she them conceiu'd, vnwares she bore: (III.vi.26–27)

These twin scenes of sexual conception and parturition are both rehearsed once more, this time with the full consciousness of all participants, in the bloody wound of Amoret's torture, which is both the virginal bloodletting of first intercourse and the ultimate act of blood flow in the culminating childbirth. We so often associate bleeding with the cruelty of mortal violence that we seldom think of it as being so basic a part of natural processes. The blood streaming through Cupid's tapestries gestures toward his hideous cruelty in the masque at Busyrane's castle, when he seems voyeuristically to enjoy her torture. But Cupid is also the infant son of Venus, the little putto who could hide himself among Diana's attendants in the Garden of Adonis, where Amoret herself is a newborn babe. Some blood flows are creative rather than destructive.

If allegory usually occludes the violence against the female that Spenser here reveals, it is because, in Teskey's terms, matter resists appropriation by the realm of abstraction. In some fundamental sense, the absolutely least abstract activity one might figure forth a female character doing is giving birth. Another version of the childbirth scene—in which violence and evil deform the good of this natural process—is the threshold moment of the entire epic, and the source of Milton's incestuous Sin. It is when the Redcrosse Knight fights with the mother-monster Error, whose progeny are first found nursing at her body; these young finally crawl back into her mouth after the battle, only to explode in self-destruction when they gorge themselves on her blood. Drinking her blood, they enact the trope so often associated with incest, that the incestuous offspring "eats" the parent's flesh. In Book I, the book of Holiness, this monstrous threshold text of physical birth and nursing becomes an evil counterpart, mothering *in malo*, to spiritual rebirth. In Canto x, just before Contemplation christens the knight St. George, he is reborn into faith after a spiritual death suffered in despair, overseen by the maternal figure of Charissa in the House of Holiness, at whose breasts numerous babes suckle. In a sense, Error's book-filled vomit reveals her as fixed, captured, a full-flown personification, her female agency textualized, with the physical aspects rendered so much *in malo* that it is truly nauseating to read.[19] The spontaneous generation Spenser associates with the River Nile makes an appearance there as well, although the shapes are monstrous and double-sexed. In contrast, the book of married chastity—which celebrates the origin of the Tudor dynasty—sees physical, material birth itself as very much a good thing. If figurative rebirth is at the core of the regeneration of Holiness, in the book of Chastity a catachrestic representation of birth —which reprises the act of intercourse—might well provide an appropriate Templar experience for the heroine. Birth is viewed not as a nauseating monstrosity but as something that—however bloody and terrifying—is mythologically sublime and can be survived, indeed quite easily so.

Britomart's witnessing of Amoret's torture is clearly pivotal for our understanding of what it is she accomplishes on her quest. She might instead have attended on the moment that envisages generativity by having her watch Genius let the souls in and out of the two gates in the Garden of Adonis. Such a scene would have given Britomart a Calidore-like vision of a ceremonious allegorized display, representing the parturition, death, and reiterative reclothing in permanent flesh of the many impermanent forms. Her own prophesied birth-giving would then be an initiating instance in one particular dynastic sequence of this process.

> For in the wide wombe of the world there lyes,
> In hatefull darkenesse and in deepe horrore,
> An huge eternall Chaos, which supplyes
> The substances of natures fruitfull progenyes.

> All things from thence doe their first being fetch,
>   And borrow matter, wherof they are made,
>   Which when as forme and feature it does ketch,
>   Becomes a bodie, and doth them inuade
>   The state of life, out of the griesly shade.
>   The substance is eterne and bideth so,
>   Ne when the life decayes, and forme does fade,
>   Doth it consume, and into nothing go,
> But chaunged is, and often altered to and fro. (III.vi.36–37)

Instead of being treated to such a vision, Britomart witnesses Amoret's torture, a bloody scene that looks a great deal like the physical act of giving birth, described in the most unabstract way possible. The actual female body in the act of childbirth works with what appears to be a perceived violence against itself: but it is a violence that, while dangerous, is ultimately unharmful, and indeed an act of love. The usual processes of childbirth are not necessarily hurtful; perhaps we tend to emphasize the far less common mishaps because the normal process involves so much blood. To understand Amoret's torture only as a metaphor of seduction created by the evil Petrarchan arts of Busyrane is to be unable fully to account for its application to Britomart's kind of chastity. She is not seduced by Petrarchan arts; she carries her own desire actively with her; she is threatened by the "wound" of love, but it is not a Petrarchan Gardante that wounds her, finally, but a powerful vision of providence that leads her to marriage and childbirth. If she is wounded again in her struggle with Busyrane, this wound only finds its ultimate expression when she has her dream of giving birth in Isis Church in V.vii.16. [20]

Before we can fully understand what Britomart learns in that vision of childbirth, however, the poem insists that we see the event *in malo* once more. The uterine dramas of Book III become even more explicit in the evil contrast Spenser provides when we encounter the next set of twins in the text of Book III. The chaste and chased Florimell flees the hyena who feeds, quite specifically, on women's flesh. The female-flesh-eating hyena suggests not only the mortal risk Florimell faces, but the specificity with which female flesh is singled out in this book. A simile describing Florimell's flight connects the specificity of this flesh to the mythological substratum of incest that has been implicit in the narrative of Adonis.

Not halfe so fast the wicked Myrrha fled
    From dread of her reuenging fathers hond. (III.vii.26)

Myrrha, the mother of Adonis, is called "wicked," as if she were to blame for the incest into which she would seem to have been lured by her father, who here seeks a just "revenge." This act of daughterly incest gets a mere fleeting reference compared to the more elaborate inset incident in which Satyrane, after catching and binding the hyena, lets it go in order to rescue the Squire of Dames from the incestuous giantess Argante. Argante's nature is incestuous at least twice over. She is not only the product of her father's incestuous coupling with his mother, Earth, she herself then engaged in incestuous intercourse with her twin brother Ollyphant (from Chaucer's Tale of Sir Thopas) while they were still in utero.

For at that berth another Babe she bore,
    To weene the mightly Ollyphant, that wrought
    Great wreake to many errant knights of yore,
    And many hath to foule confusion brought.
    While sin their mothers wombe enclosed they were,
    Ere they into lightsome world were brought,
    In fleshly lust were mingled both yfere,
And in that monstrous wise did to the world appere.

So liu'd they euer after in like sin,
    Gainst natures law, and good behauioure:
    Who not so content so fowly to deuoure
    Her natiue flesh, and staine her brothers bowre,
    Did wallow in all other fleshly myre,
    And suffered beasts her body to deflowre:
    So whot she burned in that lustfull fyre,
Yet all that might not slake her sensuall desyre. (III.vii.48–49)

The only force capable of restraining such transgressive female desire (which runs the gamut from endogamous incest to exogamous bestiality) is a force that is both female and active—like Britomart's:

But that bold knight whom ye persuing saw
    That Geauntesse, is not such, as she seems,
    But a faire virgin, that in martiall law,
    And deeds of armes aboue all Dames is deemed,
    And aboue many knights is eke esteemed,
    For her great worth; She Palladine is hight:
    She you from death, you me from dread redeemed.
    Ne any may that Monster match in fight,
But such, or such as she, that is so chaste a wight. (III.vii.52)

As a double of Britomart's, the woman warrior Palladine is carefully differentiated from the giantess's incestuous and bestial range of lust, just as Britomart's desire was distanced by Glauce from Myrrha's love for her father. It is important to notice that it is Myrrha (and not her father) and Argante (not her brother Ollyphant) who are presented as guilty of the sin of incest, as foully "eating" native flesh against nature's law. It is the female who is blamed, not because women are actually the aggressors in such couplings, but because—and this was Gayle Rubin's essential point—it is active female desire itself that is fundamentally forbidden by the taboo. It is therefore crucial that Britomart's desire for Artegall (which could not be more active) be differentiated from Argante's and from Myrrha's. Their stories, so closely installed next to considerations of the heroine's active female desire, are ways to ward off the transgression threatening in Britomart's erotic destiny.

Rather more appropriate brother-sister relations are spelled out in the narrative that forms the titular event of Book IV, the book of Amicitia or Friendship, in which Britomart finally meets Artegall when she conquers him in a joust. Lauren Silberman has noted the large change from the discourse of female agency in Book III to that in the continuation of Britomart's story in Book IV. In III, Spenser aims at understanding female agency in terms very different from the passivity required by patriarchal codes (if Florimell flees, she is, in fact, also seeking Marinell). In Book IV those codes are resolutely in place.

I am not certain, however, that the second installment of *The Faerie Queene* differs in this respect so entirely from the first (although it does differ in many other ways). The fact that Britomart wins Satyrane's tournament, with the false Florimell as the prize (an ersatz substitute for the true Florimell's lost girdle), seems designed to show just how anomalous Britomart's agency is within the structures through which she has so far been functioning. (The false Florimell contrasts with the true Florimell

not only in terms of her chastity but also of her passivity: when given
"her" own choice of victor, she selects Braggadocchio, the false knight.
She thereby negates the importance of her having been given the power
of election, and proves how useless active female choice is within the masculine structure of competitive jousting.)

Britomart's quest for Artegall makes her utterly different from the
women who are being offered as prizes in martial contests. The false
Florimell is of course no proper reward for knightly virtue, and that she
is the prize in Satyrane's tournament reveals the author's satiric judgment
on the process by which women become prizes for conquerors. The tournament arranged by Satyrane, however, is more important for the way it
comments on the first tournament to occur in book IV. That is the one
arranged by Cambell with his sister Canacee as prize: the event outlines
the necessary reasons for the traffic between men; the granting of the prize
allows them to form homosocial bonds.

Sheila Cavanagh has very importantly shown how the laws articulating the traffic in women shape the narrative that Spenser makes out of
Chaucer's unfinished Squire's tale.[21] Proceeding almost as if he had especially selected this quintessentially patriarchal figure among Chaucer's
dramatis personae in order to demonstrate the proper means for exchanging sisters, Spenser takes up the Squire's story of Cambell and Canacee as
a way of fulfilling his own imagined patriarchal legacy from Chaucer. Very
much as he dealt with the missed joke in Chaucer the pilgrim's own
romance the Tale of Sir Thopas—the basis of the entire epic thread concerning Arthur's imitative quest for the "faerie queene"—Spenser treats
the Squire's tale with the utmost seriousness.

The narrator begins with a useful summary: "whylome as antique
stories tellen us":

Couragious Cambell, and stout Triamond,
With Canacee and Cambine linckt in louely bond. (IV.2.31)

Cambell and Triamond are bound together because each is linked
with the other's sister. Triamond's sister has not been mentioned until she
arrives, like Dante's Beatrice, in an allegorical chariot announcing awe-
some authority: Cambina's very name, as A. C. Hamilton points out in a
note, means "exchange." As Cavanagh summarizes: "the happy conclusion
would not have been possible had another woman not provided" the
return gift in exchange, which closes the required circle of reciprocity outlined by Lévi-Strauss (Cavanagh, 80). The "friendship" or male bonding

that Spenser outlines with this story details the specifics of the traffic in women upon which it rests.

Until the moment when Cambina, or the principle of reciprocal exchange, enters the arena, the tournament which Cambell stages remains unstable: neither Triamond nor Cambell can win it. The lives of Triamond's two brothers live on in him and strengthen him, while Cambell is empowered by his sister Canacee's ring, which staunches blood from any wound. In this way the combatants' sibling-assisted magic is equally matched, and so the tournament remains unresolved until Cambina's arrival is heralded by a great tumult of "womens cries and shouts of boyes, / Such as the troubled Theatres oftimes annoyes" (IIII.iii.38).

Cambell's magic's ring would destroy the very purpose of his tournament, at least its stated purpose of finding his sister a husband. For if he remains the champion who cannot be bested then no one can win his sister but himself:

> Amongst them all this end he did decree:
> That of them all, which loue to her did make,
> That by consent should chose the stoutest three,
> That with himself should combat for her sake,
> And of them all the victour should his sister take.

> But yet his sisters skill vnto him lent
> Most confidence and hope of happie speed,
> Conceiued by a ring which she him sent,
> That mongst the manie vertues which we reed,
> Had power to staunch al wounds, that mortally did bleed. (IV.ii.38–40)

What Cambina's arrival permits is the chance for Cambell to give his sister to another man because now he can get a wife for himself in return. Otherwise he would keep his sister. Canacee has no choice in the matter. Indeed, the sheer symmetry of the foursquare set of couples requires and reveals no real desire on anyone's part, as if all we are meant to understand by this tournament is how the system works. The only thing motivating the set of events (aside from magic) is Cambell's desire to give his sister away.

Unlike Canacee, the false Florimell is given her choice—and she makes a poor one. The two tournaments illuminate the differing values between granting agency to an autonomous woman and the more traditional pattern of brothers exchanging sisters.[22] The second tournament, of course, is when Britomart bests Artegall, without recognizing the love object in the mirror beneath his "wild man" disguise. Her failure to know and claim him underscores how differently her desire is constructed. It is because Britomart wins but does not want the prize that the false Florimell, the ersatz lady, is allowed to choose. This juxtaposition and contrast seem necessary to distinguish sufficiently Britomart's active agency from the false Florimell's empty exercise of sham autonomy.

Perhaps not surprisingly in this context—an almost diagrammatic investigation of the workings of the traffic in women—Britomart's refusal of the false Florimell is not because she herself is a woman, but because, as a knight, she already possesses a woman she prefers, Amoret. Their relationship is not erotic, but a "friendship" between the two women; there is a full bed-sharing intimacy, but only after the revelation of Britomart's female gender. (Amoret is then "freed from feare"—which some critics have said is what happens when Britomart frees her from Busyrane). But before Britomart and Amoret can arrive at their friendship, the narrative rehearses its meditation on the comedy of same-sex female eroticism formerly seen in the scenes at Castle Joyeous.

Raising the possibility of female erotic intimacy, which Spenser treated comically in the scene with Malecasta, the narrative insists again upon what theory has guessed—that one way out of a traffic in women driven by homosocial male desires is to opt out of the compulsory heterosexuality it requires. Instances of female-to-female erotic bonding, however, haven been strangely difficult to locate in this historical period, submerged as the act must have been within an all-embracing female homosociality.

In a footnote, Linda Gregerson offers the wise speculation that the homoeroticism implicit in the relations between Malecasta and Britomart is first glimpsed, made visible one might say, as an example of male-to-male desire:

When Britomart, still armed and thus cross-dressed, first lifts her visor in Malecasta's castle, the poet describes her as. . . the simultaneously "amiable" and "manly" object of "men's rash desires" (III.i.43, 46). Which men, exactly, are we talking about here? The men guarding the castle don't appear to have rashly desired her. In other words, the attraction of female to female that resonates throughout the eroticised scenes between Britomart and Malecasta, (in which Chastity and Unchastity are complexly intertwined), is prefaced and pervaded by intimations of men's desire for men.[23]

In making this suggestion, Gregerson is relying on Stephen Orgel's arguments, which were in part suggested by Alice Jardine's theory about the allure of the "rapeable boy" on the cross-dressing Elizabethan stage.[24] But Britomart is not a stage character played by a boy, and such a formulation of male-to-male eroticism masked beneath Britomart's cross-dressing misses the chance to see if the culture has any real interest in female desire itself—whatever its erotic object.

There is a singular instance preceding Spenser, in which a woman thinks she is in love with another woman, and that is in the *Arcadia*, where Sidney's heroine Philoclea ultimately accepts her erotic attachment to someone she thinks is a woman (although it is, in fact, the cross-dressed hero, Pyrocles). Sidney's acceptance of Philoclea's desire is much like Ariosto's tone in the very passage which Spenser rewrites in the Malecasta episode. Lauren Silberman points out that Spenser takes pains to suppress any suggestion of female homoeroticism in the Malecasta episode, whereas Ariosto seemingly courts it: thus Fiordespina, who has fallen in love with the cross-dressed Bradamante, laments the impasse to which love has brought her when Bradamante gallantly lets her know her true sex.[25]

Né tra gli uomimi nai né tra l'armento,
che femina ami femina ho trovato:
non par la donna all'altre donne bella,
né a cervie cervia, né all'agnelle agnella.

In terra, in aria, in mare, sola son io
Che patisco da te sí duro scempio;
e questo hai fatto acciò che' l'error mio
sia ne l'imperio tuo l'ultimo esempio.
La moglie del re Nino ebbe disio,
il figlio amando, scelerato ed empio,
e Mirra il padre, e la Cretense il toro;
ma gli è piu folle il mio, ch'alcun dei loro. (XXV.35–36)

In all the world of nature, you invent
A female lover for a female mate!
Women their hearts to women do not lose,
Nor doe to doe, nor ewe to other ewes.

On land, on sea, in heaven, I alone
Must bear a blow of such severity;
You mean by my example shall be shown
The last extreme of your authority.
The wife of Ninus, who desired her son,
Your victim was; Myrrha with infamy
Desired her father, Pasiphae the bull,
Yet mine the maddest folly is of all.[26]

Spenser retains the issue of incest and bestiality, but in his version of the lament Britomart is comically whining that at least those women had their desires met, whereas she loves a mere image in a mirror. That Fiordespina's romantic lament is given to Glauce (to distinguish Britomart's desire from any involving incest) brings into question what actually is being erased from the list of sexual monstrosities. Any cultural meditation on female agency at this time will necessarily come up against the two tabooed means for evading the repression of that agency: active incest and the very real possibility that female friendship may include same-sex eroticism.

Britomart and Amoret's friendship at the opening of book IV is a reversal of Philoclea's predicament and even more distinctly differentiated from Malecasta's and Fiordespina's misplaced affections. The first scene in the whole of Book IV depicts the two women Britomart and Amoret becoming friends once Britomart reveals her female gender. However, before this revelation happens, Britomart goes through a bizarre charade that terrifies Amoret, as she fears that she may well be forced again to succumb to another abusive knight.

> Thereto her feare was made so much the greater
>   Through fine abusion of that Briton mayd:
>   Who for to hide her fained sex the better,
>   And maske her wounded mind, both did and sayd
>   Full many things so doubtfull to be wayd,
>   That well she wist not what by them to gesse,
>   For other whiles to her she purpose made
>   Of loue, and otherwhiles of lustfulnesse,
> That much she feared his mind would grow to some excesse.

> His will she feard; for him she surely thought
>   To be a man, such as indeed he seemed,
>   And much the more, by that he lately wrought,
>   When her from deadly thraldome he redeemed,
>   For which no seruice she too much esteemed;
>   Yet dread of shame, and doubt of fowle dishonor
>   Made her no yeeld so much, as due she deemed.
>   Yet Britomart attended duly on her,
> As well became a knight, and did to her all honor. (IV.i.7–8)

Britomart's protective charade, expressing both love and lust for Amoret, is a very different thing from her entertaining Malecasta's advances because of a naive sympathy for a fellow sufferer in love. Britomart's abuse here is oddly like Busyrane's, and it is not until her own sex is revealed that Britomart can again free Amoret from fear. At which point, Amoret

> more Franke affection did to her afford
> And to her bed, which she was wont forbeare,
> Now Freely drew, and found right safe assurance theare. (IIII.i.15)

The fact that the narrative twice arranges female-to-female erotic possibilities around Britomart, first as receiver (of Malecasta's advances) and then as aggressor (upon Amoret), suggests that at the very least such a homoerotic possibility needs to be taken into account as part of the narrative's meditation on female agency. Glauce does not include homoeroticism in her list of erotic evils (mentioning only the two abnormalities, incest and bestiality), as if the homoerotic possibility simply did not exist, at least, not in a way that could be articulated by an Ovidian vocabulary.

It is true that, in contrast to Shakespeare, the possibility of erotic attachment between women hardly exists in Spenser: the minute Scudamour realizes Britomart is female, he is relieved, for he then knows for certain that his fears about Amoret's chastity were due to "abusion."[27] It is a way of saying that nothing sexually meaningful can happen in bed between women: any possible female homosexuality is absorbed, structurally, as a matter of course into female homosociality: Amoret and Britomart in bed together, however physically intimate or even "lustful," are simply friends; male lovers, traffic in women, will be in no way threatened.[28]

Of course Spenser will reverse the typical state of affairs in the "traffic between women" by Radigund's and Britomart's fight over Artegall in Book V. Perhaps not surprisingly, Artegall is not an appropriate prize in their joust until he has rendered himself completely passive by accepting Radigund's ridiculous and unchivalric terms for their combat. Thus, he allows himself to be dressed in women's clothes and set to a peculiarly feminine kind of wage slavery. Such an unusual paralysis underscores the passivity appropriate to a prize to be given any winner. When Britomart confronts the wordless Artegall—who is as silenced as any traded woman must be—"What May-game has misfortune made of you?" we see his enslavement turned into a May-game festival pastime. It is as if Artegall were only cross-dressed for the occasion when all is topsy-turvy misrule; Britomart plays Robin Hood to Artegall's cross-dressed Maid Marian. Women-on-top festivals could be imagined in the sixteenth century, as

Natalie Zemon Davis reminded us. In Book V Spenser manages the reorganization of society back into its normal male-dominated hierarchy by making reference to such festival behavior.

By decapitating Radigund, Britomart disarms herself. She fashions herself in the kind of restraint that Radigund refused to practice when she tricked Artegall into playing by her unruly rules. Britomart will agree to play by the old rules, even though ironically it is her unorthodox, peculiarly female agency which rights the upside-down world of Radigund's Amazon kingdom, and which "the liberty of women did repeale." In some fundamental sense, the political "liberty of women" is imaginable only as an outlying alternative to the domesticity of women.[29]

In Book V, Canto vii combines Britomart's conquest of Radigund with her dream in Isis Church. The structural pairing of the two events within the same canto tells us something important about the relationship between the different aspects of Britomart's agency exercised by each episode. The childbirth dream returns to the incest implications of her imagined sexual communion with Artegall first made by her viewing of the magic mirror. Here the comparison is to an incestuous coupling specifically between a husband and wife who are also brother and sister. As David Miller has reminded us, "Britomart's passion for Artegall is tinged at first with incestuous overtones, and continues to suggest an odd convertibility between the images of parent and child."[30] Sleeping at the foot of a statue of Isis, Britomart has a vision in which she is transformed from an acolyte of that goddess into a bejeweled version of the goddess herself. She is then menaced by the crocodile beneath this statue's feet, which, grown gigantic, makes as if to devour her. But rendered meek by the statue of the goddess, the beast makes love to Britomart instead.

Which she accepting, he so near her drew,
That of his game she soon enwombed grew,
And forth did bring a Lion of great might; (V.vii.16)

When Britomart narrates the troubling dream, Isis's priest recognizes her and explains to her that the crocodile is really Osiris who sleeps under Isis's feet.

For that same Crocodile doth represent
The righteous Knight, that is thy faithfull louer,
Like to Osyris in all iust endeuer.
For that same Crocodile Osyris is,

That vnder Isis feete doth sleepe for euer:
To shew that clemence oft in things amis,
Restraines those sterne behests, and cruell domes of his. (V.vii.22)

Reprising Merlin's prophecy in terms of the myth of Isis and Osiris
achieves a number of things. First, it rehearses Britomart's maternal destiny and reveals that the endpoint of her journey will be to bear a child.
And second, it calibrates the Egyptian and English sense of dynastic generation in terms of an allegorized and secret justice. In the process of re-
making Britomart and Artegall into exemplars of Justice and equity, the
dream also imports back into Britomart's story the notion of a sacred and
enabling incest.

According to Thomas North's translation of Plutarch, "Isis and Osiris
were in love in their mothers bellie before they were borne, and lay
together secretly and by stealth."[31] While one incestuous result of this Ollyphant and Argante-like coupling may have been Typhon (a catastrophic
result), the union between Isis and Osiris most profoundly images their
bonded loyalty to each other. Thus, Isis gathers Osiris's body up after
Typhon has dismembered it into fourteen pieces, finding, according to Plutarch, all but the genital member. Isis therefore forms a counterfeit that she
names "Phallus." Plutarch also explains that Isis was pregnant by Osiris at
her own death, and argues that Isis and Osiris were daemons who, for their
loyalty, were rewarded by being turned into gods:

> For Isis the wife and sister of Osiris in revenge plagued him [Typhon] in
> extinguishing and repressing his fury and rage: and yet neglected not she the trav-
> els and paines of her own which she endured, her trudging also and wandring to
> and fro, nor many other acts of great wisdome and prowesse suffered she to be
> buried in silence and oblivion; but inserting the same among the most holy cere-
> monies of sacrifices, as examples, images, memorials and resemblances of the acci-
> dents . . . she consecrated an ensignment, instruction and consolation of piety and
> devout religion to godward, as well for men as women afflicted with miseries. By
> reason whereof she and her husband Osiris of good Daemons were transmuted
> for their vertue into gods. (1298)

In Plutarch's account, Isis's generation also has much to do with
the infinite shapes of creatures left by the receding Nile floods that
Spenser usually sees as problematic, save when he allies Chrysogonee's
spontaneous generation of Amoret and Belphoebe to its fecundating
processes. All of these usually problematic images of generation and parturition are bound up in the Isis and Osiris myth, which, because of its

parallel analogies to "Templar" scenes in the other books, seems in Book V to form the "core" to Britomart and Artegall's shared narratives.

As Gregerson has observed, Britomart's vision in the Temple of Isis is presided over by an Idol that represents a series of doubles: not only wife/husband but sister/brother and maiden/beast (96). In her useful formula, Britomart's adventure in chastity has to work its via media between the most endogamous (incest, brother Osiris/sister Isis) and the most exogamous (interspecies, human Britomart/animal crocodile) possibilities in order to articulate itself. Britomart's final dream turns the monstrous threat of Glauce's admonitions into mythic terms for imaging the concord that Britomart and Artegall's union will achieve.

The story of Isis and Osiris, as Plutarch tells it, reprises much of the material first broached by the Garden of Adonis. Isis becomes "no other thing but generation," as Plutarch explains:

For Isis is the feminine part of nature, apt to receive all generation . . . Moreover, there is imprinted in her naturally a love of the first and principall essence, which is nothing else but the soveraigne good, and it she desireth, seeketh and pursueth after . . . and howsoever she be the subject matter, and meet place apt to receive as well the one as the other, yet of it selfe, enclined she is always rather to the better and applieth herselfe to engender the same, yea and to disseminate and sow the defluxions and similitudes thereof, wherein she taketh pleasure and rejoiceth, when she hath conceived and is great therewith, ready to be delivered. (1309)

Britomart's narrative reveals the agency that women may legitimately engage in. It also depicts the violent suppression of an illegitimate political female agency when Britomart vanquishes the Amazon queen Radigund and Talus massacres the Amazon nation. Her rightful agency is not merely to be the mother of her children, but to have those children by a man whom she has seen, in some fundamental way, as her own brother. Only once does Britomart embrace Artegall, and that is in the guise of an incestuous coupling in her dream.

This is not to suggest that even Britomart's legitimate erotic agency is being presented as illegitimate, but rather to stress that the power of her eroticism, as imaged in her dream, necessarily participates in the power of incestuous desires that are predicated on the power of bloodlines and family status. For the most part, Spenser takes pains to present Britomart's eroticism in distinct (and significantly overt) opposition to the incest of Byblis and Argante. At the final moment, however, just before Britomart defeats the illegitimate power that she could all too easily exercise over Artegall (after her conquest of her double, the Amazon Radigund), she participates in a fantasy of a fruitful incestuous union between Isis and Osiris.

Britomart's agency is thus being built upon a familial power which stabilizes social hierarchy. It is the same power that brought Elizabeth I to the throne—that raised her up, uniquely, to single sovereignty. The structure of Canto vii strongly suggests that it is this endogamous agency by which Britomart is able to repeal the "liberty of women" fantasized in the stories of the seemingly outlandish Amazons.

Kathryn Schwarz has recently argued that Renaissance stories about Amazons are in the end always about the problematic construction of domesticated heterosexual desire; Britomart's story concerns how "female masculinity is governed and moralized by married chastity, and [how] married chastity is enabled by female masculinity."[32] Britomart's disguise, like actual Amazon identity, exposes "the working parts" of patriarchy's inventions. Schwarz deals in detail with Britomart's problematic masquerade with Amoret. She recognizes, as does Valerie Traub, what she takes to be the part that female homoeroticism plays in revealing the malleability of the "presumably innate," which patriarchy would stabilize if it could. Again, it seems easier to see how female same-sex desire works to destabilize the triangular traffic between men (Britomart's "masculinity" does it by many more means than female homoeroticism, according to Schwarz). But few readers take seriously the threat of incest which continues to haunt Britomart's story. As Schwarz observed, "incest and bestiality produce mothers and children and in substituting the example of Pasiphaë or Myrrha for that of Narcissus [in Britomart's glance into Ryence's mirror]. Britomart imagines desire first as a pattern of homoerotic stasis and then as a story of generative heterosexual ones" (143).

That incest can be "generatively heterosexual," in contrast to a dynastically impotent homoeroticism, may be the final point of Britomart's dream in Isis Church. At the very least, Spenser's heroine's domesticated, desiring, "masculinized" desire, contained within the rubric of active chastity, manages, finally, to borrow the power of all the erotic energy from which Spenser has so carefully distinguished it.

6

Mary Wroth

IT SEEMS ALMOST INEVITABLE that the first large verbal construct created solely by a woman in the English Renaissance should be in the genre of romance. This is not only because women were avid readers of romance and therefore writing in the genre did not feel alien to them. As I also hope to show, romance as a genre is also focused on the traffic in women in such a way that it allows a discussion of female agency and its connection to endogamy or incest more easily than other genres.[1]

Lorna Hutson has argued that the romance narratives of the sixteenth century were, in fact, less hospitable to female writers than has been previously supposed, and that, paradoxically, the kind of romances popular during the period (and seemingly aimed at a female readership) were studies in humanist discourse aimed at a redefinition of masculinity. While Hutson deals in some detail with Margaret Tyler's translation of a medieval romance (Tyler had argued that women write romances because they like them), Hutson makes a compelling case for considering Tyler's text an exemplar of what the humanist romances are *not*. In Tyler's *Mirror of Princely Deeds and Knighthood* (1578), the heroes triumph through a physical contest of some sort. In the humanist-influenced fiction that interests Hutson—Sidney's *Arcadia,* for instance—the hero wins by some feat of persuasive epideictic rhetoric. (Zelmane's and Philoclea's argument about the legitimacy of suicide is a signal instance.) But other than Tyler, the only female author Hutson discusses is Isabella Whitney, who does not write romance of any kind.[2] It is unfortunate that Hutson did not consider Mary Wroth's *Countess of Mountgomerie's Urania* (1621), a very large romance indeed (438 printed pages), for the *Urania* is a test case for any discussion of female agency and authorship in this period.

Because the *Urania* is so specifically a romance in the manner of Sidney's *Arcadia,* we do well, *pace* Hutson, to review what the genre—from its medieval to its Renaissance versions—might have had to offer a female writer. To begin with one of the most influential theories of romance as a genre: Fredric Jameson has argued that the origin of the ethical polarities endemic to romance lies in the *chansons de geste* that were popular when central authority had collapsed and "marauding bands of robbers and brigands range[d] geographical immensities."[3] According to Jameson, romance may be understood as an "imaginary solution" to the "real contradiction" that arose when these bands formed into the feudal nobility, becoming a single social class with a coherent ideology. Thus romance functions as

a symbolic answer to the perplexing question of how my enemy can be thought of as being evil (that is, other than myself and marked by some absolute difference), when what is responsible for his being so characterized is quite simply the identity of his own conduct with mine, the which—points of honor, challenges, tests of strength—he reflects as in a mirror image. (118)

Jameson argues that the fundamental ideologeme occurs when an unidentified black knight rides into the lists, refusing to say his name, until victorious (or vanquished), he proclaims himself and is revealed to be—a knight: At this point, "he becomes a knight like any other and loses all his sinister unfamiliarity" (119).

Jameson does not consider what happens when the mystery knight is revealed to be a woman (like Britomart and all the other lady warriors of Renaissance romance). As a woman the knight remains an irreducibly other "Other." While Jameson does not take up the problem of the female warrior,[4] he does suggest that the category of evil in the generic switch from *chanson* to romance suffers a "semic evaporation," no longer assigned to "this or that human agent." Instead evil is forced to become a "free-floating and disembodied element, specifically that 'realm' of sorcery and magical forces which constitutes the semic organization of the 'world' of romance" (119). In this world of magic, females do have an immense amount of power, although usually for evil. But as one of the most compelling and long-lived romances—the story of King Arthur and the Round Table—reveals, the kind of power females have in this genre is evil in a specific way. Morgan la Fay is Arthur's sorceress sister, the woman upon whom the king incestuously begets Mordred, and it is of course Mordred who destroys Camelot in the end, although the efficient cause is Lancelot's love for his beloved king's wife—a kind of incest, literalized by the king's earlier congress with his sister.

Howard Bloch takes very seriously the problematic and fundamental relation of incest to medieval romance. In his view, the complications of kinship mark the French romances at both the lexical and the structural level: the striking homophony of names (Galehot/Galahad, Mordrain/ Mordred, Gauvian/Gaheiret/Gherrhes, and Agravain) matches the interlace structure by which different plots are interwoven simultaneously into a "continually overlapping discursive grid."[5] Bloch, however, disavows the idea of a "primal incest" secreted at the origin of the Grail story. Instead he argues for a protomodern subjectivity installed by the Round Table's inturned emphasis on the egalitarian individual who has few ties to social superiors or inferiors (225–26).

Here Bloch makes a move typical of medievalists intent upon claiming a critical privilege for medieval literature, one that the traditional organization of the rift between medieval and Renaissance periods usually denies them—that is, the capacity of medieval writers to anticipate the modern. While the Round Table may move toward some notion of individualized interiority, this does not necessarily mean that the interiority anticipates any modern version of rights-bearing autonomous subjectivity. In order to make the claim, Bloch neglects a profound implication of his own argument: that the genre of medieval romance is deeply invested in questions of marriage, inheritance, and female agency, interrogating how problematic issues of power become in this context.[6]

In *Chansons de Geste in the Age of Romance: Political Fictions*, Sarah Kay follows Jameson in positing a political unconscious for genres, but argues further that the romance and the *chanson de geste* (which she calls epic) each makes clear what the other genre represses. Essentially both genres are concerned with the same social formation—the feudal aristocracy—but with different worries about its problematic internal structure. Thus, according to Kay, the *chanson* is focused on the irrepressible and repetitious intermale violence that the romance tries to avoid; conversely, romance attempts to celebrate pacific male homosocial relations. Relying on Marilyn Strathern's useful distinctions about the traffic in women, Kay argues that while romance focuses on a trafficking in women as commodities, in the *chanson* the same traffic allows women to circulate as gifts. Women thereby retain their status as persons, and as a result, somewhat paradoxically, have a kind of real social agency in the *chanson* that they lose in romance. Kay's argument is a tour de force of generic analysis that conceives the fundamental matter of the two genres to be an exchange of females in which male homosociality necessarily engages.[7] Because the genre of romance is aimed at resolving the contradictions of the feudal, knightly class—how else can this class keep reproducing itself in the face of its internal violence, except by intermarriage?—the form necessarily centers on those family connections.

If we grant that marital logics are the foundation of romance as Kay has outlined, with their ideological commitments to articulating intermarriage within a feudal elite, it is no surprise that the first major work of prose fiction to be published by a woman in English should be a romance written by a female member of the lower aristocracy.[8] It was perhaps also predictable that the work should closely pertain to particular members of her own family. Lady Mary Wroth's romance, *The Countess of Mountgomerie's Urania*, takes its very title from the wife of her first cousin, who is the brother of the man, another first cousin, to whom she bore two illegitimate children. Suggestively, the plot involves a long-deferred love affair between two first cousins. Through this narrative and its multitudinous interpolated stories, the *Urania* considers the Renaissance traffic in women in great detail.[9] And the overarching plot of the long narrative involves incest, at least insofar as first cousin liaisons were judged to be incestuous in radical Protestant continental churches (as well as in the Catholic Church).

As the niece of Sir Philip Sidney, Wroth models the narrative of *The Countess of Mountgomeries Urania* on his, just as her title mimics his dedication to his sister, the Countess of Pembroke (who was Mary Wroth's aunt as well as the mother of Wroth's first cousin lover; the countess appears in the *Urania* as the Queen of Naples). Although it is also much more, Wroth's *Urania* is first and foremost an homage to Sidney's *Arcadia*; it is therefore a rewrite of a father's brother's literary romance, a text dealing with two close cousins' protracted and comic courtships of two sisters.

The Countess of Pembroke's coauthorship with her brother had an enormous influence on her niece's bold decision to write at all. (The variety of verse forms that Wroth scatters throughout the *Urania* appears to owe much to the Sidneys' experimentation with stanza patterns in their translation of the Psalms.) Contemporaries (such as Jonson, Chapman, and Davies) saw Wroth's writing as part of a family practice.[10]

The frontispiece of the book insists upon this central fact. Because the image there is a visual presentation of the climax to the plot of the first book, set within a monument, literally, to the family relationships that frame the scene and also provide the content of the text, it deserves some comment. One reads the frontispiece before the romance. While the "cover" of this book does copy the specifics of the narrative inside, it also tells the reader how to think about the story even before she reads it. As an important work of art in its own right, the page can tell us much about the halt in the traffic in women at the heart of Wroth's narrative.

The Frontispiece

The only scholar so far to comment at some length on the title page, Shannon Miller, has analyzed the frontispiece of the *Urania* as a creation of a specifically gendered space in which the image that opens the text inscribes a movement into the "interior self."[11] Wroth's text, Miller argues,

> serves in part as a literary illustration of the new architectural emphasis in the early modern period on creating private spaces within houses for the well-to-do. The construction of a sequence of rooms to which an individual could retire developed hand-in-hand with the creation of smaller private spaces in the Renaissance . . . for a self and for that self's private thoughts. . . . Wroth negotiates the [single place from which to speak] by repeatedly expressing the interiority of women through the external object. (145)

Miller's efforts seriously to read the image of this frontispiece and her understanding of it in relation to the contents of the romance is profoundly useful. It shows, along with the analysis by Josephine Roberts, just how carefully the image reflects the details of the text it fronts.[12] It also most usefully calls attention to the architectural emphases of the frontispiece. The specificity of gender, if it inheres in the frontispiece, may well have something to do with the framing of interior and exterior spaces.

As another way into reading this page however, I want to examine it within its most restricted generic category—that is, as a frontispiece engraved in England around 1621, when the *Urania* was published. If we look at it from this historically localized perspective—first as an engraving and only secondarily as architecture—we may be able to see in more detail what the designers aimed to do. The frontispiece is an elaborate work of a very high order, clearly done on the instructions of someone who knew the text well. Engraved by Simon Van de Passe, it is a telling articulation of Jacobean reading by a highly skilled visual artist.

A member of a prominent family of engravers, Van de Passe had been employed by James I and Anne of Denmark to do portraits of them, and he had portrayed other members of the Sidney/Pembroke family as well; his engraving of the Countess of Pembroke clearly labels the book she holds as David's Psalms, depicting her as a writer and signaling the importance of this volume for her identity as an author (Figure 11).[13] Although Van de Passe did few title pages for books, he engraved a map for John Smith's 1624 voyage to New England (Figure 12) including his portraits of John Smith and Pocahontas, the latter the one by which we today know the Native American princess (Figure 13).

Thus his career is testimony to the filiations of Wroth's work; for example, the sonnet in which she imagines herself to be a "sunburnt . . . Indian" takes on greater immediacy when we realize that the poem was published in a volume the frontispiece to which had been engraved by the man who had done the only seventeenth-century image we have of such a significant, individual Native American female. Wroth herself might have seen the different skin color of Powhatan's daughter.[14]

The cartouche held aloft by the twin Corinthian double columns in Van de Passe's design announces the authorship of the *Urania* as an aristocratic family affair: "Written by the right honorable the Lady Mary Wroath, Daughter to the right Noble Robert Earle of Leicester, and Neece to the ever famous, and renowned Philip Sidney knight, And to ye most excelt Lady Mary Countess of Pembroke late deceased." In a sense, then, the frontispiece enacts the same set of filial relations that the dedication of the *Arcadia* announces. As Wendy Wall has very insightfully argued, the publication format of Wroth's romance with its appended sonnet cycle mimics the format of the Countess of Pembroke's version of the *Arcadia*. But because Wroth's sequence, unlike her uncle's, is written by one of the characters within the romance (indeed, its heroine is the author), the frontispiece may also be said to refer to the entire volume, including the sonnet sequence (although Robertson's edition does not print the cycle with the text of the romance, an omission Wall acknowledges may give a false impression of the connection between sonnet sequence and romance).[15]

The two figures in the lower left-hand corner, next to the base of the left-hand columns, are Pamphilia and Amphilanthus (both poets), coming to free the lovers trapped in the Palace of Love on Cyprus (Figure 14). The edifice in the lower middle is depicted exactly as the Bridge to the Palace is described in the text, just before the ladies become trapped in it by enchantment.

At the foote of this Hall ranne a plesant and sweetly passing river, over which was a Bridge, on which were three Towres: Upone the first was the Image of Cupid, curiously carv'd with his Bow bent, and Quiver at his backe, but with his right hand pointing to the next Towre; on which was a statue of white Marble, representing

Figure 11. Simon Van de Passe, *Mary Sidney Herbert, the Countess of Pembroke* (1618). Huntington Library.

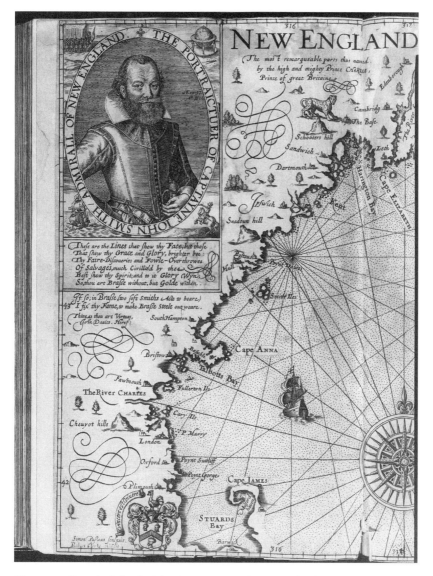

Figure 12. Captain John Smith, *A Description of New England* (London: Humfrey Lownes, 1616), 316–17. Huntington Library.

Figure 13. Simon Van de Passe, *Pochahontas* (1616). Huntington Library.

Figure 14. Mary Wroth, *The Countesse of Mountgomeries Urania* (London: Marriott and Grismand, 1621), title page. Huntington Library.

Venus, but so richly adorn'd as it might for rareness, and exquisiteness have beene take for the goddesse herselfe, and have causd as straunge an affection as the Image did to her maker, when he fell in love with his owne worke. Shee was crowned with Mirtle, and Pansies, in her left hand holding a flaming Heart, her right, directly to the third Towre, before which, in all dainty riches, and rich delicacy, was the figure of Constancy, holding in her hand the Keyes of the Pallace: which shewed, that place was not to be open to all, but to few possessed with that vertue.[16]

The image on the frontispiece—an artifact presenting before the textual fact an ekphrastic description of three statues—forecasts the importance of this scene when it occurs in the text. The reference to the Pygmalion myth from Ovid's *Metamorphoses* shows how self-consciously artful the passage is: in it Wroth prepares the stage for considering the difficulties inherent in her own female artistry, a legacy inherited from the problematic Ovid. But it is the key held by Constancy on the far right tower, which Pamphilia uses to unlock and free the prisoners in the climactic scene of Book I, that offers, as we shall see, the key to Wroth's interesting narrative technique—which the frontispiece does so much literally to foreground.

Inclusion of the "plot" on a title page is a romance device—the title page to Anthony Munday's *Amadis de Gaule*, for instance, features a scene taken from the romance: mariners on a royal ship lift a coffin from the waves (Figure 15). As the makeup of the *Amadis* page suggests, however, this vignette of the plot is presented in a very different manner; framed by the architectural structure, the Wroth scene becomes more than merely a foretaste of the story.

The only other contemporaneous title pages set up as scenes to be viewed through architectural frames were Hole's engraving of Michael Drayton's *Poly-Olbion* (1616) and his title page for a book called *The Surveyor* (1616).[17] In both cases, the perspectival view through an architectural frame mimicked the images that fronted texts articulating an expansion of the technology of chorography; both *Poly-Olbion* (Figure 16) and *The Surveyor* (Figure 17) involved the measurement and mapping of the old world, the new world, and the heavens, as Hole's title page to Rathborne's manual on surveying makes clear.

It is highly relevant that at the heart of the new technology of measuring was the desire to remap feudal landholdings.[18] This reorganization has great bearing on the redefinition of the family during the Renaissance, and points to the socioeconomic work being achieved by Van de Passe's frontispiece to the *Urania*. Hole's frontispiece for Drayton's Spenserian

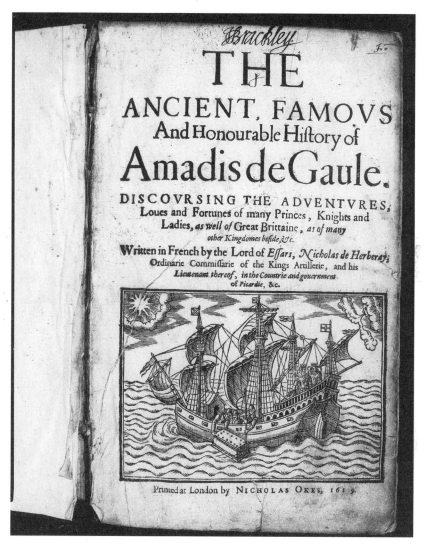

THE

ANCIENT, FAMOVS
And Honourable Hiſtory of

Amadis de Gaule.

DISCOVRSING THE ADVENTVRES,
Loues and Fortunes of many Princes, Knights and
Ladies, as well of Great Brittaine, as of many
other Kingdomes beſide, &c.

Written in French by the Lord of Eſſars, Nicholas de Herberay,
Ordinarie Commiſſarie of the Kings Artillerie, and his
Lieutenant thereof, in the Countrie and gouernment
of Picardie, &c.

Printed at London by NICHOLAS OKES, 1619

Figure 15. Nicholas de Herberay, *The Ancient, Famovs and Honourable History of Amadis de Gaule* (London: Nicholas Okes, 1619), title page. Huntington Library.

Figure 16. Michael Drayton, *Poly-Olbion* (London: M. Lownes, 1616), title page. Huntington Library.

Figure 17. Aaron Rathborne, *The Svrveyor* (London: W. Stamsby, 1616), title page. Huntington Library.

Poly-Olbion reveals a distinct generational project in the chorographical writing of the first decades of the seventeenth century, where, as Richard Helgerson brilliantly argues, the emphasis falls on the land itself, in its county and customary locality; in this land is created an authority that may vie with the absolutist authority of the sovereign.[19] It is not so much that, celebrating locality, the chorography of the first decades of the century anticipated what were to become the forces of the parliamentary party in succeeding decades, but that the embeddedness of local aristocratic rule harkened back to the medieval shires. As Helgerson argues, the only figures wearing crowns in the odd, creaturely population of Drayton's maps, are cities, whose pagan, river-nymph-like power is interspersed with depictions of local folk festivals (Figure 18).

While it is not a frontispiece, the famous *Rainbow Portrait* of Queen Elizabeth, by either Isaac Oliver or Marcus Gheeraerts the Younger around 1600–1603, offers another version of the portal-framed allegorical woman (Figure 19). Although they are sometimes difficult to see in reproductions, there are two pillars supporting an arch over Elizabeth's elaborate headdress; like the half-naked woman in the frontispiece to *Poly-Olbion*, Elizabeth wears a fascinating allegorical robe, with images of eyes and ears embroidered on the russet cloth. Along with the drop pearls, the green serpent with ruby heart in its mouth on her sleeve, and the rainbow itself with the motto *Non sine sole, iris*, the portrait is loaded with emblematic images that have attracted an enormous amount of commentary.[20] More recently, however, viewers have begun to see the erotic actuality of the female body represented on the clothes (for instance, the vaginal "ear" just at the place where the figure's genitals would be behind the cloth)— insisting that the eroticism of the portrait cannot be entirely subsumed into the imperial program that its allegorical appurtenances outline.[21]

The point to note here in juxtaposing this famous portrait of Elizabeth with the frontispiece to Drayton's *Poly-Olbion* is that the physical body of Elizabeth herself has not been entirely "captured" by the ideological program. While as queen she may have had difficulty controlling her images entirely (as in the lewd detail of the genital-like ear), Elizabeth was able to police the likeness and may have provided the costume itself.[22] The representation of the Queen with deep décolletage also insists upon her virginal status. Traub insists upon the various portraits' representation of Elizabeth's "lifelong erotic autonomy."[23] Traub takes this erotic autonomy to include the possibilities of homoerotic as well as heterosexual desire; I would like to suggest that this spectacularly allegorical portrait shows the queen as an erotically compelling virginal woman, resisting not only the traffic in women but also the allegorical "capture" that would make her the passive instrument of an ideological program over which she had little control.

To move to the frontispiece to Wroth's romance, arranged in a manner strikingly like the two Hole frontispieces, is to see another allegorical landscape like Hole's title page to *Poly-Olbion*. There is no single allegorical woman, of course, but rather four different heterosexual couples. And the landscape is not part of the costume of an allegorical personification. The title page to the *Urania* does, however, represent the allegorical scene on the bridge where real women confront allegorical statues. At the same time, the larger landscape represents a very local site: there are three visible walled gardens, many bosky rows of trees, and a most intriguing windmill. The composition tells us much about the genre of romance we will be reading. This is not chivalric romance—or indeed a chorography—but a courtly prose narrative. The walled gardens are pronounced: a set of

Figure 18. Drayton, *Poly-Olbion*, pp. 256–57. Huntington Library.

NON SINE SOLE
IRIS.

Figure 19. *Elizabeth I: The Rainbow Portrait* (ca. 1616–1663), attributed to Isaac Oliver or Marcus Gheeraerts. Collection of the Marquess of Salisbury, Hatfield House.

French parterres, an English-looking orchard, and an Italianate treillage. Not only does the depiction of the bridge with towers exactly replicate the scene of the Palace of Love on Cyprus as described in the text, but the rest of the design (in particular, the walled gardens) indicates another very important textual site—the scene of Pamphilia's first writing of a poem. This authorial scene is set in the walled garden to which she withdraws in Book I and writes on the bark of a tree. Thus the frontispiece not only stages the climax to the plot of Book I, but also represents the site of the female author's creativity (although in the frontispiece no female sits in any of the gardens writing).

The framing of the landscape within a triumphal arch with its baroque columns and ornamented pediments does not have the same perspective as the landscape that is seen through them. Josephine Roberts cites an essay arguing that this multiple perspective matches the shifting viewpoints of the narrative. While such a suggestion is provocative, I would like to offer a different explanation—that Van de Passe is actually citing another visual tradition and that what we are looking at in the frontispiece to the *Urania* is not only an image of female authority—the text is by a woman, after all—but also an idealized view of a family seat. If what we see between the two pillars in the allegorical *Rainbow Portrait* is a representation of the imperial but also erotic Elizabeth herself, what we see beyond the Palladian frame of the *Urania*'s frontispiece is a picture of the kinship from which Wroth draws her endogamous power.

In *The Villa as Hegemonic Architecture*, Reinhard Bentmann and Michael Muller point out a remarkable feature of sixteenth-century Italian villa decoration: as in Paul Veronese's mural painting for the Villa Mazur (1560–62), idealized landscapes vied with actual views visible out of the windows of particular villas, both of which impressed the viewer with the "aesthetic rationalization" involved in a reordering of the countryside to make it pay in a protocapitalist manner. In other words, just as the owner of a villa erected a classical-style building and had it decorated with images of idealized landscapes (with ruins), so the owner drained the marshes, rationalized the architecture, and in all ways attempted to make a profitable "picture" out of the land. The Italian view of such idealized landscapes was that they were, in fact, Flemish in origin.[24]

Van de Passe was Dutch, but the vocabulary of the Flemish-inflected Italian villa paintings would have been familiar to him from close range. His frontispiece for Wroth's romance shows three kinds of structures: the

Palladian structure on top of the hill, the Chenonceau-style bridge-cum-house spanning the river, and the cluster of buildings in the upper left-hand corner of the landscape. Such a jumble of buildings may well be, I would like to suggest, Van de Passe's representation of the famous Penshurst, which indeed looks like a medieval village in its collection of buildings surrounded by a low wall.

Penshurst was of course the Sidney family seat and the home in which Mary Sidney Wroth grew up. Van de Passe's structures do not accurately represent Penshurst, but his illustration shows buildings that are not Palladian in style. And insofar as it is a representation of nonclassical architecture it matches the specific attribute Ben Jonson had singled out in complimenting Wroth's father for not updating the Sidney manor. In "To Penshurst," Jonson notes that the Sidney house remains the way it has always looked.

Thou art not, Penshurst, built to envious show,
Of touch, or marble, nor canst boast a row
Of polish'd pillars, or a roofe of golde;
Thou hast no lantherne, wherof tales are told;
Or stayre, or courts, but stand'st an ancient pile,
And these grudg'd at, art reverenc'd the while.[25]

Meanwhile, at the same time that Jonson was commending Robert Sidney for not having rebuilt or renovated Penshurst, Inigo Jones, Jonson's onetime collaborator on Stuart masques, was busy redesigning the Countess of Pembroke's Wilton for her son, the Earl of Pembroke. He refurbished Wilton in the Palladian style, adding pillars and the famous "cube" rooms. Thus, while the frontispiece is no depiction of any real family seat, it does resemble the idealized landscape of gardens imagined by the country house poem and includes in its images the two very different kinds of architectural styles, Palladian and non-Palladian, so famously embraced by the Sidney-Pembroke family. The landscape resembles what might have been glimpsed through the windows of a rebuilt Jacobean mansion such as Wilton, with classical structures dotting the landscape, but with a medieval Penshurst-like village in the distance.

In 1616 Ben Jonson had published *The Forrest*, whose first two poems have as their subject matter Mary Wroth's family: the first, "To Penshurst," and the second to her husband, Robert Wroth. As the names of Jonson's volumes suggest—*Forrest* and *Underwoods*—this landscape is itself the site of a special kind of authority. Rightly seen as one of the greatest creators of a masquing art that celebrates royal absolutism, Jonson is also, as we see in his country house poem, engaged in articulating projects that would later in the seventeenth century celebrate another site for more local authority. Both Jonson's poems to the Wroths image the pinnacle of life as a pastoral setting in a bosky countryside, in which the ideal is Penshurst, a natural feature in itself.[26] Jonson specifically mentions the poetry-writing legacy of the Sidneys, inherited from Sir Philip, as witnessed by a tall tree in the Penshurst gardens—"There, in the writhed barke, are cut the names / Of many a Sylvane, taken with his flames" (15–16). (The *Urania* presents Pamphilia's first poem as carved on a tree.)

Not only Wroth but her cousin William Herbert, Earl of Pembroke, is directly addressed in the Jonson volume (while Jonson's entire *Works* is dedicated to him); each also is the dedicatee of a play (the *Alchemist* is dedicated to Mary Wroth, *Catiline* to Pembroke). The Earl of Pembroke and Mary Wroth earn a couple of Epigrammes each as well.[27] The family's literary capital is blazoned in Jonson's volume.

As I have noted earlier, "To Penshurst" is not, as has been claimed, the first "country house poem" to be published. The tradition began in the sixteenth century and Jonson's poem must share seventeenth-century honors with Emilia Lanyer's "A Description of Cooke-ham," published in 1611, five years before "To Penshurst" was included in Jonson's collected works. The shared generic context of these otherwise very different poems is demonstrated by the fact that Lanyer, although she does not make quite the extensive survey of Cooke-ham that Jonson does of Penshurst, nevertheless titles her poem with the generic label "description." Her poem participates quite consciously in the chorographic project that Helgerson outlined as an alternative to absolutist power: their common product was a "description," a "survey," or a "chorography" (131).

It is perhaps only dynastic accident that eventually makes one of the dramatis personae in Lanyer's poem into a Herbert. Long after the poem was written, its addressee Ann Clifford married Philip Herbert following the death of her husband Dorset; such a match again reveals the importance of the Sidney-Pembroke family. And, as we have seen, Lanyer fully understood the importance of another Sidney woman to her woman-centered project in *Salve Deus Rex Judaeorum*, when she dedicated one of her prefatory poems to a dream of Mary Sidney.

Recently Kelly Boyd McBride has argued for the special concern of "country house discourse" to explicate the way aristocratic legitimacy is founded in that landscape. McBride details how Elizabeth Talbot Shrewsbury's (a.k.a. "Bess of Hardwick") and Ann Clifford's building practices used the "semiotics" of country house discourse to "communicate an authority which is seemingly always already there."[28] While less appreciative of the particular ways aristocratic legitimacy can be enhanced by the stasis of a high-born woman who returns to her natal home and rebuilds it, McBride realizes that in both these women's cases, exercise of power was not in the service of any kind of "cultural revolution." Bess of Hardwick chose to build Hardwick Hall on the property where she was born, and which she had bought from her impecunious brother.

Susan Frye emphasizes that the gigantic initials E.S., which crown Hardwick Hall, make a signature for the house in terms of Elizabeth's final marriage, the one that elevated her to the title of Countess of Shrewsbury. Frye rightly argues that such initials bespeak Bess's exercise of her "maternal textuality" (also displayed in the same initials embroidered on the hangings within the hall), but notes that she also shared the exercise of a similar textuality with the myriad initials of lesser-known women, whose only "writings" are these embroidered letters stitched all over the textile artifacts left by Tudor and Stuart women.[29] "Elizabeth, Countess of Shrewsbury"'s use of her married initials on a building situated on her natal land makes a nice analogy to Weiner's "paradox" of "keeping while giving." Elizabeth Talbot exercised her agency by bringing back to her native place the status and wealth she had acquired through marriage: even though she had been "trafficked" away in these marriages, she was able still to keep close to her natal origin.

Ann Clifford famously fought for and won her rights to her own patrimony. While she did not build but merely repaired her ancestral castles, McBride stresses that she also chose to *inhabit* them. Ann Clifford may have married Philip Herbert, Earl of Mountgomerie, later in her life, but she is clearly remembered by her family name, Clifford (just as "Bess of Hardwick" is a name that insists on a female identity congruent with her family of origin). Their building activities exhibit the same kind of endogamous focus on the natal family, and they enhance both the woman's agency and the family's prestige.

Donald Wayne has read the "semiotics" of Jonson's poem along with that of Penshurst Place itself, outlining the Sidneys' dynastic designs in laying claim to a feudal past to which they had, in fact, no legitimate connection. The garden of Penshurst "was primarily the operator of a transformation and of a transvaluation of the notion of nobility from a concept based in hereditary descent and wealth to one based in natural virtue."[30] The gardens of the *Urania* frontispiece, then—depicting some of the most

unusually distinct features in the chorographic articulation of the aristocratic landscape—might well rehearse the language of the cartouche. As in
Lanyer's female-centered poem in praise of the ancestral seat of a mother
and daughter (one who would pursue her own inheritance), we see the
country estate as the site of a female authority firmly lodged within the
aristocratic family. Mark Girouard has argued that women were not present in the country house in sufficient numbers to be a meaningful part of
its historical importance up through the end of the sixteenth century. As
the examples of Bess of Hardwick and Clifford show, however, to judge
from such demographics is to misunderstand the importance of the few
highly born women who were there.[31] The Sidney-Pembroke family is doubly represented by the women in the frontispiece to the *Urania*; women
are present in propria personae, and also in the title insisting on the relationship between niece and aunt. The conjuncture of the two families is
also represented by two kinds of architecture recalling the Herberts' Wilton and the Sidneys' Penshurst. These two families were joined together by
two women, in one generation by Mary Sidney and in the next, if less legitimately, by Mary Wroth.

The frontispiece also includes a generically resonant reference made
by a windmill. This windmill does not appear in the verbal description of
the Palace of Love in the text, nor do windmills figure in any representations of Penshurst. Clearly Van de Passe, or whoever gave him directions
for the engraving, is responsible for it. As one contemporary reader's
response to the text—the engraver's—the windmill begs many questions
about how we might go about interpreting its presence in the landscape.

Van de Passe grew up in the Low Countries and so would have been
familiar with the omnipresent windmill. But it is unlikely that the windmill is there simply to make the landscape realistic from a lowlander's
point of view. Van de Passe's father Crispin, a famous engraver in his own
right, had done the plates for one of the most famous Dutch emblem
books, Gabriel Rollenbach's *Nucleus emblematum selectissimorum*. These
plates were recycled in George Withers's 1635 *A Collection of Emblemes
Ancient and Modern* (Figure 20). Nowhere does the windmill appear as an
icon in an emblem (although it does function as such in two other traditions of emblems).[32] As mere landscape filler in Crispin Van de Passe's
designs, the windmill travels with images of the punishment of sin: the
windmill sits on the horizon with gallows (Figures 20 and 21) or as an
image of the fickleness of fortune (Figure 22). Neither seems to have a
very resonant set of connections to the plot of the *Urania*.

One emblem in Henry Peacham's *Minerva Britannia* (1612) demonstrates just how difficult it is to trace the significance of visual references. Thus, for example, an emblem of Urania, the muse of astronomy, shows a windmill which seems to stand as an image of the forces of mundane nature (the "muddy lake") that lies beneath the interests of a heaven-pointing Urania (Figure 23). If any emblem stands behind the *Urania* frontispiece it should be this one; however, there is no moment in the book when the character Urania is focused upon the heavens. Indeed, Wroth's point is that Urania is a woman who does not know who she is, and she certainly is no personification of interest in celestial bodies. Again, there seems to be little resonance between the Peacham image and the image in the frontispiece.

A far more compelling set of connections to this windmill may well lie elsewhere. I would suggest that it is an attempt to call attention to the

Figure 20. George Withers, *A Collection of Emblemes Ancient and Modern* (London: Augustine Matthews, 1635), f. 33. Huntington Library.

parodic nature of Wroth's romance, just as Miguel Cervantes's *The History of Don-Quichote* had satirized the conventions of chivalric romance as seen from the point of view of a more realistic early seventeenth-century society.[33] The 1612 frontispiece to the English translation of the first part of Cervantes's novel, featured a very prominent windmill (Figure 24). This engraving was repeated in the title page to the second part, published in 1618. The windmill on the 1621 *Urania* may thus very well have been intended to call attention to Wroth's Cervantes-like parodic critique of a number of her precursors' stories. Because Edmund Blounte, the printer of the translation of *Don Quichote*, also printed the first folio of Shakespeare's works, which was dedicated to William and Philip Herbert, we might well detect a connection between the printer of Cervantes's fiction and William Herbert, the model for the hero Amphilanthus in Wroth's romance.[34] Herbert himself may well have been involved in suggesting

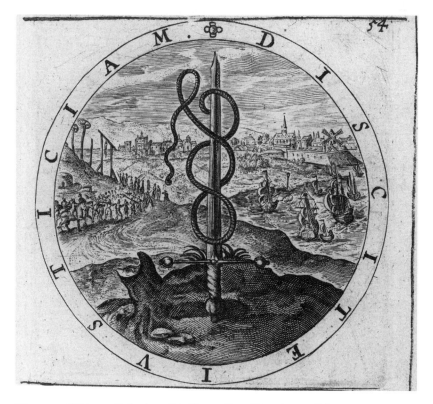

Figure 21. Withers, *Collection of Emblemes*, f. 54. Huntington Library.

the windmill to Van de Passe as a means for signaling Wroth's use of Cervantes and thus the parodic bent of the text.

Wroth is not, of course, a comic writer in the vein of Cervantes; there is no obvious tilting at windmills in her courtly inversions of romance conventions, while the literary self-consciousness of the title page, as we have seen, is far more subtle than Cervantes's own inclusion of a dedicatory sonnet from *Amadis di Gaul* in the opening pages of *Don Quixote* (the closest Wroth comes to this kind of comedic play is having one of her own characters be the author of the sonnet cycle appended to the text). Josephine Roberts points out that in the opening pages of Wroth's romance there is a Cervantes-styled rewriting of a famous episode from book I of Spenser's *Faerie Queene*, when the heroine is menaced by a ravenous beast. But

Figure 22. Withers, *Collection of Emblemes*, f. 73. Huntington Library.

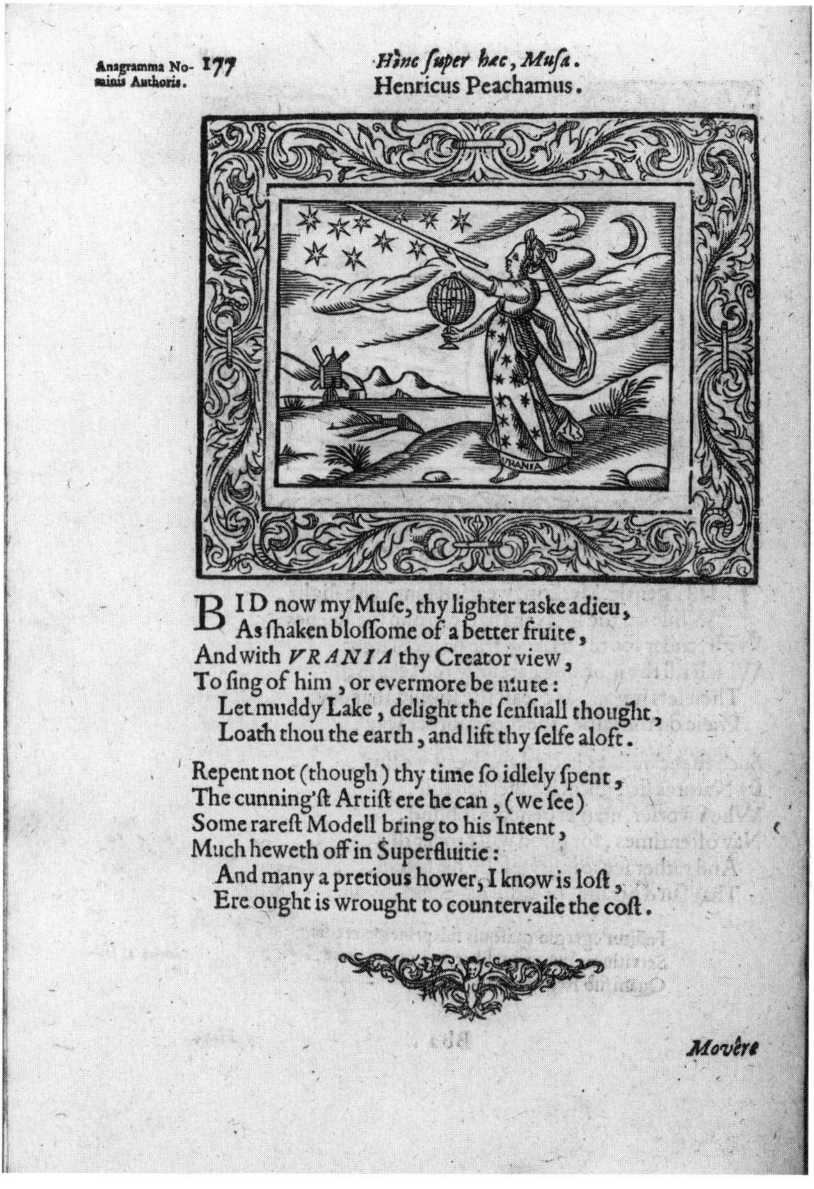

Anagramma Nominis Authoris. 177

Hinc ſuper hæc, Muſa.
Henricus Peachamus.

BID now my Muſe, thy lighter taske adieu,
As ſhaken bloſſome of a better fruite,
And with *VRANIA* thy Creator view,
To ſing of him, or evermore be mute:
Let muddy Lake, delight the ſenſuall thought,
Loath thou the earth, and lift thy ſelfe aloft.

Repent not (though) thy time ſo idlely ſpent,
The cunning'ſt Artiſt ere he can, (we ſee)
Some rareſt Modell bring to his Intent,
Much heweth off in Superfluitie:
And many a pretious hower, I know is loſt,
Ere ought is wrought to countervaile the coſt.

Movère

Figure 23. Henry Peacham, *Minerva Britannia* (London: Walter Dight, 1612), no. 177. Huntington Library.

THE
HISTORY OF
DON-QVICHOTE.
The first parte.

PRINTED FOR ED: BLOUNTE

Figure 24. Miguel Cervantes, *The History of Don Qvichote* (London: Edmund Blount, 1612), title page. Huntington Library.

unlike the lion that charges Una in Canto iii of Book I, the wolf that men-
aces Urania is not subdued by her chaste beauty. Instead two shepherds
rush onto the scene and kill it:

one might imagine, seeing such a heavenly creature, did amase her and threaten
for medling with her: but such conceits were vaine, . . . the true reason being . . .
the hasty running of two youths who with sharpe speares, soon gave conclusion
to the supposed danger. (19)

Also like Una, Urania is accompanied in the first scene by a lamb, but
this lamb is no guarantor of innocence, virtue, and Christological reference. Instead, in the second chapter, when the heroine finds that the
father of the two young shepherds is starving, she cooks the lamb for supper. This may not be as humorous as Cervantes's raucous rewriting of
chivalric codes of hospitality when he has Pancho tossed in a blanket for
not paying the inn bill, but Urania's practicality of cooking her lamb
for dinner does do away with some of the nonsense hovering around
the symbolic magic of female chastity and virtue in such romances. The
windmill is there to announce a subtly ironic slant on a subtler kind of
romance, including the reality of dealing with gender relations (as imaged
in the three sets of couples on the frontispiece), seen from the wry and
very different perspective of a woman.[35]

The frontispiece is, in a very real sense, a visual illustration of the
place of halt in the traffic in women, where female authority can find a discursive space for itself to expatiate and display. In the process the exercise
of that female agency elevates the status of the family and increases its cultural prestige.

The *Urania*

The very first scene of Wroth's romance is a conscious revision of the
opening scene of Sidney's *Arcadia*. Because the niece's rewrite of her
uncle's text recasts a scene that he himself had revised once before, it will
be useful to look at Sidney's totally new beginning to the *Arcadia*. As
niece to the Countess of Pembroke, Mary Wroth would have been one of
the privileged readers of the manuscript version of the *Old Arcadia*. She
would have had easy access to this particular version and would thus have
been able to assess the nature of the vast revisions in the text, both Sidney's own and, doubtless, the countess's also.

The move she makes to revise the text is similar to the one she evinces with Urania's cooking of the lamb for dinner. Where, in the opening scene of the *New Arcadia*, Sidney presents two shepherds lamenting the absence of a shepherdess named Urania, who never appears anywhere in the narrative, Wroth begins with the lament of the shepherdess herself, also named Urania, who has just learned that she is not really a low-born shepherdess but an aristocrat. Wroth's shepherdess's change in class status is similar to Sidney's male shepherds' sense of their own class transformation. Their love of Urania has elevated them from their base-born state as pastoral tradesmen to the status of true poets. As one rhetorically asks the other,

> Hath not the desire to seem worthy in her eyes made us, when others were sleeping, to sit viewing the course of the heavens; when others were running at Base [a ball game], to run over learned writings; when others mark their sheep, we to mark ourselves? Hath not she thrown reason upon our desires and, as it were, given eyes to Cupid? Hath in any but in her, love-fellowship maintained friendship between rivals, and beauty taught the beholders chastity?[36]

Urania's own absence from the *New Arcadia*, like Laura's and Stella's absences from the sonnet sequences that immortalize them, underwrites male writing. Her nonpresence here also marks the new authority for Sidney's revision.[37] Love of Urania has so ennobled Strephon and Claius that Musidorus, even in the midst of his frenzy over the fact that Pyrocles has been lost in a shipwreck, notices their distinct and unshepherd-like worthiness. They have shifted class, been raised into nobility by their love for Urania. As a new muse of revision and by her very withdrawal—by their remembering of her—Urania, muse of the stars, names the generic leap in class that Sidney's own *Arcadia* makes from (unpublished) family comedy to fully public, heroically ambitious narrative.[38] The new opening scene is a substitute for the straight narrative description of Basilius's quasi-comic withdrawal from political activity in the *Old Arcadia*. It is a withdrawal that Urania's absence mimics, but now without any problematic emphasis on a senex illegitimately withholding his daughters from a proper traffic in women—a senex therefore vulnerable to any machinations the comic heroes might think up to circumvent his folly (cross-dressing and lower-class disguise). In Sidney's revision, Virgil's Fourth Eclogue leaps to mind rather than Plautus: Urania's absence, unlike Basilius's, means politically serious prophecy rather than private pastoral shenanigans.

In the opening scene of *The Countess of Montgomerie's Urania*,

Wroth's Urania is not merely not absent, she is also alone. This singularity accentuates the gendered nature of her predicament.

Alas Urania said she . . . of any misfortune that can befall woman, is not this the most and greatest which thou art falne into? Can there be any neare the unhappinesse of being ignorant, and that in the highest kind, not being certaine of mine own estate or birth?[39]

Whereas Strephon and Claius celebrate their high aspiring knowledge while lamenting Urania's absence, Wroth's Urania loses the base of her identity by learning that she is high-born:

Why was I not stil continued in the beleefe I was, as I appeare, a Shepherdes, and Daughter to a Shepherd? My ambition then went no higher then this estate, now flies it to a knowledge; then was I contented, now perplexed. O ignorance, can thy dulness yet procure so sharpe a pain? and that such a thought as makes me now aspire unto knowledge? How did I ioy in this poore life being quiet? blest in the love of those I took for parents, but now by them I know the contrary, and by that knowledge, not to know my selfe. (1)

Their love for the absent Urania allows Sidney's shepherds to gain a self-awareness that is the truest sign of humanist discourse for it carries a sense of self-worth beyond class. They celebrate the elevation in their status. In contrast, Wroth's shepherdess Urania laments her elevation in class. This is, she says, the worst that can befall *woman*. Wroth places the female character center stage, elevates her class, but has her speak a complete lack of self-knowledge. If she does not know who her family is, she does not know herself. Undomesticated in her grief, unfamiliar, unknown, "her very soul turned into morning" (2), Urania speaks extempore an English sonnet in which she laments her similarity to Echo:

Unseene, unknowne, I here alone complaine
To Rocks, to Hills, to Meadowes, and to Springs,
Which can no helpe returne to ease my paine,
But back my sorrowes the sad Eccho brings. (1)

Although the poem is about Echo, it is not an echo-poem, such as, for instance, Philisides's hexameters in the Second Eclogue, to which Urania's poem bears resemblance. There is no enacted response to Urania's lamentations, and therefore no real dialogue between Echo and the speaker, whereby conventionally Echo recasts the last words of the male poet in order to create her own meaning.[40] This missing "female" part of the text is doubtless significant. There is no description by Wroth of what Echo does, but rather an insinuation of an uncanny resemblance between the speaker and the self-less nymph, whose voices, however doubly resounding, tend to collapse into a single "monefull voice," in a self-consciously bonded female experience.

Thus still encreasing are my woes to me,
Doubly resounded by that monefull voice,
Which seems to second me in miserie,
And answere gives like friend of mine owne choice.

It is not so much that Echo reflects the speaker's misery, as that the speaker and Echo are shown to be so similar in their grieving that together they become a unit to which alternate features of the landscape are "others."

Thus only she doth my companion prove,
The others [Rocks, Hills, Meadowes, Springs] silently doe offer ease:
But those that grieve, a grieving note doe love;
Pleasures to dying eies bring but disease.

Then, finally, in the couplet the speaker identifies herself with Echo's death-in-life lack of existence:

And such am I, who daily ending live,
Wayling a state which can no comfort give.

This is recognizably Petrarchan discourse, the language of a lover lamenting the absence of the beloved; but here Urania speaks not to bewail a lost lover, but rather a lost sense of self as a (female) member of a family. One could say that Wroth subtly stages here her own imitation of her uncle's text (Philisides is Philip Sidney's persona for himself), and that she dramatizes her differently gendered mimicry of a tradition by allying herself with one possible lyric female voice within that tradition — the character of Echo. Importantly, however, Wroth's use of Petrarchan discourse to have a female speaker lament her own lack of self-presence paradoxically works to insert that female into the generically well-defined position of the Petrarchan speaker. It is a way of saying that even though she is but a late echo of an already defunct genre, Wroth is appropriating quite self-consciously its discursive possibility for expressing a self, commenting as she does so (in the figure of Echo) on the very lateness of her start.[41] Without a family for context, and therefore without a definite class position (although we are right, generically, to expect this orphan to be ultimately revealed as an aristocrat), the speaker is momentarily free to define her subject position by all that it lacks.

The details of the two opening scenes are so coherent in their pointed reversals that we must acknowledge the clarity of Wroth's insertion of gender difference into the tradition she revises. Urania had asked if hers were not the worst "Of any misfortune that can befall woman." What can we expect from this Perdita-like beginning for a heroine? That Urania will rush off into her narrative, armed like a pastoral Britomart with a desire to find, not a male lover, but her female identity, that in doing so she will possibly be cross-dressed, or if not, then protected by her lower-class disguise (as Celia is in *As You Like It*)?

The very first thing Urania does is, in fact, very Britomart-like. When she comes upon a knight lamenting his lost beloved, she stirs him out of a Scudamour-like sobbing passivity and into heroic action. *But* she does not accompany him on his quest, nor does she engage in any further questing female action of her own. Instead, another kind of narrative makes its way back to the privileged pastoral spot where Wroth, just as Sidney before her, has opened her text. Thirty pages into the romance we learn that there is a most royal prince, indeed the hero of the story, who along with all his noble cousins seeks his lost sister. Urania, one quickly guesses, cannot but be that same lost sister. And indeed she is. In this way, shortly after the abrupt short-circuiting of what modern readers might hope for in a female-authored quest, Urania is not only found, she is soon lost again.

Wroth shuts her heroine up in Venus's Tower of Love. She is trapped there because her paramour Parselius (the confrere who found her) has momentarily lost sight of her importance to him. Because Parselius rushes off into a spurious vision of heroic achievement and male bonding, Urania is lost to the text entirely. Imprisoned in her tower, she remains absent from the narrative for a hundred pages, and does not reappear until her brother, the renowned Amphilanthus and his most loyal lady, Pamphilia, arrive on the isle of Cyprus and release her from her enchantment (I.i.l42) in the climactic scene represented in the frontispiece.

Rather like Spenser, Wroth gives the reader multiple heroines. The titular character, Urania, is not the heroine of the romance; Pamphilia, for whom Urania functions as friend and foil, holds that privileged position.[42] But even Pamphilia is quite un-Britomart-like. Britomart rescues Amoret unaided by anyone else; in contrast, Pamphilia releases lovers from their enchantments in the company of Amphilanthus. Both of them are necessary in order for the enchantment to be undone. Pamphilia tries to enact a Britomart-like rescue at the climax of the printed part I, but she fails. Again, it seems almost is if Wroth were inserting the reality of gender difference into each narrative turn to see what other eventuality would be the outcome. Urania cooks Una's symbolic lamb for supper; Pamphilia fails where Britomart succeeds. The differences are quite instructive. Wroth's detailed revision of the scene of Amoret's torture thus deserves a careful scrutiny.

In Spenser's scene, the enchanter Busyrane is a sadistic sonneteer who writes strange characters with Amoret's heart's blood. In Wroth's variation on this episode the rescuer is the poet, the torture victim is male, and the torturers are icons of female sexual infamy, rivals to the heroine. While the fact that the victim is male means that Wroth is unable to consider the issue of childbirth—which, I have suggested, is embedded in the heart of Spenser's episode—the names of the characters Wroth gives the torturers are very suggestive. Musalina, although she is a fully developed character in the text and one of Pamphilia's main rivals for Amphilanthus, has a name that allies her with the muses. She may thus name the questions of Petrarchan discourse overtly addressed in Spenser's scene. The other torturer is Lucenia, who like Musalina is a fully developed character in the fiction and therefore more than merely her name. But, like Musalina's, her name has a specific resonance; Lucenia recalls Saint Lucena, the Roman saint of childbirth. If such an allusion were intended by Wroth (it is not clear that it was, as Wroth's character Lucenia has nothing to do with children or childbirth elsewhere in the text), then it would be possible to claim that Wroth, as a female reader of Spenser's scene, had, in fact, intuited the physiological events implicit in the scene of Amoret torture.

Britomart is of course successful in her rescue of Amoret from torture, while Pamphilia is not; Pamphilia's impotence recalls Scudamour's when he cannot pass the flames. Wroth's rewrite of Spenser here is just as specific and close as her rewrite of her uncle Sidney's opening:

Pamphilia adventured, and pulling hard at a ring of iron which appeared, opned the great stone, when a doore shewed entrance, but within she might see a place like a Hell of flames, and fire, and as if many walking and throwing pieces of men and women up and downe the flames, partly burnt, and they still stirring the fire . . . the longer she looked, the more she discernd, yet all as in the hell of deceit, at last she saw Musalina sitting in a Chaire of Gold, a Crowne on her head, and Lucenia holding a sword, which Musalina took in her hand, and before them

Amphilanthus was standing, with his heart ript open, and Pamphilia written in it, Musalina ready with the point of the sword to conclude all, by razing that name out, and so his heart as the wound to perish. (I.iv.494)

Wroth's rescripting of Spenser's already literalized set of conceits in Amoret's torture, by making the written name "Pamphilia" visible on Amphilanthus's fleshly heart, is authorized by Spenser's own practice, as we have seen, in the first poem of the *Amoretti,* where his beloved reader is asked to read what has been written by tears in "heart's close bleeding book."[43] The bits and pieces of burnt male and female lovers' flesh derive from the dismembering tradition of the Petrarchan blazon, which is clearly one influence on this baroque scene of torture.[44] But what is most striking about Wroth's revision of Spenser's scene is that the moral values are completely reversed. Pamphilia tries vainly to come to Amphilanthus's rescue but she is unable to do so, not because she may, like Scudamour, be implicated in some way in causing the torture, nor because she has no powers of aggression (nothing comparable to Britomart's magic—and some have thought phallic—lance), but because only *false* lovers are able to enter such an arena. All-loving Pamphilia is too true and constant (read "chaste") to pass through the flames:

so with as firm, and as hot flames as those she saw, and more bravely and truly burning, she ran into the fire, but presently she was throwne out again in a swound, and the doore shut; when she came to her selfe, cursing her destinie, meaning to attempt again, shee saw the stone whole, and where the way into it was, there were these words written:

Faithfull lovers keep from hence
None but false ones here can enter:
This conclusion hath from whence
Falsehood flowes, and such may venter. (I.iv.494)

Britomart had ignored the script over the doors in Busyrane's palace and had gone in a "bold Britonesse." Pamphilia has all the courage necessary to do the same. The problem is that the enchanted site rejects her because of her very virtue. This site is the polar opposite of the enchanted palace of Venus on Cyprus, where, by virtue of her virtue, Pamphilia is able to open the doors and free the lovers. She is unable, however, to remain for long within this "hell of deceit." It is as if Poverty, or Chastity itself, were trying to enter Deduit's Garden of Love in the *Roman de la rose*. Such virtues must remain arranged as statues on the outside of the garden wall, decorating it, but incapable of entering it. As Wroth's contrasting sites attest, her use of landscape allegory insists upon the defining character of the moral virtue of constancy (the titular virtue for the incomplete seventh book of Spenser's epic). Pamphilia is the heroine of the *Urania* because she is the truest, most constant lover, the most all-loving. Wroth's huge romance, then, is rewriting Spenser's satirical Squire of Dames dilemma as well as the constancy test of the Argalus and Parthenia episode in the *Arcadia*.[45] One might also say that Wroth rewrites the "Mutabilitie Cantos" as well, so insisting that the female is the principle not of Mutability but of Constancy. As we shall see in the repeat of the Amoret-torture scene, when it is Pamphilia's (and not Amphilanthus's) chest that is torn open, Pamphilia's experience in the earlier scene in Venus's palace remains central to Wroth's manipulation of Spenser's allegorical techniques.

One of the greatest differences between Spenser's and Wroth's handling of female agency is Wroth's refusal to use cross-dressing as a device. In a genre in which cross-dressing is the norm, no lead character undertakes any gender-disguise in the *Urania*. It is as if Wroth were insisting that gender is not something one can put on and off with one's clothes. Wroth grants us a savvy—and, as far as I know, culturally unique—female viewpoint on the stage convention of male cross-dressing. She sees through it, noting in passing of one male character that he is so unmoved by a female character's pleas that "he was no further wrought, then if he had seen a delicate play-boy acte a louing woman's part, and knowing him a Boy, lik'd onely his action" (I.i.60). The fact that Wroth is here commenting on a female character's unpersuasive play-acting nor merely broaches the problematic issue of role playing open to either gender in Elizabethan and Jacobean court society, but also subtly comments on the artifice of Sidney's basic plot device. Pyrocles's cross-dressing somehow manages to fool everybody but Gynecia. Indeed, Wroth mocks the theatricality of the woman who would, Britomart-like, pursue her lover actively. She extols in her place the domestic and withdrawn nature of Pamphilia's unexpressed desire, unexpressed in all ways except in poetic discourse with herself. This withdrawal into a private, yet quite open outdoor space indicates just how hospitable the aristocratic familial site was for female agency.[46]

As representative of Wroth's authorial agency, Pamphilia's writing is doubly a family practice; in a signal episode of Pamphilia's authoring a poem, Wroth both rewrites one of Sidney's poems from the *Arcadia* and re-creates a scene celebrated by Jonson as central to Penshurst's allure. Having retreated to a private garden essentially to brood, Pamphilia instead writes a sonnet on a tree—much like the tree at Penshurst which Jonson had praised for being the site of so many lovers' names. Her poem begins, "Beare part with me most straight and pleasant Tree, And imitate the Torments of my smart" (I.i.75). The lament is a rehearsal of Pamela's in the *Arcadia*: "Do not disdain, O straight upraised Pine, that wounding thee my thoughts in thee I grave" (650). But it is important to note the overarching difference between the two contexts for these poems: in Sidney's text, Pamela has happily allowed herself to be taken off by Musidorus, trusting to his self-restraint and loyalty. Her poem is part of a love duet, for he writes a companion poem on other trees. Also, her poem insists upon her virtue, which is indeed a problematic matter at the moment; having allowed herself to be carried off, she has put her virtue profoundly at risk. Immediately after the recitation of the poems in the *Old Arcadia*, Musidorus plans to rape Pamela; he does not follow through on his intentions only because he is interrupted by the sudden appearance of a peasant mob (this scene was thoroughly revised by the Countess of Pembroke before being published in her version of the *New Arcadia*).

By contrast, in the *Urania*, Pamphilia writes her poem when she has withdrawn to her private garden to continue engraving on a tree a poem she had started earlier. Sidney's poem emphasizes the difference, the implicit agon, between the speaker and the tree, who vie with each other in virtue, however much they share a superficial similarity. In contrast, Wroth's poem insists upon the pain that Pamphilia shares with the tree. Again, as in the case with Urania and Echo, Wroth collapses rather than creates differences: the sympathetic speaker shares with the tree a similar torment.[47]

In Sidney's Italian sonnet, Pamela opens with a conceit that stresses the straightness of both tree and her virtue. However, because her thoughts are more deeply wounded than the tree, she cannot think that "My inward hurt should spare thy outward rine":

Do not disdaine, O straight upraised pine,
That wounding thee, my thoughts in thee I grave;
Since that my thoughts, as straight as straightness thine,
No smaller wound—alas! far deeper have. (650)

The sestet presents the twist that, however opposed tree and speaker are, "Yet still, fair tree, lift up thy stately line"—a line that includes not only the long-lived tree's height, but now the stately verses about Pamela's virtue that the tree continues to testify. The poem then closes with a couplet that tightly draws the paradox of the female in Pamela's position; in typical Sidney fashion, it overturns the logic of the first twelve lines and leaves the conceit of the tree utterly behind:

My heart my word, my word hath giv'n my heart.
The giver giv'n from gift shall never part.

The crux of the entire plot of the *Old Arcadia* is that the proper bestower of Pamela's hand—that is, her father, Basilius—has specifically refused to give her away, having withdrawn in terror because of a prophecy that had forecast some misfortune connected with Pamela's courtship. Turned (impossibly) into both giver and gift, Pamela may wish to bestow herself where she desires, but in so doing, she risks all—as the attempted rape and rebellion subsequently reveal. Sidney's tree-poems artfully outline the problem Pamela faces: even though the "root" of her desire is virtuous and constant, her virtue can offer no solution to the problem posed by her attempt to be the giver of herself as a gift. The illogic of the couplet's "paradox" makes the problematic Elizabethan traffic in women explicit. A woman cannot legitimately be both the giver of a gift and the gift itself.

Although Pamela comes up against something of the traffic's systemic limit in the last two lines of her poem, Sidney ventriloquizes through her a very active speaking subject. In contrast, although Wroth's Pamphilia commands her tree to do any number of things, her poem enforces stillness, positing a similarity rather than a dramatic agon between arborial addressee and speaker. Wroth's speaker is nearly as immobile as the tree itself as she asks the tree to join in sympathy with, and to imitate, the speaker in her pain.

Beare part with me most straight and pleasant Tree,
And imitate the Torments of my smart
Which cruell Love doth send into my heart,
Keepe in thy skin this testament of me: (*Urania*, 75)

Sidney's Pamela—herself a cruel mistress who denies Musidorus—confesses that she has given herself her own wounds ("Thus cruel to myself"); Wroth's Pamphilia more traditionally complains that she has been a passive subject of love's mastery. In the second half of Wroth's

octave, it is indeed difficult to say at first what is being engraved—the tree
or the speaker:

Which Love engraven hath with miserie,
Cutting with grief the unresisting part,
Which would with pleasure soone have learnd loves art,
But wounds still cureless, must my rulers bee. (*Urania*, 75)

Only as we read further do we understand that what love has engraved is
the "testament" of the grieving speaker and not the tree. Wroth's sestet
pursues a similarity between object and subject that Sidney's poem
neglects until its final paradoxical closing couplet. Drawing an analogy
between the sap of the tree and a lover's tears, she makes use of this
baroque comparison in the prose introduction to the poem; thus Pamphilia "finished a Sonnet, which at other times shee had begunne to en-
grave in the barke of one of those fayre and straight Ashes, causing that
Sappe to accompany her teares for love" (I.i.74). In the poem itself, the
sap actually becomes the tree's tears; its weeping is similar to the speaker's
heart's blood that "drops."

   Thy sap doth weepingly bewray thy paine,
My heart-blood drops with stormes it doth sustaine,
Love senceless, neither good nor mercy knows
Pitiless I do wound thee, while that I
Unpitied, and unthought on, wounded crie:
Then out-live me, and testifie my woes. (*Urania*, 75)

   These blood drops recur throughout the poetry of the *Urania*, becoming something of a signature as well as, perhaps, as acknowledgment
of Spenser's precedence in the Amoret episode in sadomasochistic son-
neteering. The ultimate difference between Wroth's tree and speaker,
however, is that the tree will live on but the speaker, a mere mortal, will
not. The implication is that the speaker expects to "die" of love's torments
sooner rather than later. The notion of the long-lived tree—testimony to
Pamela's long-delayed gratification of desire—here in Wroth's poem not
only serves as a kind of love death, but also implicitly speaks to the
immortality of the verse. Sidney's Pamela does not expect to be remembered as a poet. Wroth's Pamphilia at least considers the possibility.
   Soon after she has written this poem, Pamphilia is startled by a noise
in the bushes and spots Antissia secretly "close by her," just as Musidorus

had eavesdropped on Pyrocles/Zelmane in the *Arcadia* when the latter had been reciting his poem on his cross-dressed predicament: "Transformed in show, but more transformed in mind" (*Arcadia*, 131). Unlike Musidorus, however, Antissia already knows that Pamphilia is in love. With the sensitivity wrought by fellow-suffering, she recognizes all the signs in Pamphilia, though the poet is reputed to be above such folly. What Antissia wishes to know is not whether Pamphilia loves, but whom she loves: "My curiositie . . . was, and is, lest it should bee hee whom I affect," that is, Amphilanthus (67–78 [*sic*]). Pamphilia, the most discreet of princesses, heroic in her silent suffering, refuses to confess that she loves Amphilanthus beyond his just deserts as a most worthy prince. But, she asks, even if she should, theoretically, love him,

> what then? Were it any more then my extremest torment, when I should see his affections otherwise placed? The impossibility of winning him from a worthy love, the unblessed destiny of my poore unblessed life, to fall into such a misery; the continuall afflictions of burning love, the fier of just rage against my owne eies, the hatred of my brest for letting in so destroying a guest, that ruines where he comes; these were all, and these alone touching me in all disquiets. What need should they have to molest you, since so perfectly you are assured of his love, as you need feare no occasion, nor any body to wrong you in that, wherein he will not wrong his worthy choice and constancy? (*Urania*, 79)

Their conversation ends with Antissia confessing "I am contented." And the scene closes when, "So rising, and holding each other by the arme, with as much love, as love in them could joine, they tooke their way backe towards the Palace" (79).

But Antissia is only momentarily satisfied by Pamphilia's evasions and has not, in fact, been taken in by the latter's pretense; she still suspects what is all too true, that Pamphilia loves Amphilanthus and is beloved by him. Later she witnesses a secret meeting in this same garden between Pamphilia and a man whom she takes to be Amphilanthus. In fact, the man is not Amphilanthus (that is, Urania's brother), but instead one of Pamphilia's own four brothers, who, dressed as a servant, has been engaged in his own Musidorus-like courtship; now he has returned in secret to his father's court, where he wishes to remain unknown, or rather, known only as the Unknown Knight (as he has been commanded by his lady to call himself). As a result, Pamphilia needs to act as secret messenger between her disguised brother and their father, the king of Morea, who—behaving very differently from the noncomic literary tradition—remains remarkably mute and remote in Wroth's text.

The king's lack of immediate authority over his progeny is demonstrated in an episode when Dalinea arrives at his court to announce not only her prior marriage to his son Parselius, but the birth of their child. The king is distressed to hear of this marriage—which Parselius has not bothered to mention, for he has been paying bigamous court to Urania—and he calls his son in to explain. But before Parselius can lie to his father, Dalinea announces herself and reminds him of their marriage. Not addressing her directly, Parselius asks his father to call in Leandrus, Dalinea's brother. He then confesses all, to both his father and Leandrus: "This Sir is true, and humbly I aske pardon for my fault, which I had meant more priuately to have confess'd; and you Leandrus pray now pardon me, your Sister hath lost nothing" (203)

The king for his part "forgave them, and with fatherly affection wept, and kissed her, and the babe: then did Leandrus embrace them both, shee asking pardon, and Parselius too he did forgive, and so all were content." Urania, for her part, is "untouch'd with love or anger" by these radical shifts in everyone's emotions. With characteristic cynicism the narrator comments, "mourning was cast aside and all the joy express'd that clothes or Triumphs could produce." Pamphilia, for her part, "admiringly" (that is, in some puzzled wonder) "beheld Urania and her Brother," and prays "Protect me from such distress" (203).

It is impossible to overstress the strange plethora of brothers and the even more bizarre patriarchal silence of fathers in the *Urania*. In the latter case, it differs radically from the *Arcadia*, where fathers are much in evidence: if Basilius is a bad father to his daughters, withholding them from a proper traffic in women, then Euvarchus is the patriarch par excellence, exhibiting his patriarchal governorship most pertinently at the point when, Abraham-like, he would sentence to death his own son Pyrocles to satisfy the exigencies of the Law. The son's life is saved by the comic deus ex machina of Basilius's resurrection when the misadministered love potion simply and finally wears off.

In the *Urania*, Parselius owes as much to Leandrus' forgiveness as he does to his own father's: the responsibility for patriarchal order is shared between fathers and sisters' brothers, and the general pressure of the narrative grants the brother the greater share of power over women. The women silently suffer not only their wayward lovers' but also their brothers' wayward actions.

As we have seen, Sidney kept insisting on his male right to advise the queen on whom she might and might not marry, acting, that is, the male patriarchal family member, assuming her lack of freedom to dispose of herself where she might wish. Lady Mary Wroth is herself the eldest offspring of the marriage between Robert Sidney and Barbara Gamage; Queen Elizabeth had tried to stop the wedding (just as she had tried to stop the Sidney-Walsingham match), but her letter interdicting the nuptials arrived a few hours too late.[48] Somehow the Sidneys always managed to evade her patriarchal powers. If even Queen Elizabeth could not control the traffic in women in her own court, far be it from such as Mary Worth, or Urania, or Pamphilia to think of doing so. And no one ends up with the "right" person in the second part of the *Urania*.

In her study of identity and difference in *The Subject of Tragedy*, Catherine Belsey has argued that women in Britain "for most of the sixteenth and seventeenth centuries were not fully any of [the] things . . . posited of the subject of liberal humanism—unified, autonomous, author of [their] own choices." Able to speak, indeed to write, they were "permitted to break . . . silence [only] in order to acquiesce in the utterances of others. . . . [They] were denied any single space from which to speak for themselves."[49] The confusing contestation for control over the "subject position" of women at this period and its troublesome impact on even so self-conscious an author as Mary Wroth is signaled by the bizarre pronoun slippages that, as we have seen, mark Urania's opening soliloquy. However, as Wroth's fictional representative of the self-possessed "poet," Pamphilia's writing practices are not only more self-conscious, they are also more coherent than Urania's. Significantly, Wroth stages an interchange between the two women characters about this very issue of self-possession, one which may bear on their different authorities not only as writers but as "authors" of their own choices. We will not, however, understand the peculiar pressures on Urania's position (or what, finally, Wroth might be alleging by positing a contrast between the two women) unless we take into account Urania's dramatic experience of her brother's culturally granted power to "trade" her—that is, to help her select a suitable suitor.

I noted above that Urania seems less upset than she might have been when Dalinea comes to claim Parselius. The reason for her coolness is that prior even to hearing this revelation of his unfaithfulness to her, Urania has been cured of her love for him. The cure aptly dramatizes the power given to brothers in this romance. After rescuing his newly found sister Urania from her imprisonment on Venus's island, Amphilanthus sets about obeying an obscure and alarming prophecy. He takes Urania to the island of St. Maura, where, he has been told, he must pitch her into the sea. Stoically, she doesn't object.

Deerest Urania, I must throw thee into the Sea; pardon me, Heaven appoints it so. My deerest brother, sayd she, what need you make this scruple? You wrong me much to thinke that I fear death, being your sister, or cheerish life, if not to joy my parents; fulfill your command, and be assured it is doubly welcome, comming to free me from much sorrow, and more, since given mee by your hand . . . he tooke her in his armes, and gently let her slide, shewing it rather to be her slipping from him, then letting her fall, and as shee fell, so fell his heart in woe, drownd in as deepe an Ocean of despaire. (192)

As it turns out, there is no need for his sorrow; Urania is rescued very quickly by "two men in a boat" who dive in after her; they are her brother's friend and kinsman—Parselius and the man destined to be Urania's husband (Steriamus). After all three are rescued from the waves, "Amphilanthus embraced them, and with teares of joy welcom'd his sister, and his friends, who now well understood the operation of that water; for Parselius knew nothing of his former love to her, only the face of Urania, and being assured of her neernesse to him in blood [they are first cousins], rejoyced with them. . . . Urania's desires were no other, then to goe into Italy to see her father" (193).

Cast away by her brother, taken up by his friends, shipped off to her father—Urania enacts how women are the bonds between men, the cultural glue, as it were, that holds society together through their exchange between groups of men. At this point, Urania begins to move (if as yet imperceptibly) from Parselius to Steriamus (who has begun to forget that he was in love with Pamphilia, Parselius's sister, as he moves on to Urania, Amphilanthus's sister). If fathers trade in both sons and daughters—that is, arrange matches for both—the gendered (as opposed to the generational) nature of patriarchy becomes clearest in the very different relations of power between brothers and sisters. Brothers as well as fathers can trade in their female relations. Indeed, if it had been Wroth's conscious intention specifically to focus on the gendered nature of patriarchy, the way it treats females differently from males, she would have had almost programmatically to distinguish between the authority of fathers and brothers. Patriarchy allows fathers to traffic in upper-class youth of both genders—as William Cecil, Lord Burleigh notoriously manipulated the system of wardship in male heirs to his personal profit. But patriarchy does not merely allow one generation to traffic in another, it allows males to traffic in women. By multiplying the number of brothers and sisters in her text, Wroth points to that brother-sister relation that most specifically marks the gendered nature of the system of transfer. If fathers trade both sons and daughters, only brothers trade sisters. Sisters do not trade brothers.[50]

The humane warmth and affection of the interchange between Amphilanthus and Urania show how deeply Wroth accepts the natural affective bond between brother and sister. The intimacy and strength of the tie, the sense of physical connectedness between the two, demonstrate the emotional richness of the bond, a richness Wroth fully dramatizes. These are not "abnormal" relationships like that of the Duchess of Malfi and her diabolical brothers, or that of the incestuous siblings in *Tis Pity She's a Whore*. However, the normality of sibling relationships in the *Urania* does not mean that Wroth is incapable of catching a glimpse of the problematic position in which the far greater power of brothers puts sisters such as Urania. Unlike the Duchess or Annabella, Urania may not die at her brother's hands, but she is happily willing to do so.

Wroth most directly critiques the traffic not through the figure of Urania, however, but the (perhaps more problematic) position of Pamphilia. Although at first orphaned, Urania is the character Wroth uses instead to analyze the experience of the female reassuringly traded out by her brother, relieved of her passion for a close family member. Pamphilia, in her royal isolation (she is a queen in her own right), allows Wroth to focus on a sovereign female who actively chooses an erotic attachment across the very kinship tie Urania is made to relinquish. Before we can understand the specifics of the analysis she undertakes of the Jacobean traffic in women, as she contrasts Urania's and Pamphilia's experiences, we need a better sense of the specifics of Wroth's own unusual family situation.

The central and overarching relationship of mutual passion in the *Urania* is one between two first cousins, Pamphilia and Amphilanthus. Josephine A. Roberts has persuasively argued that this pairing is a reflection of Wroth's long-term affair with her own first cousin, William Herbert, son of Mary Sidney Herbert, a notoriously amorous young man, to whom Wroth bore two illegitimate children. Some have, of course, also identified Herbert as Shakespeare's Mr. W.H., the only "begettor" of the sonnets. A positive identification of William Herbert with Amphilanthus, however, rests on rather more solid ground than equating him with Shakespeare's beloved young man, not merely because both familial and erotic relationships are the same in the poem and in life, but also because Wroth makes Amphilanthus the author of a poem independently identified as Herbert's in a number of contemporaneous manuscript collections.[51]

This poem is presented only in the unpublished manuscript second half of the romance. Thus, although he is famous for his poetry throughout the entire narrative, Amphilanthus never actually produces a poem in the published volume, almost as if Wroth can neither risk identifying him in public, nor deny the identification by supplying him with a poem of her own composition. In the manuscript segment of her work, however, Wroth does risk the familial identification by reproducing "Had I loved butt att that rate."

It is difficult to assess whether or not the affair between Wroth and her cousin would have been thought by their associates to be actually incestuous; it did, in any case, produce two illegitimate children, a girl and a boy. Illegitimacy was not necessarily an insurmountable problem in itself with this class at this time (Penelope Devereux's five illegitimate children—whom she reared quite openly with her lover Charles Blount—are a case in point), and Wroth's having Herbert's children would not necessarily have been a terrific scandal. Statutes passed under incest-obsessed Henry VIII had decreed first-cousin marriage to be licit in the Church of England of the time—but the Catholic Church and, more important, continental Protestant churches still considered it well within the prohibited degrees. It is possible that the Sidney family's radical religious feelings may have made them less than easy with the situation, as, I suppose, we would be today with our own rather vague sense of the interdiction against first-cousin marriage. Of course, whole human societies are organized along lines of just the kind of cross-cousin marriage that Wroth's relationship with Herbert would have entailed. As Christine de Pizan pointed out, incest is only incest when society decrees it to be so.

Whether or not the relationship between Wroth and Herbert was felt to have been actually incestuous, their affair lies close to one end of an endogamous extreme; it was clearly very discursively empowering for her. Similarly in the romance, Pamphilia is granted a choice of her own sexual partner (loving her first cousin) that runs counter to the prevailing social norm (in the case of Wroth, the social norm of legitimate Protestant marriage).

Assuming that "by contracting a relationship close to the forbidden degree of consanguinity, [Wroth] could both defy convention and enfold herself back into the family romance," Gary Waller associates such a transgression with her writing: her "defiance of literary and social conventions and her battles for both publication and privacy mark her writing as an area in which, however tentatively and with whatever opposition, resistance to patriarchy can be sensed."[52]

Urania criticizes Pamphilia for loving her brother Amphilanthus, but not because theirs is an unsuitable match (although Urania has just been cured of a parallel attachment to Pamphilia's brother by Amphilanthus's ministrations in St. Maura); Urania's point is rather that Pamphilia deserves someone better than her inconstant brother. (Although apparently acceptable, an official union between the two is never contemplated by anyone, even though both principals are unmarried and later—in the manuscript continuation—freely marry others.) Because Amphilanthus has been constantly inconstant to her, so Urania reasons, Pamphilia too should be allowed a change in her affections. Urania argues against Pamphilia's obstinate refusal to do so:

'Tis pitie said Urania, that ever that fruitlesse thing Constancy was taught you as a vertue, since for vertues sake you will loue it, as having true possession of your soule, but understand, this vertue hath limits to hold it in, being a vertue, but thus that it is a vice in them that breake it, but those with whom it is broken, are by the breach free to leave or choose againe where more staidnes may be found. (400)

Urania does not, of course, specifically single out herself as a happy instance of those who find greater contentment in change, although Amphilanthus did save her a period of sorrow by pitching her over the cliff, thereby drowning out memories of her unsuitable love. For her part, Pamphilia insists on the willful activity of her desire, irrespective of anything Amphilanthus might or might not do to deserve her devotion. Pamphilia's position seems at first glance to be quite masochistic; however, upon closer scrutiny of its specific terms, it demonstrates rather that she has a will of her own, and that she exercises full command over it in order to institute her own active desire as her possession of herself. Urania charges her with something like having been captured by the abstraction "constancy" which has taken "possession" of her. Pamphilia insists that her virtue is under the mastery of a different force, the god of love.

To leave him for being false would shew my love was not for his sake, but mine owne, that because he loved me, I therefore loved him, but when hee leaves I can do so to. O no deere Cousen I loved him for himselfe, and would have loved him had hee not loued mee, and will love though he dispise me. . . . Pamphilia must be of a new composition before she can let such thoughts fall into her constant breast, which is a Sanctuary of zealous affection, and so well hath love instructed me, as I can never leave my master nor his precepts, but still maintaine a venturous constancy. (400)

As paradoxical as it may sound, Pamphilia's point is really that if she loved Amphilanthus only as a return for his loving her, her desire would have its origin in the male's desire and would remain a mere reflective repetition of it. In order to locate an active desire in her female self, she needs her own will to be autonomous. While she appears to depend on him, taking her identity from loving him constantly, she in fact insists upon an identity impervious to any action he might take. Her constancy is, finally, an act of willful self-definition. She "will love though he despise me." The "master" whose instructions she follows is love itself, the Amor of an older tradition of love poetry, not the boy Cupid but a mature Lord of Love such as the one who instructed Amant in the *Roman de la rose*. Pamphilia defines herself by the constant breast she maintains — and the anatomical location of the "sanctuary" she celebrates here is the same place where Amoret's torture takes place, and, consequently, Wroth's rewritings of that scene of torture.

Pamphilia's tenacity derives not merely from a biographical choice clearly made by Wroth herself in her illegitimate alliance with her inconstant cousin William Herbert. Rather this pivotal conversation between the two lead female characters in her narrative has deeply embedded connections to Wroth's rewrite of Spenser's allegory in *The Faerie Queene*. When Pamphilia remarks that she cannot let thoughts of a new lover "fall into her constant breast" until she is of a new composition, she borrows for herself the authority of a personification without, I would like to suggest, sacrificing her own female agency. Much in the manner of Spenser's replicative, self-interpreting text, her comment refers back to a most important moment at the climax of book I, the scene of disenchantment that forms the subject matter of the romance's frontispiece. The question of the relationship between Pamphilia's identity as woman and the crucial virtue of constancy is at the crux of both scenes.

When Pamphilia releases the prisoners in the Castle of Love on Cyprus by giving to Amphilanthus the key that the statue of Constancy has just given to her, the personification of Constancy as represented in the statue on the bridge disappears into Pamphilia's breast.

Both then at once extremely loving, and love in extremity in them, made the Gate flie open to them, who passed to the last Tower where Constancy stood holding the keyes, which Pamphilia tooke; at which instant *Constancy* vanished, as metamorphosing her self into her breast; then did the excellent Queene deliver them to Amphilanthus, who joyfully receiving them, opened the Gate. (169)

Here it is almost as if, to use Gordon Teskey's formulation, the allegorical abstraction Constancy has effected a "capture" of Pamphilia, transforming her "constitution" irremediably. It seems to be on the basis of this moment that Pamphilia later says that she must become of a different "constitution" in order for other thoughts to fall into her breast so that she would become able to love someone other than Amphilanthus. The infusion of Constancy into Pamphilia has marked her "constitution." Because Pamphilia's breast later becomes the site of her own baroquely imagined torture, Constancy's transformation into that breast allows us to see how carefully Wroth prepares her rewrite of Spenser. Her series of scenes seem almost explicitly to address Teskey's understanding of what is at stake in the negotiations of female authority with allegorical personifications. The mediating text in the first disenchantment episode is Ovid's *Metamorphosis;* it is again recalled in Constancy's "metamorphosing her self" into Pamphilia's breast. It appears first in the description of the statue of Venus, which is compared to Pygmalion's masterpiece. (Wroth rewrites Ovid constantly in the *Urania,* regendering, as Roberts points out, Ovid's tale of Arethusa and Byblis.[53])

To recall the myth of the transformation of Pygmalion's statue into a real woman is to move in reverse along the path Teskey calls the "halfway process" of capture, that is, the movement is away from abstraction toward materiality. This is also true of the relationship between Constancy and Pamphilia: Constancy vanishes, transformed into the breast of a real woman, almost as if Wroth herself might be meditating on Shakespeare's rewrite of the Pygmalion myth in *The Winter's Tale*—where the statue can move because it has always been a real, aging, female body. In each of these rehearsals what gets insisted upon is that the woman is real, the artwork is not.[54] Pamphilia is half-captured, not by constancy, but by Love. This very half capture has made her into a poet. She is not the dead and lifeless work of art but the artist who creates poetry out of her sufferings as a constant woman. When we hear Pamphilia and Urania debate the problems surrounding "this word constancy," as Urania derisively terms it, she gives Pamphilia the opportunity to articulate her own ontological status in relation to the term.

The ultimate revision of the moment of torture—which again insists on the unreality of the artwork in contrast to the living woman—is the vision Amphilanthus has of Pamphilia in the hell of deceit. Already replicating the scene in which Pamphilia saw Amphilanthus being tortured by women (with his heart ripped out of his chest cavity and Musilina trying

to erase Pamphilia's name from its surface), Amphilanthus's vision is a
return to the original gender arrangements of Spenser's scene in which
Amoret is tortured by Busyrane.

> A Ring of iron hee then saw, which pulling hard, opened the stone; there did
> he perceive perfectly within it Pamphilia dead, lying within an arch, her breast
> open, and in it his name made, in little flames burning like pretty lamps which
> made the letters as if set round with diamonds, and so cleare it was, as hee dis-
> tinctly saw the letters ingraven at the bottom in characters of bloud; he ran to take
> her up, and try how to uncharme her, but he was instantly throwne out of the
> Cave in a trance, and being come again to himself, resolving to dye, or to release
> her since her found her loyalty, he saw these words onely written in place of the
> entrance.
>   This no wonder's of much waight,
>   'Tis the hell of deepe deceite. (655–56)

Pamphilia here seems to have been turned into a dead icon of "loyalty," as if the "capture," in Teskey's sense, had been total. Here too we get,
fully literalized, the "characters of blood" in Busyrane's kind of writing.
The narrative itself, however, undercuts this vision; it is not, finally, "of
much weight," for the vision is false, of "deep deceit." It is not that Pamphilia is false, but that she is not dead. She is, in fact, alive, whole, and still
loving Amphilanthus. If only inconstant lovers can be "in" the hell of
deceit, the place is capable of offering only deceitful visions. What Amphilanthus sees is a false vision, rather like the false vision created by Archim-
ago that leads the Redcrosse Knight astray in Book I of *The Faerie Queene*.
Through its falsity, however, Amphilanthus understands the truth, that
Pamphilia is constant. Her constancy, however, is not a dead thing, but
fully agented. A few paragraphs after this vision, Pamphilia appears in the
narrative, unharmed in any way. Amphilanthus may imagine Pamphilia
constant and dead; but she is, in fact, quite alive. The conclusion of the
first enchantment in Book I had hinted at Pamphilia's freely chosen
agency, for there the force named by another term takes the place of Constancy in effecting the happy outcome. The narrator explains how the
prisoners in the Tower of Love are finally released.

> [Pamphilia and Amphilanthus] then passed into the Gardens, where round about
> a curious Fountaine were fine seates of white Marble, which after, or rather with
> the sound of rare and heavenly musick, were filled with those poore lovers who
> were there inmprisoned, all chain'd one unto another with linkes of gold, enam-
> eled with Roses and other flowers dedicated to *Love*: then was a voice heard, which
> delivered these wordes: "Loyallest, and therefore most incomparable Pamphilia,

release the Ladies, who must to your worth, with all other of your sexe, yeeld right preheminence: and thou Amphilanthus, the valliantest and worthiest of thy sex, give freedome to the Knights, who with all other must confessee thee match-lesse: and thus is *Love* by love and worth released." (170)

Wroth may well be punning on her own name in insisting upon the "worth" that pairs with love in order to release the prisoners. Because "worth" is predicated of her preeminence among women, we are invited to see Wroth's authorial character present in Pamphilia's achievement. Paradoxically, Pamphilia's "worthiness," like Stella's "richness" in Sidney's sonnet cycle, is declared by the husband's name. Like Bess of Hardwick's initials "ES," Wroth's name further signifies her identity as a widow. Both women bring their married status back to the natal family site. "Worth" names her true value, her constancy to her first-cousin lover and it is a virtue of equal force with Amphilanthus's heroic bravery.

Within the fiction of the romance, Pamphilia is as famous for her poetry as is Amphilanthus. When she complains of his infidelity and insists on her own constancy in poem after poem, she borrows the authority of the personification of the virtue, but she bases her own agency on her refusal to respond to the fluctuating demands of male desire. Hers is an active volition that is to be distinguished from the personified abstraction she not so much refuses to become (like Dante's Francesca), in Teskey's for-mulation, but that she contains within herself to make it a defining char-acteristic of her own will.

What Wroth has done, then, is to reformulate a transgressive active female desire, dressing it up in a traditional female virtue, patient con-stancy. Out of this maneuver, she creates Pamphilia's authority, institu-tionalized in the poems of the sonnet cycle appended to the *Urania*. These poems stage the halt of the traffic in women as Pamphilia again and again voices her desire for her first cousin, the privileged son of her father's (and uncle's) sister. As the author not merely of the first work of pub-lished prose fiction written by a woman, but of the only sonnet cycle pub-lished by a woman in English during the Renaissance, Wroth constructs herself not merely as a writing subject but as an author. In staging that authority as a regendered imitation of her uncle's various texts, she imi-tates in her fiction the erotic choice she made in her life: she will not be traded out, but remains within the protection of a family that persis-tently authorized its females' desire to write, thereby increasing its own remarkable status.

7

Shakespeare's Cordelia

AGAINST THE AUTHORITY OF ALL the sources of *King Lear*, Cordelia dies at the end of the play. Bale's use of her in the preface to his edition of Elizabeth's *Glass* (1548) as an exemplum indicating women's fitness to rule had followed the traditional story about Lear: Cordelia outlived her father and reigned alone for a time after he died.[1] Readers have long complained of the peculiar cruelty of her death. Samuel Johnson for one found the pain of reading the scene so great that he had to force himself to read it a second time when he was editing the play.[2] Many critics have struggled to make sense of what seems a particularly relentless dramaturgical pathos, the outcome of a death sentence ordered by Edmund which he disavows a moment too late, creating a final tragedy which was not entirely necessary. The fact that Shakespeare goes against the entire shape of the story as it had traditionally been told only makes the matter worse.

Jonathan Dollimore has argued that the timing of Cordelia's and Lear's deaths are "precisely subversive: instead of complying with the demands of formal closure . . . the play concludes with two events which sabotage the prospect of both closure and recuperation."[3] Because Albany has just been moralizing on the deaths of Goneril and Regan about which "This judgment of the heavens, that makes us tremble, Touches us not with pity" (V.iii.230–31), the audience is prepared to see the next events as a divine judgment. Albany continues moralizing while Lear enters carrying Cordelia's dead body:

All friends shall taste
The wages of their virtue, and all foes
The cup of their deservings. (V.iii.302–4)

Is the dead Cordelia in his arms one of Lear's "deservings"? Dollimore's point is that the deaths of Lear and Cordelia "sabotage" the "supernatural" intelligibility of society which Edgar also intones when he explains the justice of Gloucester's blindness:

The gods are just, and of our pleasant vices
Make us instruments to plague us:
The dark and vicious place where thee he got
Cost him his eyes. (V.iii.170–73)

Janet Adelman finds in Cordelia's death the intelligibility of, at least, Lear's sufferings: "if Cordelia's death comes to Lear as the prerequisite for his new emotional openness, it comes to Cordelia herself as a punishment for the desire he has invested in her. For the mother that threatens to suffocate Lear by his sheer need of her must herself be suffocated: that is the price Cordelia pays for acquiring the power of the displaced and occluded mother."[4] Although Adelman nowhere calls this desire "incestuous," Lear's desire for a maternal Cordelia can be so termed, as Richard McCabe indeed does: "So far as family relationships are concerned, the opening scene is one of the most embarrassing in the Shakespearean canon."[5] According to McCabe, Cordelia would avert an incestuous relationship by her silence, her resistant "nothing," but in the final scene McCabe finds that she looks perilously as if she had answered Lear's indecent request:

Cordelia has effectively abandoned her husband in her father's interest thereby according him the "kind nursery" he had sought all along. . . . Lear speaks as though he had finally lured Cordelia into the sort of total commitment demanded in the opening scene. (178)

McCabe insists that in fact Cordelia does not waver—her "personal attitude remains constant," he bluntly states—although how he knows this is not made clear. Instead, Cordelia dies, with the cruelty that seems so entirely undeserved.

Stanley Cavell puts the blame squarely on the nature of Lear's love for Cordelia—"too far from plain love of father for daughter": Cordelia herself is perfect, "she alone" possessing the capacity for compassion Lear needs, "transcending personal morality."[6] Cordelia must die, according to Cavell, because, even after all the purgative sufferings Lear has endured, he repeats the sin of his first desires: the play shows us "that the reason consequences furiously hunt us down is not merely that we are half blind, and unfortunate, but that we go on doing the thing which produced these consequences in the first place. What we need is not rebirth, or salvation, but the courage, or plain prudence, to see and to stop" (81). While Cavell never calls Lear's desires incestuous, he does insist upon critics' sharing in

Lear's refusal to "see" what the real position of a character is at a given moment, and in this, readers share Lear's own tragedy, which is a willful "refusal to see," or rather more largely, the "avoidance of love" that is, the willingness not only to see, but also to be seen by another.

What critics of such diverse persuasions agree on here is the pain of Cordelia's seemingly unwarranted death, and the need to exonerate her of any complicity in the sin for which her death might (or might not) be punishment. Their shared testimony is witness to the remarkable power of the scene to overwhelm the audience with pain: perhaps its dramatic power to move may finally be the real reason for its existence as spectacularly effective theater. All attempts to account for the cruelty of its power may simply be our understandable efforts to deflect so great a pain.

Another more easily readable—but perhaps also partly unfair—double death might clarify a little the historical paradigm Cordelia's death fulfills. In the *History of Pericles, Prince of Tyre*, word comes that the incestuous Antioch and his unnamed daughter have been killed by a bolt of lightning:

When he was seated in a chariot
Of an inestimable value, and
His daughter with him, both appareled all in jewels,
A fire from heaven came and shriveled up
Their bodies e'en to loathing, for they so stunk
That all those eyes adored them ere their fall
Scorn no their hands should give them burial. (8.7–13)[7]

It may seem unfair that the nameless daughter has to die, but in this version of the incestuous couple she is also at fault. Our twenty-first-century sensibilities do not allow us to blame someone who is clearly a victim, but we differ from the Renaissance in this. Helicanus moralizes:

for though
This king were great, his greatness was no guard
To bar heav'n's shaft, but sin has his reward. (8.14–16)

While this scene is from the part of *Pericles* most scholars agree Shakespeare did not write, it has the authority of close proximity to *Lear* and may grant us insight into conventional Elizabethan/Jacobean cultural response to the daughter's guilt and its appropriate punishment in a case of flagrant incest. It may help us to understand how the Renaissance did indeed assume that the sin was shared between the couple and therefore that Cordelia's final complicity in her father's fantasy makes her also guilty.

By this kind of reasoning she is just as deserving of the mechanically applied justice as Goneril and Regan. She is not at all like them, of course, for they are evil and cruel and she is good and kind: but the play punishes her fulfillment of Lear's fantasy just as it does Antiochus's daughter's compliance.[8]

I propose this placement of Cordelia's predicament not in order to deepen or enrich our understanding of her "character"—indeed, I think we of the early twenty-first century are ultimately incapable of "understanding" Cordelia as being in any way guilty of any sin or crime, much less one deserving death as its punishment. The notion of divine punishment seems a bit otiose in and of itself. The following argument is offered to help outline what the parameters for female agency were at this point in time and how these cultural limits affected actual women writers of the period. The need to understand another Shakespearean character in a slightly different way is far less pressing than the need to understand the unread women authors of the Renaissance, and if attempting to reperceive Cordelia, however alien it makes her, helps us towards this understanding, it is worth taking the risk.

Cordelia has most agency in the play when she comes back from France at the head of an army: but that is also when she is fulfilling Lear's fantasy of rescue and communion. She has the least amount of agency— is banished from the stage in chosen silence—when she seems to us to be enacting her most autonomous independence from her father, Yet she expresses this seeming "autonomy" only by her obedience to the rules enjoining the mandatory traffic in women, contenting herself to be the bond "between men."

> Haply when I shall wed
> That lord whose hand must take my plight shall carry
> Half my love with him, half my care and duty. (I.i.98–100)

Cultural moments differ; while we may never be able to teach ourselves to respond to earlier poetry as C. S. Lewis once asked us to, by finding the seventeenth-century cavalier within us, we can come to recognize the vast difference which separates us from the late sixteenth and early seventeenth centuries. If the very limits on Tudor and Stuart women's freedoms make them irremediably strange to us, by understanding that difference we may begin to appreciate how unreliable a picture of the period our sense of the transcendent genius of Tudor and Stuart male authors may have provided us. Our century tends to find the (female) victim of incest innocent, in contrast to the active blame the Renaissance play of *Pericles* puts on Antiochus's daughter; Shakespeare's revision of Gower's medieval version of the story elides the pains taken there to reveal the daughter's victimization by her coercive father:

> sche was tendre and full of drede,
> Sche couthe nought hir Maidenhede
> Defend, and thus sche hath forlore
> The flour which sche hath longe bore.
> It helpeth noght althogh she wepe,
> For thei that scholde hir bodi kepe
> Of wommen were absent as thanne;
> And thus this maid goth to manne,
> They wylde fader thus devoureth
> His oghne fleisshe, which non socoureth,
> And that was cause of mochel care
> Both after this unkind fare
> Out of the chambre goth the king,
> And sche lay stille, and of this thing,
> Withinne hirself such sorghe made,
> Ther was no wiht that mihte hir glade,
> For feere of thilke horrible vice.[9]

Even with this understanding of her innocence, however, the medieval tale, like the Renaissance play, still incorporates the daughter with her father in the sin's punishment (showing how similar these two periods are to each other, and how different from our modern moment):

> Antiochus, as men mai wite,
> With thondre and lyghthnynge is forsmite
> His doghter hath the same chaunce,
> So be thei bothe in o balance. (9.999–10002)

The later Renaissance play gives no insight into the daughter's state of mind, save for a single remark she makes, when she hopes that Pericles might succeed at his quest. Insofar as the daughter demonstrates her agency at all in the play, it is through the riddle itself, which is cast in her voice, a different approach from that taken in Gower's text where the riddle is a garbled medley of both father's and daughter's voices:

> With felonie I am upbore,
> I ete and have it noght forbore

Mi modres fleissh, whos housbond
My fader forto seche I fonde,
Which is the Sone ek of my wif. (VIII.405–9)

If the answer to the "I" who eats mother's flesh is the daughter, Gower
has prepared the reader to understand that this is only due to the father's
sin, he being the first to "devour his own flesh" in coercing his daughter:
"the wylde fader thus devoureth / His oghne fleissh." In contrast, the riddle in the Renaissance play is entirely in the voice of the daughter: she is
the speaking subject of the sentences, voicing her active desire:

> I am no viper, yet I feed
> On mother's flesh which did me breed.
> I sought a husband, in which labour
> I found that kindness in a father.
> He's father, son, and husband mild:
> I mother, wife, and yet his child.
> How this may be and yet in two
> As you will live resolve it you. (1.107–14)

As if it were not the patriarchal duty of her father to find her a husband,
the riddle assumes the daughter's absolute agency: "I sought . . . in which
labor I found." Led by the strength of this stated subject position, Pericles
punningly addresses the daughter herself as if she were the one who had
to be answered (as well as being the answer to the riddle):

Fair glass of light, I loved you and could still,
Were not this glorious casket stored with ill.
. . .
You're a fair viol . . .
But being played upon before your time,
Hell only danceth at so harsh a chime.
Good sooth, I care not for you. (1.124–29)

Her "vile" crime, of course, is that she has been the passive recipient of
untimely attention—but still she has been the crime's instrument. When
not led by the language of the riddle—which gives agency to the daughter—Pericles in soliloquy names the incestuous agent as the one the
twenty-first century would agree he is, the father:

If it be true that I interpret false,
Then were it certain you were not so bae
As with foul incest to abuse your soul,

Where now you're both a father and a son
By your uncomely claspings with your child—
Which pleasure fits a husband not a father
And she, an eater of her mother's flesh
By the defiling of her parents' bed. (1.167–74)

The idea of incestuous cannibalism, as it were, intercourse with a father being equated with the eating of human flesh, underscores the nature of the taboo being broken. As Mary Douglas has argued in *Purity and Danger*, dietary rules and incest laws are twin means by which a society polices its permeable borders, where the bodily difference between inside and out, allowed and disallowed, are most ambiguous and ambivalent.[10]

As if to understand the provisional nature of taboos, Gower's version of the tale opens with a disquisition on the periodic lawfulness of incest: it had been necessary during antediluvian times to increase the number of humanity ("Forthi that time it was no Sinne / The Soster forto take hir brother"; 8.68–69), and also after the flood, it not becoming illicit until the Third Age, when "ther was people ynouh in londe" (8.101). The story of Apollonius of Tyre is an exemplum of how a man should dread to feel lust within his "Sibrede" or kindred; in fleeing the incestuous couple in Antioch, Apollonius demonstrates how one should behave as a properly exogamous potential husband and father.

Apollonius-Pericles's exogamous activities may make clear by contrast what Shakespeare's Lear does that is so contrary to proper patriarchal behavior. I say "Shakespeare's Lear" because in the contemporaneous play, which may have been a source for Lear, the king behaves in a much more properly exogamous fashion. This play does not have to be a source for *Lear*, I would argue, in order to be useful in providing an illustrative contrast, outlining as it does what would have been deemed, if not "normal," then dramatically verisimilar behavior to contemporaneous society. Along with *Pericles*, the two plays can provide a useful yardstick to measure where Lear seems to transgress even those norms allowed fictional characters.

The True Chronicle History of King Leir

Unlike King Lear, Leir intends to make no invidious distinctions among his daughters' dowries, to whose husbands he plans to give "nor more, nor less, but even all alike" (1.37);[11] this is the appropriate treatment of daughters, who get equal divisions of the inheritance, primogeniture

applying only to male heirs. The jealousy among the sisters in the drama-
tized chronicle history is stirred up not by their father but by someone
else entirely, the evil councilor Skalliger, who lies to Regan and Gonorill
that their father will give the greatest dowry to the one "whose answer
pleaseth him the best." Indeed, Leir concocts the idea of the love test only
in order to trick Cordella into choosing among her suitors.

I am resolv'd, and even now my mind
Doth meditate a sudden stratagem
To try which of my daughters loves me best
Which till I know, I cannot be in rest.
This granted, when they jointly shall contend
Each to exceed the other in their love,
Then at the vantage will I take Cordella,
Even as she doth protest she loves me best.
I'll say, "Then, daughter, grant me one request:
To show thou lovest me as thy sisters do,
Accept a husband whom myself will woo." (I.75–85)

Leir's wish to choose a husband is the farthest thing from Shakespeare's Lear's desire to give a "more opulent" third to Cordelia because he
intends to place his rest on her "kind nursery." Leir himself requires from
Cordella only that she be as accepting as her sisters of his choice for her
husband; because they have already acquiesced to his choices (which, they
imply, are their own as well), they are free to pretend greater love to their
father, but again, even their pretenses insist that their love is best shown
by a free acceptance of his choice of husbands. There is no hint of incest
in this scene—nor is there any hint elsewhere in the plot; rather, the tragicomedy revolves around the older daughters' knowing manipulation of
Leir and their sister, and Leir's enraged decision to dispossess himself in
order to disinherit Cordella once she has refused to go along with the
game. Lynda Boose comments that the Leir play reveals a more clear-cut
set of motivations on the part of its characters than *King Lear*, and this
is doubtless the case.[12] Cordella's agency is that of a romance heroine,
who, in refusing to let her father choose her husband, is left fatherless,
orphaned, and so able—rather like similarly orphaned Perdita—to choose her
own husband, who she thinks is low-born. Or, rather, as Florizel does in
The Winter's Tale, the disguised king of Gallia wins Cordella's love after
he has fallen in love, listening to her vow to earn her living as a seamstress.

While this position accords most closely to our sense of autonomous,
undomesticated, wage-earning feminist agency, we need to be cautious.

The vow is a means for down-classing Cordella, underscoring with the most obvious signal possible (class change) her now spectacularly un-fathered status. Cordella thinks of herself as inhabiting the status of some-one of "mean estate"—as if her tale were Griselda's—owing all to her husband. And indeed, she does, so that her husband counsels her to "For-get thy father and thy kindred now" (Sig.E2ʳ). In a sense, this out-of-class place outlines a discursive position of halt similar to that achieved by in-cest, where the daughter is not traded out by the father so she is free to choose her own lover. Yet even this utterly disinherited Cordella articu-lates what it is to be the perfect wife by being the perfect daughter—just as her imperfect sisters err most in the chronicle history first by being bad wives. Like Cordelia in the opening scene of Shakespeare's play, Cordella elegantly describes how the traffic in women is supposed to work when she complains to her husband the king:

Not that I miss my country or my kin,
My old acquaintance or my ancient friends,
Doth any whit distemperate my mind,
Knowing you, which are more dear to me
Than country, kin and all things else can be.
Yet pardon me, my gracious lord, in this,
For what can stop of the course of nature's power?
. . .
As easy is it for the slimy fish
To live and thrive without the help of water;
. . .
As I am able to forget my father. (xvi.29–45)

When Cordella and the king of Gallia go to aid King Leir, they do so together, both indeed recognizing that it is the husband's will which is the active agency; the king of Gallia promises to go to war:

If ere my heart do harbor any joy
Or true content repose within my breast,
Till I have rooted out this viperous sect
And repossess'd my father of his crown,
Let me be counted for the perjur'dst man
That ever spake since the world began. (sig.Hᵛ)

In the romance play, then, the two kings, Gallia and Leir, are bound to-gether by the woman's love whose affections they share between them. Cord-ella's desire to aid her father thus initiates the affective bond between men.

Pericles, Prince of Tyre

Leir's mistake is not, like Lear's, to engorge all of his daughter's love, but to trick her into letting him choose a husband for her. The problem is a delicate one, which the romance of *Pericles* also addresses in Pericles's courtship of Thaisa. When Pericles finds himself in Tarsus, beloved of Thaisa, her father Simonides comically enacts the "blocking" father's usual reluctance to grant his daughter to another man. Like Prospero and Miranda, father and daughter ideally must approve the same suitor.

> King Simonides . . . Now to my daughter's letter.
> She tells me here she'll wed the stranger knight,
> Or never more to view nor day nor light.
> I like that well. Nay, how absolute she's in't,
> Not minding whether I dislike or no!
> Mistress, 'tis well I do commend your choice
> And will no longer have it be delayed. (9.13–18)

Even though he approves of Pericles as a suitor, Simonides pretends until the last—and rather ridiculous—moment that he objects to the match:

> I'll tame you, yea, I'll bring you in subjection.
> Will you not having my consent
> Bestow your love and your affections
> Upon a stranger—(aside) who for aught I know
> May be, nor can I think the contrary,
> As great in blood as I myself,
> Therefore hear you mistress: either frame your will to mine—
> And you, sir, hear you: either be ruled by me—
> Or I shall make you man and wife. (9.96–105)

Immediately after Simonides's parody of the comic senex and his abrupt transformation into the good father, the play stages a dumb show of the announcement that Antiochus and his daughter have been slain by a bolt of lightning. Simonides's objection to Thaisa's exercise of her own choice —which seems to him too "absolute"—is colored not only by concern for her choice of a foreigner, but by his worry that she may also be moving out of her class. He intuits Pericles's class correctly, however, and so looks with favor on the match.

Strangely, Pericles turns out to be a very different kind of father from Simonides. He marries off Marina with such abruptness in the final scene that he doesn't even think to ask how she might feel about it. This

abruptness seems to short-circuit the agency the play has so painfully
established for Marina by all her professorial lecturing and teaching in the
brothel. Almost as if it were comically literalizing all the contradictions in
the traffic in women, the play reveals how a woman may gain agency for
herself by halting the traffic in women. When Marina refuses to be sold as
a prostitute, the social status she gains—lecturing in the brothel—allows
her ultimately to enact a healing of her father the riddling terms for which
sound like incest. Marina may provide us another important contrast to
Cordelia in the multiple distinctions she poses to the nameless daughter
of Antiochus, victim of her father's incestuous desires.

The pirates who make off with Marina begin the process of comic lit-
eralization of the bond a woman represents between men: "Half-part,
mates, half-part!" (15.142). So too they comically register the profit to be
gained in exogamous practice: they elect not to make use of her sexually
themselves because they can sell her to a greater profit if her virginity is
intact. When she is finally set up in the brothel, of course, she manages by
her eloquence to maintain her virginity, to keep herself untrafficked in.
Gower's narrative explains that Marina is a notable poet; in the city of
Mytilene in *Pericles*, however, she is a preacher:

First Gentleman. Did you ever hear the like?
Second Gentleman. Nor, nor never shall do in such
a place as this, she being once gone.
First Gentleman. But have divinity preached there—
did you ever dream of such a thing?
Second Gentleman. No, no. Come, I am for no more
bawdy houses. Sha'll go hear the vestals sing?
First Gent. I'll do anything now that is virtuous,
but I am out of the road of rutting for ever. (19.1–9)

Her eloquence—her very speech—becomes something like a substitute
commodity for the sexual congress she does not provide. Lysimachus (her
husband-to-be) is dazzled by her wit and confesses "Though I brought
hither a corrupted mind, / Thy speech had altered it." (19.128–29)

When it is clear that her virtue is ruining all the trade of the brothel,
and Boult cannot bring himself to deflower her in order to make her useful, she suggests a money-making scheme similar to Cordella's:

If that thy master would make gain by me,
Proclaim that I can sing, weave, sew, and dance
With other virtues which I'll keep from boast:

And I will undertake all these to teach.
I doubt not but this populous city will
Yield many scholars. (19.205–10)

Her remarkable agency, underwritten by her eloquence, is further emphasized by Pericles's corresponding speechless state. When he is told that
his daughter is dead, his response is to become mute. Thus when the
third tempest of the play brings him by providential chance to Mytilene,
the place his daughter resides, the locals offer to bring him to a special
young woman of the town who is capable of curing his peculiar disease of
silence:

We have a maid in Mytilnee, I durst wager,
Would win some words of him. (21.32–33)

Whereas similarly unusual female eloquence by Portia in the lawcourt is
protected by masculine cross-dressed disguise, here the very halt in the
traffic in women enables and is enabled by Marina's remarkable eloquence. Her eloquence is synonymous with her virtue and will heal her
father's silence.

   One of the sources for the play—and the source from which Shakespeare gets the name Marina—may well be the story of Saint Marina, who
as a young woman defied her father's plans to marry her to a rich suitor,
hiding from him by cross-dressing and entering a monastery. There the
"brother" becomes famous for great healing powers; when Marina's father
comes to the monastery for solace, he is sent to the spiritually gifted monk
who promises the father that he shall see his long-lost daughter. When the
brother dies before this event happens, the father comes to rail at the
monk's corpse, only to share in the monastery's revelation that the brother
is, in fact, a woman—Marina, his daughter (as a letter clutched in the
corpse's hand makes clear).[13]

   Standing behind the scene of the reconciliation between Marina and
Pericles, the story of Saint Marina insists that Marina's halt in the traffic
in women by virtue of her eloquence is similar to the agency underwritten by cross-dressing in the legend of the saint. Cross-dressing similarly
allows a number of Shakespeare's heroines to experiment with female
agency; it is a freedom which the language of incest would also appear to
underwrite: the moment of healing in *Pericles* is presented in the language
of metaphorically incestuous begetting just as the analogous moment in
the saint's legend is the revelation of the cross-dressed body.[14]

Why Shakespeare should have changed the name of the hero of the Gower story from Appolonius to Pericles has also been cause for discussion. If, as some have suggested, the name comes from Philip Sidney's *Arcadia*, the connection puts the play squarely within the tradition of Elizabethan cultural meditations on female agency and the traffic in women occasioned by Elizabeth I's anomalous (and as we have seen, quite incest-specific) autonomy. Sidney's romance not only provides a different version of cross-dressing when Pyrocles disguises himself as an Amazon, it also flirts, as we have noted, with a comically conceived endogamous desire whereby three separate family members are in love with the same cross-dressed man. As Leonard Tennenhouse has provocatively suggested, the romance proved to be a resource for an astonishingly vast number of theatrical redactions because it spoke so crucially to the overriding issue of the period, Elizabeth's problematic female inheritance of authority.[15]

Pericles's address to Marina once he recognizes that she is his lost daughter, makes use of the incestuous language of the play's opening to insist not upon punishment but upon miraculous recovery:

O Helicanus, strike me, honored sir,
Give me a gash, put me to present pain,
Lest this great sea of joys rushing upon me
O'erbear the shores of my mortality
And drown me with their sweetness! O, come hither,
Thou that begett'st him that did thee beget,
Thou that wast born at sea, buried at Tarsus,
And found at sea again. O Helicanus,
Down on thy knees, thank the holy gods as loud
As thunder threatens us, this is Marina! (21.178–87)

The multiply begotten relationship that Pericles celebrates with his new-found speech posits it as, if not the last moment of ecstasy in this play, then the highest (he does not hear the music of the spheres when he is rejoined to his wife Thaisa but only when he is rejoined to his child). It is profoundly like the joy celebrated in Elizabeth's translation of Marguerite's soul's union with God, or the absolutely perfect love of the doubly incestuous brother and sister (who are also father and daughter) lamented by the sinning mother in story 30 of the *Heptameron*.

So powerful is the threat of incest amid all this joy, and so necessarily different must Pericles be from his avatar at Antioch, that his first word after insisting that his courtier will know his daughter as "thy princess" is to ask of a strange man who stands nearby, "Who is this?" In a mere forty-three lines, he has contracted with this stranger to wed his new-found daughter to him. From the moment of his sentence to Lysimachus, the previously eloquent Marina remains absolutely silent, although Pericles addresses a number of remarks to her ("List, my Marina" 21.216).[16]

If we contrast this moment of father-daughter confrontation with that between Lear and Cordelia we see some crucial differences among the similarities, all of which point to the refusal of the scene in Lear to do what the scene in *Pericles* does with such startling abruptness to protect itself against the taint of incest. Indeed, the revisions of the scene, an apparent streamlining of the stages of Cordelia's return to England from Quarto to Folio version, insist upon her greater, singularly autonomous, unhusbanded agency.

In the Quarto version Cordelia comes with her husband, the king of France; in the late Folio version she is alone, with no mention at all made of her husband. It may be that having a foreign king accompany Cordelia looks more like an invasion, the repulse of which is legitimate—thereby making the evil party, at least in their warring (they do win), in the right: in the Quarto, for example, Goneril spurs on a reluctant and censorious Albany by asking, "Where's thy drum? France spreads his banners in our noiseless land" (16.52; later, Albany specifically comments on the fact of foreign invasion: "it touches us as France invades our land"; 22.26–29). The Folio cuts all these references, thereby denying the evil party any kind of legitimacy in defending their homeland. The Folio's change, however, not only denies the evildoers any moral right, it also serves to underscore Cordelia's entry as herself the head of the (nonforeign) army. In the Folio version she shares no agency with her husband or even with his surrogate (in the Quarto "Monsier la Far" acts as general; 17.9). The stage directions in the Quarto insist on Cordelia's daughterly domesticity—she is nurse: "Enter, CORDELIA, DOCTOR, and others"—as if Cordelia were here most of all a precursor to Marina, who comes to minister to a father's failing mental health. The Folio's stage directions for act IV, scene 3, specifies a military accompaniment: "Enter with drum and colors, CORDELIA, GENTLEMEN, and soldiers."

At the same time that Cordelia's agency is given greater stress, the streamlining of the plot in the Folio version tends generally to deny agency to the husbands of Lear's daughters: thus in the Quarto Albany expresses horror at the sisters' treatment of Lear, articulating his own male bond with his brother-in-law as well as the feudal bond of retainer to prince: "Could my good-brother suffer you to do it— / A man, a prince by him so benefacted?" (26.43–44). The Folio cuts this concern.

Cordelia's heightened military responsibility in the Folio seems to be in lieu of lengthy characterizations of her response to news of her father's suffering in the Quarto, so summarily cut (and replaced in the conflated text still printed by the Norton version of the Oxford Shakespeare). As well as making the last scenes run more quickly (which is doubtless the real dramaturgic reason for the cuts), they deny us the chance to imagine Cordelia crying offstage "queen / Over her passion whom, most rebel-like, / Sought to be king o'er her" (17.14–16), with the famous passage about her tears and smiles like sunshine and rain together. So too in the Quarto Kent describes Lear's reluctance to confront his daughter because of his great guilt.

A sovereign shame so elbows him: his own unkindness,
That stripped her from his benediction, turned her
To foreign casualties, gave her dear rights
To his dog-hearted daughters—these things sting
His mind so venomously that burning shame
Detains him from Cordelia. (17.43–48)

good ordlypts
of QDF

His unkind treatment of his daughter includes his turning her out to "foreign risks," the very thing she had asked for in the opening scene. The Folio's cuts, then, generally deny us a sense that Cordelia has a legitimate life elsewhere, married, with a husband with whom she shares Lear as "our" father.

Falling as it does on Cordelia's unhusbanded agency, the emphasis of the Folio version of the final communion accentuates the intimacy Lear's prison fantasy establishes for the two of them, father and daughter, sequestered together, relieved of the responsibilities of governing: this is just like the "kind nursery" Lear had imagined at the beginning, a desired communion destroyed by Lear's rage at Cordelia's refusal to comply with his command to love him "all." Here Lear is triumphant: "Have I caught thee?" he asks her. All we are vouchsafed of insight into Cordelia's motives at this moment is her ambiguous remark about good intentions: "We are not the first / Who with best meaning have incurred the worst" (5.3.3–4). It is her last speech in the play.

That the "worst" here is incest—whatever Cordelia's better intentions—needs to be shown. While many readers have sensed that Cordelia here complies with a desire she rejects in the opening scene—and it is a desire which she herself brands incestuous when she criticizes her sisters' hypocrisy—it is useful to ask whether or not the play actively makes an effort to signal this problem in the final scene. The incest at issue in this climactic scene is, of course, that pointed out by Edmund in his metaphorical claim that the two sisters and he marry in death: "I was contracted to them both: all three / Now marry in an instant" (5.3.202–3). The bodies of the two (doubly) incestuous sisters (first in hypocritically claiming to love their father and second in courting the same man) are brought onstage just before Lear arrives carrying Cordelia: such a parallel may be offered to show the contrast between the two, but if Goneril, Regan, and Edmund marry at death then so, it may be supposed, do Lear and Cordelia.

Perhaps the greatest dramaturgical signal the play makes toward incest as part of its high tragic theme is that which generically separates the tragicomedy of *King Leir* from Shakespeare's tragedy: the secondary plot of Gloucester's blinding, the story Shakespeare imported from Sidney's *Arcadia* but which may owe its remarkable cultural resonance to Greek tragedy, at least as Greek tragedy was filtered down to the Renaissance through Seneca's redactions of the plays. Late nineteenth-century criticism found the connection between Gloucester's blinding and Seneca's traditionally grotesque physicality too obvious to need comment. In 1893 John Cunliffe says of *Lear*, "in addition to wholesale slaughter and physical horrors such as the putting out of Gloster's eyes," the play "contains some resemblances worth noting."[17]

This resemblance seems, however, quite crucial, in particular the possibility that a theater-going public would have seen in the figure of a mutilated, blind man being led by his child a reminiscence of Oedipus, the tragic Theban king. Such a signal would have great bearing on Edgar's comment about Gloucester, that "the dark and vicious place" where he begot Edmund "cost him his eyes." This remark—part of the language of divine retribution which Dollimore sees as being subverted by the cruel unfolding of the scene—signals what is at stake, a series of Oedipal infractions which deserve punishment.

The story of the father blinded and forced to wander alone, only to be rescued by a kinder legitimate son, is, as the father tells it in Sidney's *Arcadia*, an exemplum of what happens to a man who is morally blind to begin with. The king of Paphlagonia narrates his story to the two princes, Pyrocles and Musidorus, as they wait out a tempestuous storm: he ends by asking them to kill him, just as he has asked his loyal son to do, pleading with him to lead him to the top of a rock, beneath which they now shelter, where he might jump to his death. The son refuses, causing the father to summarize: "only therein since he was born showed himself disobedient unto me."[18] There is no source listed for this story, a narrative nested within another narrative (as Musidorus tells Pamela about the princes' earlier adventures). In Sidney's hands, the moment becomes another instance of the corrosive power of despair and the need to take counsel against it. The scene is therefore preparation for the long dialogue between Pyrocles and Cleophila about Stoic virtue, in which she attempts to dissuade him from committing suicide.

Shakespeare's version, like Sidney's, emphasizes despair, but makes the father's desire for death into a means by which a child is able to cure a parent. Edgar's ruse in bringing his father to an imaginary Dover cliff and having him leap off it is a remarkably complicated dramaturgical moment which plays the force of narrative against theater, as Edgar discursively creates a landscape for the blind Gloucester which the audience cannot see: the imaginary narrative of cliff ascent, desperate fall, and miraculous landing from so great a height is juxtaposed to what the audience actually sees, Gloucester merely flopping to the floor. The bathetic contrast enacts the comic belief (in miraculous salvation) which Edgar would create in his despairing father. But the moment also plays with considerations of what happens when narrative is turned into theater. The manipulation of theatrical devices (Edgar alters voice, playing at least two parts) calls attention to the very theatricality of the moment, just as Sidney's narrative calls attention to its own narration (two separate people tell the story within the story Musidorus relates).

The most famous theatrical moment (which Sidney would have known) of a blind man being led by a child is, of course, Oedipus led by Antigone. It was a story which would have been well known to the learned members of Shakespeare's audience. For example, *Jocasta*, George Gascoigne's adaptation of Seneca's redaction of Euripides' *Phoenician Women*, had been presented at Grey's Inn in 1566. In this redaction of the Theban story, Antigone chooses not to marry Creon's son, but to lead her blind father through the wilderness in his banishment:

OEDIPUS: O yes, dear daughter, leaue thou me alone
Amid my plagues: Be mery while thou maist.
ANTIGONE: And who shall guide these aged feet of yours,

That banisht bene, in blind necessitie?[19]

Antigone is not the only daughter to be leading a blind father in this play; in an earlier scene blind Tiresias enters led by his daughter Manto. It is almost as if the blind father led by the dutiful daughter becomes an emblem of the Theban cycle itself, a shadow emblem, as it were, of Sidney's claim that keeping in one's memory the emblem of Aeneas carrying his father Anchises will make one a more heroic individual. I mean to suggest not that Shakespeare intuited a Senecan source to Sidney's story, but that the image of the blind man being led by his child would have had a far more specifically Oedipal resonance in Elizabethan culture, and by "Oedipal" I mean here, with distinct historical specificity, the story of Oedipus as Seneca had retold it in numerous plays, variously reprinted and imitated throughout the sixteenth century.

According to Robert Miola, by the end of the sixteenth century there were more than fifty separate printings of Seneca's collected plays. Nor would printings of the plays in Latin have had the widest dissemination.[20] Seneca's *Oedipus* had been translated by Alexander Neville, a fifteen-year-old Cambridge scholar, and printed in 1563; it was printed again in a collection titled *Seneca, his tenne tragedies* by Thomas Newton in 1581, and had thereby a wide circulation. As did other translators of other plays in the volume, Neville changes a lot of the play, not least making Oedipus the executioner of his mother as well as of his father (in Seneca's original she kills herself).[21] Neville thus punishes Jocasta with greater force. Bruce Smith remarks that, as is usual with Elizabethan redactions of classical plays, Neville changes a Greek sense of fated tragedy and the ironic gap between divine knowledge and human action into a more clear-cut moralized humanist concern that punishment should provide justice: for his recasting of Seneca's hero, "Neville has his eye on the choosing protagonist of morality-play tradition, and in his direct-address harangues, Oedipus confronts the audience not as Seneca's sublimely isolated sufferer, marked out by fate for a destiny all his own, but as chastened Mankind who willfully has worked his own destruction: 'Alas, the fault is all in mee.'"[22] Clearly Neville's Oedipus feels Jocasta shared some of the blame.

The 1581 print of the play, interestingly, provides brackets around the lines describing Oedipus's self-blinding: two sets of triplets, amid the fourteener couplets, call attention to the extra emphasis the verse form gives the moment of blinding.

With fiery flaming spotted cheekes
    his breast he often beats,

And scratch and teare his face he doth
    and Skin asunder treats.
That scarse his eyes in head could stand
    so sore he them besets.
. . .
When sodenly all franticklike
    himselfe from ground he reares,
And rooteth out his wretched Eyes,
    and sight asunder teares. (92)

The last two fourteeners are bracketed in the text, a visual cue that the climactic moment has been reached, the text providing something which a reader would want to be sure not to miss.

The third tragedy in Newton's 1581 text makes Oedipus's blindness central to the opening scene: the first act of the *Thebais*, translated by Thomas Newton, opens with Oedipus pleading with Antigone to leave him so that he may blindly stumble and fall to his death:

Dear Daughter, unto Father blynde
    a Staffe of steady stay,
To weary Syre, a comfort greate,
    and Guide in all his way:
And whom to have begotten,
    I may glad and joyfull bee:
Yet leave me now, thy haplesse Syre,
    thus plunged in misery.
Why seekest thou meanes, still to direct
    my stalking steppes aright?
Let mee I pray thee headlong slide
    on breaknecke tumbling plight.
. . .
Leave of thy hold, let lose thy hand,
    good daughter, let mee goe:
Let foultring foote light where it will,
    let it (this once be so).
Ile trudge, and runne, Ile skudde, and faunge,
    Ilse haste to the hill
Of raggy stiepe Cytheron, there
    I hope to worke my will (41)

He even threatens her with incestuous rape:

Depart a mayd and Virgin hence,
    for feare of afterclaps:

Since villany to Mother shewde,
    its good to doubt mishaps. (42)

Antigone is unswayed, answering with an acute analysis of her difference
from her brothers:

My Brothers twayne let them contend,
    and fight for Princelye swaye
Of wealthy Thebes: where whilom raignd
    King Labdacke many a day.
The greatest share and portion
    that I do loke to have
Out of my Father's kingdome, is
    my Fathers lyfe to save. (42)

Antigone finally manages to cure Oedipus's desire for suicide by offering
to leap with him off a "huge Promontory that elboes into Sea." Her offer
anticipates Edgar's trick with uncanny similarities:

Heere beaten with the tyde
Bee craggy Cliffes, let's goe to them:
    Here runns a gulphy streame
With force afore it dryving stones
    as bigge as mountaigne beame.
What say you? shall we drench our selves
    within this fomy Flood? (43)

It seems entirely possible that, when Edgar moralizes about his father
Gloucester, speaking to his brother about "The dark and vicious place
where thee he got / Cost him his eyes," at least some members of the
audience would have found such Senecan moralizing familiar. Quite possibly some might have thought of the blind Oedipus, led by the faithful
Antigone, when Edgar leads blind Gloucester to the "cliffs" of Dover.
Oedipus's family is not unlike Gloucester's: two sons battled each other
to the death, Eteocles having denied Polyneices his right. In another play
based on the myth, Gascoigne's *Jocasta*, Antigone reveals to her blind father
their two corpses, placing his hands over the sons' bodies just before she
guides him offstage.[23]

Janet Adelman makes a parallel argument about the relevance of
Gloucester's blinding to Lear's Oedipus-like problems and his incestuous
desire for Cordelia, but she does so by psychoanalytic means. Moving
through the verbal associations among the terms used for the bleeding

empty eye sockets themselves—as Edgar describes them, "bleeding rings, / Their precious stones new lost" (5.3.189–90)—Adelman's point is that, as an image of castration, they figure forth the regendering of Lear as a man overwhelmed by the feminine force he would suppress, the "mother," which chokes him.[24] The "dark and vicious place" where Gloucester begot Edmund is the "female sexual 'place'," where, according to Adelman, the play locates darkness and evil itself, a further emanation of which is the "eyeless" storm in which Lear also wanders lost and ill-seeing.

Adelman's subtle means for connecting the two plots is their shared repression of the "occluded maternal presence":

> The pattern of repression and return visible in Edmund's illegitimacy and in the blinding of Gloucester is played out again in the Lear plot, where the presence of daughters *per se*—daughters instead of sons—has a function equivalent to the presence of the illegitimacy in the Gloucester plot, that of returning the father to the occluded maternal place. (107)

Although she mentions in a footnote the traditional Freudian understanding of blinding as a punishment for incest, she does not, in fact, make that argument, pointing instead to the Renaissance assumption that blindness was a result of excessive sexual activity in general. Rather, she mines the play for remarkable parallels that underpin the connection between the two plots:

> the one acts out the subjugation that has been implicit in the other: in the blinding of Gloucester, the punitive female power of the storm—the power of the dark and vicious place—is given a local habitation and a name. We begin the rush into the storm with the womanish tears Lear attempts to suppress, the tears that threaten to stain his "man's cheeks" (2.4.80); we end with a Gloucester vulnerable as a woman, a Gloucester whose man's cheeks are stained with the blood and jelly of his weeping eyes. We begin with the "eyeless" storm (3.1.8) and end with the blinded Gloucester. (112)

Such a brilliant reading of the dense verbal texture of the play can only be enhanced by a recognition that a Renaissance audience might well have seen some of these same thematic concerns by means of a distinct dramaturgical allusion to the theatrical image of Oedipus as they would have received it from the Senecan plays.

I would also like to suggest, however, that Adelman's argument parts company with a historical reading of the situation of incest in the play when she laments the loss of Cordelia's agency in the final act. Adelman sees Cordelia's return to nurse her father as, in fact, complicity with her father's incestuous fantasy, but she blames Shakespeare for this, not, as I think Shakespeare's society would have, Cordelia.

> Insofar as the Cordelia of 1.1 is silenced, insofar as we feel the Cordelia who returns more as an iconic presence answering Lear's terrible need than as a separate character with her own needs, Shakespeare is complicit in Lear's fantasy, rewarding him for his suffering by remaking for him the Cordelia he had wanted all along; Shakespeare too requires the sacrifice of her autonomy. (125)

Far differently from my reading of the opening scene, Adelman sees Cordelia's refusal to respond to Lear's request as a demonstration of her autonomous agency. Paying less attention to the remarkably traditional *content* of Cordelia's objection to her father—that she intends merely to be the bond between men—Adelman marks this moment as one which reveals Cordelia's "selfhood." In contrast, I have argued that this moment reveals Cordelia's specific lack of protomodern autonomy, as she does not even name a specific beloved. She intends to have her desire follow all the established laws for female desire and to become a mere conduit between men. So too, Cordelia herself says that she is silent, associating her own silence with an obedience to patriarchal laws and the injunction against incest, which, she nicely points out, her sisters transgress when they claim to love their father "all."

In the final scene, Cordelia's agency is no longer sacrificed; she has come back, after all, at the head of an army. This remarkable change in Cordelia, which Adelman laments as a *loss* of agency, is actually the assumption of the same kind of agency her sisters exercised when they spoke the language of incest. Incest opens the space for female agency because the traffic is halted; Cordelia's presence on stage—finally answering her father's transgressive desire for her—after she has been banished in silence, reveals the paradigm at work. As I have suggested, the parallel between Cordelia's and Lear's virtually simultaneous deaths and the destruction in *Pericles* of Antiochus and his unnamed daughter would imply that the Renaissance auditor could entertain a different perception of female agency—and that therefore not only Lear but also Cordelia herself is punished by Cordelia's death.

Adelman's argument about Cordelia, a profoundly moving and subtle late twentieth-century reading of the dramatic predicament posed by Shakespeare's revision of the traditional story, sees the sacrifice of Cordelia's autonomy as something every human being requires, even the modern feminist reader who responds to Lear's investment of Cordelia's maternal presence with her own needs for a similar sacrifice. Because Cordelia's initial "no" to Lear ultimately announces the "betrayal inherent in individuation itself," Cordelia becomes the "mother" who we all wish would love us best, all, never-endingly (and who, tragically, never does): "I too inhabit the terror of finitude and the desire for merger with the infinitely kind nursery that can undo the pain of separation. . . . I participate with [Lear and Shakespeare] in the destruction of Cordelia's self-hood" (126).

If, however, what is released in the play is Cordelia's own desiring agency, if we can continue to see her as a daughter and not join with Lear in seeing her as mother, then her heroism is her fulfillment not only of Lear's fantasy but of her own distinctly gendered activity, a woman rescuing her father. Adelman rightly asks, "What literally kills Cordelia?" and answers that it is Edmund's rage at Lear's redefinition of his punishment as bliss. Try as she might, Adelman (as everyone else) is incapable of seeing Cordelia's death as something that happens "specifically to her, not only to Lear." She is murdered for the "desire he has invested in her" not for anything she does herself. If we grant her agency and do not deny it here, we must admit that her love aims at an incestuous end. There is a way, then, to absolve Shakespeare of the sacrifice of female agency. The Folio, after all, makes her the head of an army, invader of England, looking like some female Bolingbroke. In concerted coherence with its cultural moment, the text of the play presents female autonomy as inherently transgressive against the passivity required by the proper traffic in women. The incestuous halt of this traffic allows women a space in which to act. Returning home husbandless to rescue her father at the head of an army, Cordelia demonstrates a truly heroic agency. While we do not, therefore, have to deny Cordelia agency in the final scene, we do have to accept the Renaissance definition of her transgressive desire, for which she is punished with death.

Epilogue: Milton's Eve

To take up Milton's Eve in relation to Cordelia is to juxtapose a quintessential daughter with a wife. But Eve is also Adam's—and God's—daughter, and as the bizarre nuclear family of Sin, Satan, and Death makes clear, incest dogs, as it were, female sexuality in the poem. Minaz Jooma has brilliantly but problematically argued for the complicated connections between Eve's transgressions of eating the forbidden fruit and the rebellions of incestuous sons (Satan, Adam) against the Father.[1] Building on Mary Douglas's anthropological argument about the linkage among physical bodily orifices for representing the transgression of boundaries in the social body, she alerts us to the connections between Sin's experiences of maternal rape and cannibalism in Book II and the ingestion of the forbidden fruit in Book IX.

Jooma's argument in "The Alimentary Structures of Incest in *Paradise Lost*" is complex, but its essentials can be rehearsed briefly. Jooma explains the anthropological theory which makes sense of Gower's understanding that the incestuous family member eats another family member's flesh—a connection replicated in the riddle which opens Shakespeare's *Pericles*: the daughter is an "eater of mother's flesh."

Jooma begins by understanding that, as in Douglas's argument, "eating and incest occupy an ambiguous space: as each occurs at a body orifice which inside/outside divisions may blur" (27). Milton's rewrite of Spenser's Error episode makes this connection entirely too clear. Jooma points out that when Sin is first raped by her father, Satan, and then gives birth to Death, who then rapes her again, we see a triple incest. Progeny of the last rape, the hellhounds then crawl back into Sin's womb and gnaw her there. The multigenerational incest, as it were, is turned into maternal cannibalism. Jooma then asks what this particular tangle has to say about the relationship between Adam and Eve:

as Adam and Eve stand in precisely the same relation to one another (father begettor to daughter-begot) as Satan and Sin, doesn't the union of Adam and Eve become as problematic as that of Satan and Sin? Isn't Adam, like Satan, a father who hermaphroditically conceives a daughter and engages in sexual relations with her to make of her a mother? And doesn't the union in each case ultimately result in the birth of a predatory deathliness? (32)

Jooma answers her questions by arguing that Eve's eating of the "Father's fruit" signals her "presence as a hungering daughter" and her refusal to continue to minister as mother to others' appetites (such as Adam's, or Raphael's). Moreover, her seduction by Satan insists upon her eating as a means of exercising not only her own desire, but also her capacity for speech.

Speechlessness both denies the articulation of desire and underlines the more explicit injunction against orality implied in the forbidding of the fruit which yields the father's knowledge. As each of the injunctions is aimed at the willing- ness of children to hear and to obey the Father's word, the oral/aural method of Satan's seduction of Eve (first entering the serpent through the mouth to give it voice and then crouching at Eve's ear) becomes powerfully charged. If it is the Father's higher discourse that has by-passed Eve in the confabulation between God and Adam prior to her creation . . .it is access to orality that Satan's "persua- sive words" at first seem to promise. (38)

Jooma does not point out that attention is first aroused by the fact that the Serpent can speak the "Language of man pronounced by tongue of brute"—a fact which only underscores Jooma's point about Eve's autonomously desiring agency and access to speech. Were Eve to be as incestuous as Jooma argues, she would be this book's clearest example of female agency and rebellious, autonomous speech enabled by incest. Yet, while Jooma's argument very nicely demonstrates that Eve's agency allows for an Oedipal rebellion similar to Sin's, she does not take up the pro- foundly problematic question of the difference between Sin's and Eve's ontological status as a characters in the text. Her equation between them, while complicated and theoretically elegant, ignores certain problematic issues associated with Milton's presentation of Sin as an allegorical figure.

Milton takes Sin's experiences from Spenser's Error episode in the first canto of *The Faerie Queene*, but he radically changes its import by making the monstrous hellhounds, offspring of Death's rape of his mother, rape Sin again. Error's brood simply crawl back into her mouth, while Sin's gnaw at and cannibalize her womb. Error's children only gorge on her blood (and, distended to the breaking point, pop themselves to death) after the Redcrosse Knight has slain her. Milton's move against Spenser is, as I have argued elsewhere, a brilliant typological revision of Spenser's personification allegory. Milton has Sin sit at the "mouth" of hell, that is, the place to which Error's "mouth" refers typologically, into which her progeny retire. The exchange of womb for mouth reemphasizes the incest, of course, which Sin's very birth as sign of Satan's Oedipal revolt also signals. But it also alters the allegorical landscape, making what is typological in Spenser (the mouth is a typological sign for hell's gate) into a literal site in a landscape imagined as real.

Milton's reliance on and rewrite of Spenser's Error insists upon the function of personification in Spenser's semiotic system. As Gordon Teskey has argued, the problem of gender in the figure of personification has much to say about the suppression of actual female agency. In a sense, Sin's status as a personification allows her to articulate the incestuous evil of female agency without claiming for it the transgressive activity, which would make it properly dangerous. Having been captured by the idea of "incest" itself, Sin cannot exercise a proper agency. Triply incestuous, as daughter and mother, Sin ought to have—at least in terms of the theory outlined by this book—an immense amount of her own autonomous agency. However, in an almost textbook demonstration of the opposite, she is the spokeswoman for obedient passivity: the language she speaks uses virtually no active verbs. She is, again as I have argued elsewhere, the antithesis of active free will.[2] Because free will is so important an issue in this poem, the passivity of the grammar can be no accident. As a personification, moreover one functioning locally within a landscape allegory, she must also remain in her place, as a boundary marker. Milton famously complicates the structure of such allegorical narrative when he has Satan in one bound overleap "all bound" when he first enters Paradise, or when he complains, "myself am hell." But Sin, the personification, is a sign for the place at which she sits. Her only freely chosen action in the poem is to open the gates to let Satan pass. She cannot close them.

In contrast, Eve initiates an immense amount of action in the poem, not merely the fall itself, but the reconciliation afterward, when she asks Adam for forgiveness. In her terms the whole future history of the human race as well concerns her, not Adam ("the seed of woman"), and very strangely, she has the last spoken word in the poem.

While Jooma is therefore right to insist upon the importance of incest schemes in Milton's poem, I think she overstates the case against Eve, making it difficult to see how different Eve is from Sin. Assuming that "Satan's relation to Eve duplicates . . . his relation to his own daughter

Sin" (in promising them both "elevation through alimentation"), Jooma explains that Satan's "seduction of the daughter is bound to succeed" (39). Most problematically, when Jooma's argument ends up denying any real agency to Eve, it reasserts the poem's official program of containing her. The poem offers, however, other ways to understand Eve's agency as active, autonomous, and not incestuous. Milton's Eve is in this way not the most perfect example of my argument, but rather the exception that proves the rule.

The most important and obvious point is that Satan is not Eve's father. Sin chooses to open up hell's gates for Satan because she knows, quite rightly, that Satan, not God, *is* her author. So, too, the poem seems to take great pains to set up crucial differences within the parallels between the unholy trinity of hell and the father/daughter dyad of Adam and Eve in paradise. Sin vaunts to Satan that she is a perfect image of him: "Thee . . . oft/thyself in me thy perfect image viewing" (II.763). Eve notoriously needs to be taught that she is the image of Adam, and actually prefers, narcissistically, the image of herself in the mirror of the lake's surface (just as Britomart's look in the mirror needs to be allied to, but differentiated from, the glance of Narcissus). So, too, in Adam's narration of the birth of Eve, the poem takes great pains to make it seem as if Eve is a gift given between the male agents, God and Adam. Thus Adam thanks God for Eve:

Giver of all things fair, but fairest this
Of all thy gifts . . . (8.493–94)

Insofar as we think of God as Eve's creator and that she is given by him to Adam, and not that Adam is her "father" (he would actually be her mother), her desire is taught to conform to the necessary and Cordelia-like passivity that makes her a bond between men. However, given the oddity of Adam's own incestuous bond with her (he knows she is his child, even if she has to learn it), her passivity in responding to his call (being thus led to him) is part of her response to his incestuous desire. Rather than being that which gives her agency, the incestuousness of her relationship to Adam denies to her the autonomy of her own desire, which is at first to turn away from him. Thus, unless we think of Satan as in some way Eve's brother (as are all sons of God), he becomes a substitute bridegroom when Eve practices a kind of fallen exogamy, "deflowered" (in Adam's words) by Satan's seduction. While Jooma is certainly right to see Adam's and Satan's revolts as parallel transgressions against the Father, each preferring the female image of himself to obedience to God, Eve and Sin are not in exactly the same position. Eve's agency, therefore, needs to be seen in a slightly different way from Sin's radical passivity when she follows Satan's will and rebels with him against God. What I think we see opening with Eve is a different kind of (potentially protomodern) agency for women, where the possibility of freestanding female autonomy is glimpsed on the horizon, only to be shut down as completely as possible. Eve's argument about making an equal division of their labor, and the need to earn their living as if they were wage laborers in Book IX sounds far more "modern" than Adam's understanding of their feudal relationship with God, who does not need their work. Eve in Eden assumes she is already a citizen of the modern, protocapitalistic world and must be corrected by Adam.[3]

It probably should not surprise us that Eve exercises, when she can, a nonincestuous, modern-looking autonomous female will. One of Milton's most notorious and radical arguments was his provocative stance on divorce and his insistence that marriage not be defined as it had been in custom, as only a means for assuring the continuation of the family line through the creation of offspring. Profoundly anti-kin—at least in the divorce tracts—Milton sees the proper function of marriage (the traffic in women) to serve a single end, the psychological comfort of the male mate. *Paradise Lost* does, of course, define wedded love with the customary understanding of the traffic in women as bonds between men:

Hail wedded love, mysterious law, true source
Of Human offspring, sole propriety
In Paradise of all things common else.
. . .
Founded in reason, loyal, just, and pure,
Relations dear, and all the charities
Of father, son, and brother first were known. (IV.760–67)

But in the divorce tracts marriage has nothing to do with the creation of kinship, culture, or charity among men; indeed the atomistic nature of the patriarchal households that form the basis for the legitimacy of the new polis Milton imagines means that the nation is constructed by connecting the rights of all the (male) heads of households together in their shared consent (or not) to government. Not surprisingly, Milton, the regicide is anti-absolutist; his stance on the family (and divorce) is also forward-looking and anti-traditional. It ought not to surprise us, then, that the

subtle details of his use of incest and female agency should be so different
from the traditional system of in-marriage, which creates cultural capital
for an aristocratic kinship network. Cordelia exercises most agency when
she fulfills her father's incestuous fantasy by returning to rescue him at the
head of an army; in contrast, Eve exercises the most agency when she is
consorting with a creature of another species (while she thinks it is a snake,
it is actually an angel: the exogamous extreme applies in both cases).

We also do Eve—and the poem—an injustice when we look only at
the kind of events that transpire during the fall; after the fall, Eve initiates
the reconciliation necessary for Adam and Eve to experience the fall as a
possible "felix culpa." Eve intuits the possibility of forgiveness by crying
"Forsake me not thus Adam" (X.914). She spontaneously takes the prostrate position, which Adam learns from her (and which the poem repeats,
word for word). She is thus the first to intuit the proper mode of divine
address thereafter, that is, of prostrate and humble supplication as well as
praise.

What this very briefly sketched argument has tried to do is to offer
one more instance of the incestuous and agented daughter in Sin, but also
to drive a wedge between Eve and Sin, however parallel their situations
seem to be at first. I have argued elsewhere that the pun on her name,
"Sin-sign," signaled the metaphoricity of fallen language as opposed to a
different (less metaphorical) prelapsarian language, as if once again incest
and female access to speech are connected.[4] Victoria Kahn has argued that
Sin's status as "sign" does not mean, however, that postlapsarian language
is riven by a punning duplicity that is somehow different from the language of God's command, which is unitary.[5] Kahn's point is that language
cannot "fall" into polysemy after the fall, because language is always already semiotically riven. The interdiction is itself, according to Kahn, as
problematically semiotic as Sin. The tree is also a "sign," just as the "fruit"
of the forbidden tree already has multiple meanings even before it has
born fruit in the fall.

I would argue, however, that as a personification Sin must necessarily be understood to be a different kind of sign from the tree. Although
both are signs, they work quite differently, if only because the tree is not
a personification. The tree is an object, indeed, which possesses utterly
no narrative agency in the poem. Sin has agency, but as Samuel Johnson
long ago noticed, when Satan and Sin speak to each other, the "allegory
is broken" for two ontologically different kind of characters interact. It is
important to understand the difference in the ontological statuses of Sin

and tree within the fiction, even if both are assigned the function of signs. In Teskey's useful term, Sin is an agent who has been "captured" by an abstraction and she is given a feminine gender. While the tree is a "sign" of Adam and Eve's obedience, it is not so in the same sense that the falling angels take Sin for a sign. In a sense, the magic of the fall does not inhere "in" the tree of the Knowledge of Good and Evil. The knowledge does not reside in its apple. Satan's disobedience produces the birth of Sin as its visible result; in authoring the actuality of disobedience, Satan has created the possibility of sinning. Perhaps Sin names at that moment the potential for all the fallen angels to make the same choice, a potential which had of course always existed, but which takes on bodily form when Satan wills his disobedience.

Adam and Eve do not fall because the apple somehow poisons them; rather, they fall because they disobey God and then realize that they have done evil. It is in the realization that they are now separated from God that they finally understand the goodness they formerly experienced in an entirely different way, when that goodness is lost (by evil). Sin's noticeable rhetoric of passivity ("and in the general fall, I also"), names the refusal to accept responsibility which is fundamental to sinfulness; Satan's hardness of heart in his soliloquy to the Sun in Book IV enacts that signal passivity and refusal to accept responsibility for one's own actions. In a sense, it is this very passivity that is the force by which she is captured, for more than anything Sin marks by her nature the inability to exercise free will and choice. Such a shirking of responsibility is obvious in the immediately biblical buck-passing of postlapsarian Adam and Eve, which indeed continues until Eve begins to take (however wrongly) all responsibility for the fall. Eve's supplication of Adam to forgive her for transgressing against him is an action of taking responsibility for one's own deeds, an act of which Sin would never be capable.

In a sense, the ontological universe in which Sin sits at Hell's gate insists on the lack of change, on stasis, within that world. Her incestuous female agency then insists on the halt at the boundary, even—and perhaps especially—when she is building the bridge to earth for her incestuous father, with her incestuous son Death. When they build the bridge, they in essence simply expand the stationary boundary, for it now reaches to the new world. The apple might well have done the job of conferring the knowledge of good and evil to Adam and Eve. Thus Satan even boasts that he accomplished his mission, "the more to increase / Your wonder with an apple!" (X.486–87). Many readers may be tempted to make the same reductive mistake—that it was the apple which caused the fall—but it is a reading against which the poem offers many warnings. Adam's and Eve's first, mistaken postlapsarian responses make them feel sexual desire differently which they attribute to tasting the apple. Satan's very boast that he did it "all" with an apple suggests that the understanding is suspect.

In a book arguing that *Paradise Lost* is in fact a baroque allegory of the sort Walter Benjamin analyzes in the *Trauerspiel*, Susan Gemelli Martin has argued that Sin's ontological status as a personification does not make her different from the other dramatis personae in the poem. Martin explains of Sin and Death, "Far from behaving like fictions . . . these allegorical agents demonstrate a range of deliberative and material freedom as temporally real and as limited as Satan's own."[6] I have argued that Satan's own agency becomes largely attenuated after his transformation into a hissing serpent in hell in Book X.[7] He fades into matter for pagan myth, not true history. I would suggest that the difference between Martin's and my own sense of the "effects" that allegorical personifications can have in a narrative that is not thoroughly allegorical may be similar to the difference Teskey points out between true personification and the half-way operation he sees in the figures of Spenser's Amoret and Dante's Francesca. As Alma tells Guyon in Book II of *The Faerie Queene*, "Shamefast you are, Shamefastness itself is she." Just so, the statue of Constancy in Wroth's *Urania* is a lifeless representation of an abstract virtue; when the statue moves to hand over the key to Pamphilia, it has begun the process of metamorphosing into Pamphilia's breast, which instantiates Pamphilia as a constant woman. Unlike, for example, the metamorphosis of Spenser's Malbecco, who turns into the abstract word "Jealousy," Constancy's movement does not mean that Pamphilia is "captured" in Teskey's useful term. Thus Sin (the personified abstraction) never arrives, in propria persona, in Paradise. Sin (with a little "s") does; and this little "s" sin acts by infecting the race of mankind, rather like some biological process of disease—another of the "real" effects of the fall, caused by man's actual transgression. In such a way, too, Michael teaches Adam not to dream of a "local fight" between good and evil, such as one might wish to see in a psychomachia, or chivalric tale, but in the internal psychological process of individual moral choices.

To put such weight on the status of Sin as an allegorical abstraction not only allows us to see the distinctions the poem makes with her narrative about the truth status of pagan poetry (the birth of Athena is the demon-inspired version of the origin of fallen wisdom), but it also enables us to use Jooma's argument about Sin's incest, without going on to see so much similarity between them that we must fold Eve's autonomous agency into Sin's incestuous passivity. Sin is entirely captured by the abstraction of obedience to evil; Eve makes a disobedient choice and thereby sins. Jooma's argument ultimately strips Eve of her agency because her disobedience is merely a means to enable Adam's Oedipal rebellion. It thus fails to appreciate the power of the autonomy which has been Eve's all along.

Most strangely, Eve is given the last word in the poem; because it concerns the *protoevangelum*, the only moment in Genesis which casts forward to a prophetic future, when the "Woman's seed" shall bruise the serpent's head, it is of course appropriate that she voice the prophecy. The woman whose seed will bruise the serpent, is, of course Mary, Mother of Jesus, the Son of God. As we have seen, it is this second Eve who, in fact, becomes a powerful voice for the incestuous holy family, the trope which underpins the force of the theological metaphor with which we began. Eve's speech within the poem, and especially at the fall, has struggled to articulate an exogamous-tending, freestanding agency, different from the passivity of incestuous Sin. Eve's last words, which look forward in time to the woman who, as passive vessel, mothers the seed, merely begin to sound like Marguerite de Navarre's, like Elizabeth's, and also like Mary Wroth's language of incestuous desire.

Notes

Chapter 1. Halting the Traffic in Women

1. I take the famous phrase from Gayle Rubin's now classic article, "The Traffic in Women: Notes on the 'Political Economy' of Sex," in *Toward an Anthropology of Women*, ed. Rayna Reiter (New York: Monthly Review Press, 1975), 157–210.

2. Janet Adelman, *Suffocating Mothers: Fantasies of Maternal Origin in Shakespeare's Plays*, Hamlet *to the* Tempest (New York: Routledge, 1992), 103–29, argues that *Lear* collapses the father and the son into a single figure, investing Lear's relationship with his daughters with infantile fantasies "so unmediated in their intensity that they are relatively disorganized," and engaging the play in the "maelstrom of what Freud called primary process thinking." For Adelman, Cordelia's "muted strivings for autonomy . . . are the first challenge to Lear's omnipotence. Goneril and Regan become the principle of female autonomy run mad" (118). For a fuller discussion of the play see Chapter 7.

3. Richard McCabe, *Incest, Drama, and Nature's Law, 1550–1700* (Cambridge: Cambridge University Press, 1993), 178. For a fuller discussion of the issue of incest in *Lear* and *Pericles*, see Chapter 7.

4. Judith Butler, "Is Kinship Always Already Heterosexual?" *differences: A Journal of Feminist Cultural Studies* 13, 1 (2002): 14–44.

5. *The Faerie Queene*, III.vii.47–52. Ollyphant is the name of the giant whom Sir Topas pursues in Chaucer's parody of chivalric romance, "The Tale of Sir Topas," the poem from which Spenser takes his overarching plot of Arthur's pursuit of Gloriana, the Faerie Queene. Argante's incest is thus connected to Spenser's intended cultural containment of the authority of another faery queen, that is, Queen Elizabeth I. See Chapter 5.

6. Suzanne W. Hull, *Chaste, Silent, and Obedient: English Books for Women, 1475–1640* (San Marino, Calif.: Huntington Library, 1982).

7. Patricia Parker, *Literary Fat Ladies: Rhetoric, Gender, Property* (London: Methuen, 1987). For a discussion of the restraint of female speech in another play by Shakespeare as it compares with a closet drama by the first woman to publish a play in English, Elizabeth Cary, see my "Staging Gender: William Shakespeare and Elizabeth Cary," in *Sexuality and Gender in Early Modern Europe*, ed. James Turner (Cambridge: Cambridge University Press, 1993).

8. Myra Jehlen, "Archimedes and the Paradox of Feminist Criticism," *Signs* 6 (1981): 582.

9. Pierre Bourdieu, *Outline of a Theory of Practice* (1977; rpt. Cambridge: Cambridge University Press, 1993), argues conversely, making practices the test

of the "fallacies of the rule"; Bourdieu does not concern himself with incest per se, but with the case of parallel cousin marriage as an instance of the way practices and unofficial strategies must be taken into account in understanding how society works.

10. Claude Lévi-Strauss, *Elementary Structures of Kinship* (London: Eyre and Spottiswoode, 1969), 115–16.

11. Eve Kosofsky Sedgwick, *Between Men: English Literature and Male Homosocial Desire* (New York: Columbia University Press, 1985).

12. Rubin, " Traffic in Women," 210.

13. Sigmund Freud, *Sexuality and the Psychology of Love*, ed. Philip Rieff (New York: Macmillan, 1963), 239.

14. Jacqueline Rose, in Jacques Lacan, *Feminine Sexuality: Jacques Lacan and the École Freudienne*, trans. and ed. Jacqueline Rose (New York: Norton, 1966), 45.

15. See also Jacques Lacan, *Écrits: A Selection*, trans. Alan Sheridan (New York: Norton, 1977), 66.

16. Rose, in Lacan, *Feminine Sexuality*, 45n.

17. Luce Irigaray, *Speculum of the Other Woman*, trans. Gillian C. Gill (Ithaca, N.Y.: Cornell University Press, 1985), 124.

18. Luce Irigaray, *This Sex Which Is Not One* (Ithaca, N.Y.: Cornell University Press, 1985), 112.

19. Julia Kristeva, "Stabat Mater," in *The Kristeva Reader*, ed. Toril Moi (New York: Columbia University Press, 1986), 180–81.

20. Kaja Silverman, *The Acoustic Mirror: The Maternal Voice in Psychoanalysis and Cinema* (Bloomington: Indiana University Press, 1988), 105.

21. The legitimization of female celibacy in saints' lives and in the foundation of monasteries for women are twin sites for the agency of women throughout the Middle Ages: convents may have been places for an entire range of female homosocial activities, including the homosexual. See Judith Brown, *Immodest Acts: The Life of a Lesbian Nun* (Oxford: Oxford University Press, 1986); theoretically, however, they are places where sexual desire is sublimated within a discourse of virginity. For a fuller discussion of female asceticism, see Caroline Walker Bynum, *Holy Feast and Holy Fast: The Religious Significance of Food to Medieval Women* (Berkeley: University of California Press, 1987).

22. In a later article, "Thinking Sex: Notes for a Radical Theory of the Politics of Sexuality," Rubin explores the history of homosexuality and specifically rejects her earlier bundling of sex and gender: "it is essential to separate sex and gender analytically," in *Pleasure and Danger: Exploring Female Sexuality*, ed. Carole S. Vance (Boston: Routledge, 1984), 308; in this essay Rubin understands taboos against intergenerational sex and incest as part and parcel of the taboos against homosexuality.

23. Sedgwick is careful to explain that she is not arguing that patriarchal power "is primarily or necessarily homosexual, as distinct from homosocial" (20): she does, however, insist that "in any male-dominated society, there is a special relationship between male homosocial (including homosexual) desire and the structures for maintaining and transmitting that desire" (25).

24. Jonathan Goldberg, *Sodometries: Renaissance Texts, Modern Sexualities* (Stanford, Calif.: Stanford University Press, 1992), 37.

25. Goldberg is drawing on the germinal work done by Leah Marcus, who was the first to argue for the "political uses of androgyny," in "Shakespeare's Comic Heroines, Elizabeth I, and the Political Uses of Androgyny," in *Women in the Middle Ages and the Renaissance*, ed. Mary Beth Rose (Syracuse, N.Y.: Syracuse University Press, 1986), 135–53.

26. Judith Butler, *Gender Trouble: Feminism and the Subversion of Identity* (London: Routledge, 1990).

27. Judith Butler, *Antigone's Claim: Kinship Between Life and Death* (New York: Columbia University Press, 2000), 72–73.

28. Lorna Hutson, "Why the Lady's Eyes Are Nothing like the Sun," in *Women, Texts, and Histories: 1575–1760*, ed. Clare Brant and Diane Purkiss (London: Routledge, 1992), p. 21.

29. Karen Newman, "Directing Traffic: Subjects, Objects, and the Politics of Exchange," *differences: A Journal of Feminist Cultural Studies* 2, 2 (1990): 41–54.

30. See also her *Fashioning Femininity and English Renaissance Drama* (Chicago: University of Chicago Press, 1991), 104–7.

31. Naomi Miller, *Changing the Subject: Mary Wroth and the Figurations of Gender in Early Modern England* (Lexington: University Press of Kentucky, 1996). Jonathan Goldberg has written on women writers in *Desiring Women Writing: English Renaissance Examples* (Stanford, Calif.: Stanford University Press, 1997) but does not take up the theory of homosociality to understand their practice, beyond broaching the issue of female-to-female desire. While he does explore with some seriousness the question of incest in the case of Mary Sidney, he does not make a theoretical connection to the problem of homosociality. For Goldberg, the two projects remain distinct, the discourse of male homosexuality and female writing being only parallel practices of previously silenced minorities. See *Sodometries*, 81–101; and especially the "Introduction" to *Queering the Renaissance*, ed. Goldberg (Durham, N.C.: Duke University Press, 1994), 5, where Goldberg comes very close to juxtaposing Sedgwick's notion of homosociality with Carla Freccero's understanding of female groups, which register an "alternative social scene."

32. Some such reasoning may be behind the importance of lesbianism to contemporary feminist theory.

33. Valerie Traub, *The Renaissance of Lesbian Desire in Early Modern England* (Cambridge: Cambridge University Press, 2002), chapter 6. Traub's argument is that a new social construct, which she terms "domestic heterosexuality," was profoundly threatened by the power of female friendship, and so the figure of the chaste femme had to be made more threatening: hence its absorption by the figure of the tribade.

34. Valerie Traub, "The (In) Significance of 'Lesbian' Desire in Early Modern England," in *Queering the Renaissance*, ed. Jonathan Goldberg (Durham, N.C.: Duke University Press, 1994), 62–83.

35. Kathy Psomiades, "Heterosexual Exchanges and Other Victorian Fictions: *The Eustace Diamonds* and Victorian Anthropology," *Novel* 33 (1999): 93–118.

36. Marilyn Strathern, *The Gender of the Gift: Problems with Women and Problems with Society in Melanesia* (Berkeley: University of California Press, 1988).

37. Annette B. Weiner, *Inalienable Possessions: The Paradox of Keeping-While-Giving* (Berkeley: University of California Press, 1992). The earlier book is Weiner, *Women of Value, Men of Renown: New Perspectives in Trobriand Exchange* (Austin: University of Texas Press, 1976).

38. For a discussion that also relies on a careful rereading of the Rubin argument as applied to Renaissance texts, see Karen Newman, "Portia's Ring: Unruly Women and the Structures of Exchange," *Shakespeare Quarterly* 38, 1 (1987): 19–33.

39. Catherine Gallagher, "Embracing the Absolute: Margaret Cavendish and the Politics of the Female Subject in Seventeenth-Century England," in *Early Women Writers: 1600–1702*, ed. Anita Pacheo (London: Longman, 1998), 133–46.

40. Rosemary Kegl, "Margaret Cavendish, Feminism and *The Blazing-World*," in *Feminist Readings of Early Modern Culture: Emerging Subjects*, ed. Valerie Traub, M. Lindsay Kaplan, and Dympna Callaghan (Cambridge: Cambridge University Press, 1996), 124–25.

41. Ranjana Khanna in *Dark Continents: Psychoanalysis and Colonialism* (Durham, N.C.: Duke University Press, 2003) analyzes the important figure of the silent female "subaltern" in postcolonial theory as a site for enabling a new ethical discourse of transnational feminism.

42. Margaret Hannay argues that manuscript coterie publication may have been a more prestigious means for circulating writing by women. See "The Countess of Pembroke's Agency in Print and Scribal Culture," in *Women's Writing and the Circulation of Ideas: Manuscript Publication in England, 1550–1800*, ed. George Justice (Cambridge: Cambridge University Press, 2001), 17–49.

43. See Jennifer Summit, *Lost Property: The Woman Writer and English Literary History, 1380–1589* (Chicago: University of Chicago Press, 2000), 63–107, for a discussion of Christine's reception in England. See also Nancy Bradley Warren's argument, in *Spiritual Economies: Female Monasticism in Later Medieval England* (Philadelphia: University of Pennsylvania Press, 2001), about female piety. She makes an interesting case for early English printing of Christine's work in the construction of English masculinity at the Tudor court (239 n1).

44. I am grateful to Anne Lake Prescott for pointing out the existence of the manuscript at Blois. For the tapestries, see Susan Groag Bell, "A New Approach to the Influence of Christine de Pizan: The Lost Tapestries of 'The City of Ladies,'" in *Sur "Le Chemin de long étude": Actes du colloque d'Orléans, juillet 1995*, ed. Bernard Ribémont (Paris: Champion, 1998), 7–12.

45. Maureen Quilligan, *The Allegory of Female Authority: Christine de Pizan's "Cité des dames"* (Ithaca, N.Y.: Cornell University Press, 1991), 69–86.

46. Giovanni Boccaccio, *De mulieribus claris*, ed. Vittorio Zaccaria, vol. 10 of *Tutte le opere di Giovanni Boccaccio*, ed. Vittore Branca (Milan: Mondadori, 1967), 36; the translation is from *Concerning Famous Women*, trans Guido A. Guarino (New Brunswick, N.J.: Rutgers University Press, 1963), 6.

47. Christine de Pizan, *The Book of the City of Ladies*, trans. Earl Jeffrey Richards (New York: Persea Press, 1982), 40.

48. Lévi-Strauss, *Elementary Structures of Kinship*, 475. Another way out of this impasse is chronicled in the *Mahabharata: A Swayamvara Marriage*, in which the high caste woman is given as a reward to a lower caste man who has achieved some great feat. Another is for the woman to give herself as a gift. See Lévi-Strauss, 475–76.

49. See Augustine, *The City of God*, trans. Marcus Dodds (New York: Random House, 1950), 15.498. See also Marc Shell, *The End of Kinship: "Measure for Measure," Incest, and the Ideal of Universal Siblinghood* (Stanford, Calif.: Stanford University Press, 1988), 30.

50. Hélène Cixous, "The Laugh of the Medusa," *Signs* 1 (1976): 875–93; reprinted in *The Signs Reader: Women, Gender, and Scholarship*, ed. Elizabeth Abel and Emily K. Abel (Chicago: University of Chicago Press, 1983), 289.

51. Of course, as Annette Weiner argues, those exchanges always included more complexity and placed more value on women's gift-giving than the theory made room for.

Chapter 2. Elizabeth I (with a Note on Marguerite de Navarre)

1. Jasper Ridley, *Henry VIII: The Politics of Tyranny* (New York: Viking, 1985), 151–53, 157–80.

2. Marc Shell, *Elizabeth's Glass, with "The glass of the Sinful Soul" (1544) by Elizabeth I, and "Epistle dedicatory" & "Conclusion" (1548) by John Bale* (Lincoln: University of Nebraska Press, 1991), 14 explains the doctrine of "carnal contagion." See also Jack Goody, *The Development of the Family and Marriage in Europe* (Cambridge: Cambridge University Press, 1983), 176–77 on the equation of affinity with consanguinity (that is, believing having sexual relations with two sisters is incestuous).

3. Ridley, *Henry VIII*, 214.

4. Ridley, *Henry VIII*, 270.

5. Shell, *Elizabeth's Glass*, 16–22. I am profoundly indebted to Shell's edition for my own reading of Elizabeth's translation.

6. Wallace MacCaffrey, *Elizabeth I* (London: E. Arnold, 1993), 50.

7. Susan Doran, *Monarchy and Matrimony: The Courtships of Elizabeth I* (London: Routledge, 1996), 24: "were she to accept the legitimacy of a papal dispensation in this case, Elizabeth would be *de facto* recognizing the validity of her father's marriage to Catherine of Aragon and hence her own bastardy."

8. For a discussion of the problems attendant upon Seymour's courtship, see Sheila Cavanaugh, "Princess Elizabeth and the Seymour Incident," in *Dissing Elizabeth: Negative Representations of Gloriana*, ed. Julia Walker (Durham, N.C.: Duke University Press, 1998), 9–29.

9. Carrolly Erickson, *Bloody Mary: The Remarkable Life of Mary Tudor* (New York: Quill, 1978), 330. For a discussion of the argument mounted against the marriage in terms of its incest, see 337–38.

10. Shell, *Elizabeth's Glass*, 19.

11. Katherine Parr was an author herself; she had published her *Lamentation*

of a Sinner in 1547. Janet Mueller finds in a number of male English Protestant divines the models for Katherine's prose; she does not, however, take into account the text Katherine's stepdaughter had presented to her. See Janet Mueller, "A Tudor Queen Finds Voice," in *The Historical Renaissance*, ed. Heather Dubrow and Richard Strier (Chicago: University of Chicago Press, 1988), 115–47; and also "Complications of Intertextuality," in *Representing Women in Renaissance England*, ed. Claude J. Summers and Ted-Larry Pebworth (Columbia: University of Missouri Press, 1997), 24–41.

12. For a discussion of the odd scholarly silence about the content of Marguerite's poem, see Shell, *Elizabeth's Glass*, 6–7.

13. In what follows, I aim to practice a "sociology of the text," as outlined by D. F. McKenzie, *Bibliography and the Sociology of Texts* (London: British Library, 1986), who argues that bibliography "has an unrivaled power to resurrect authors in their own time, and their readers at any time. One of its greatest strengths is the access it gives to social motives: by dealing with the facts of transmission and the material evidence of reception, it can make discoveries as distinct from inventing meanings. In focusing on the primary object, the text as a recorded form, it defines our common point of departure for any historical or critical enterprise" (p. 19). My emphasis will be on the "social motives" one may decipher in the repeated recycling of two royal female authors' texts about incest. While I do not assume that we can thereby avoid "inventing" meanings, we are allowed a different view onto the material.

14. Pierre Jourda, *Marguerite d'Angoulême, duchesse d'Alençon, reine de Navarre (1492–1549): étude biographique et littéraire* (Paris: Champion, 1930), 172–78, chronicles the events leading up to the Sorbonne's censure of *the Miroir*.

15. See Jourda, *Marguerite d'Angoulême*. Joseph L. Allaire suggests that the Sorbonne may have been offended by Marot's announcement that the psalm had been translated from the Hebrew and not from the authorized Vulgate version, which the Sorbonne protected. Marguerite de Navarre, *Le Miroir de l'âme pécheresse*, ed. Joseph L. Allaire (Munich: W. Fink, 1972), 20–21. Allaire also points out that Marguerite neglected to cite the Vulgate but quoted the Bible in the French translation by Lefèvre d'Étaples, who was known to favor reforming the church.

16. Michel Jeanneret, *Poésie et tradition biblique au XVIe siècle* (Paris: Corti, 1969), 28.

17. Marguerite de Navarre, *Le Miroir de l'âme pécheresse*, ed. Renja Salminen (Helsinki: Tiedeakatemia, 1979), 171–72; all citations are to this edition.

18. Shell, *Elizabeth's Glass*, 117.

19. I am grateful to Margreta de Grazia for pointing out Elizabeth's intensification.

20. Jourda, *Marguerite d'Angoulême*, 182.

21. Marguerite de Navarre, *The queen of Nauerres Tales* (London: John Oxenbridge, 1597). All modern English translations from the *Heptaméron* are from *The Heptaméron*, trans. P. A. Chilton (London: Penguin, 1984).

22. Elizabeth Archibald, *Incest and the Medieval Imagination* (Oxford: Oxford University Press, 2001), 142–44, discusses Martin Luther's version of the same tale. Carla Freccero, "Queer Nation, Female Nation: Marguerite de Navarre, Incest, and the State in Early Modern France," *MLQ* 62, 4 (2000): 29–47,

argues for the pivotal importance of the incest in Marguerite's Story 30 to the formation of the early modern state.

23. Goody, *Development of the Family*, 137.

24. Goody, *Development of the Family*, 146. A table of prohibited marriages (listed in William Clerke's 1594 *The Triale of Bastardie*) cites such convoluted interdictions as (under the category "the unequally collaterall line and second degree"), "A man may not marrie his Father's brother's wife."

25. David Herlihy, "Making Sense of Incest: Women and the Marriage Rules of the Early Middle Ages," in *Law, Custom, and the Social Fabric in Medieval Europe*, ed. Bernard S. Bachrach and David Nicholas (Kalamazoo, Mich.: Medieval Institute Publications, 1990), 1–16, argues that Goody's position is untenable because no contemporary made the argument about the Church's incest agenda. It is not, however, necessary for a process to be consciously comprehended by contemporaries in order for it to have real historical force. Herlihy counters that the purpose of exogamy made "the marriages and the households of the poor resemble those of the rich" (12–13). By so denigrating elite families, the incest rules aimed at a social leveling which controlled secular dynastic pretensions. But this, of course, is precisely Goody's point—by leveling social difference, the Church aimed to undo the creation of social hierarchy at which intermarriage aimed, according to Weiner. So too, Herlihy's argument against Goody claims that the Church was not interested in limiting the number of heirs to a fortune because married as well as unmarried people granted money to the Church. Such a rebuttal fails to take into account the far greater amounts an unmarried person would have bequeathed than someone who had children. If there were no heirs for whom a parent needed to provide, the entire fortune could have passed to the church. A parent, however pious, would not be likely to leave a child homeless for the benefit of the Church.

26. Elaine Pagels, *Adam, Eve, and the Serpent* (New York, Random House, 1988), 16.

27. Georges Duby, *The Knight, the Lady, and the Priest: The Making of Modern Marriage in Medieval France*, trans. Barbara Bray (New York: Pantheon, 1983), 48.

28. I am indebted to Martin Kauffman, Department of Western Manuscripts, Bodleian Library, for aid in handling the volume. See also Margaret H. Swain, "A New Year's Gift from the Princess Elizabeth," *Connoisseur* 36 (1973): 258–66.

29. Lisa M. Klein, "Your Humble Handmaid: Elizabethan Gifts of Needlework," *Renaissance Quarterly* 50 (1997): 459–93.

30. Mary Tudor also undertook to translate Erasmus's paraphrases of the Gospel of John for her stepmother Katherine Parr. This text was printed in 1548, during the same year but not by the same people as those who printed Elizabeth's translation of Marguerite's more Protestant-leaning text. Both are available in *Elizabeth and Mary Tudor*, ed. Anne Lake Prescott, The Early Modern Englishwoman: Printed Writings, 1500–1640, Series 1, Part 2, vol. 5 (Aldershot: Ashgate, 2001). Prescott argues that Mary Tudor probably did not complete the translation, having become uncomfortable with the pro-Protestant sympathies of her stepmother.

31. Klein, "Your Humble Handmaid," 460.

32. Jennifer Summit, *Lost Property: The Woman Writer and English Literary History* (Chicago: University of Chicago Press, 2000), 168–71 discusses the embroidered volume containing the *Glass* as a signal instance of female coterie publication which marked Elizabeth's poetic practice throughout her life.

33. See Ann Rosalind Jones and Peter Stallybrass, "The Needle and the Pen," in *Renaissance Clothing and the Materials of Memory* (Cambridge: Cambridge University Press, 2000). Jane Donawerth, "Women's Poetry and the Tudor-Stuart System of Gift Exchange," in *Women, Writing, and the Reproduction of Culture in Tudor and Stuart Britain*, ed. Mary E. Bruke, Jane Donawerth, Linda L. Dove, and Karen Nelson (Syracuse, N.Y.: Syracuse University Press, 2000), 3–18, understands Elizabeth's gift to function within a female circulation system that ran in tandem with a male-dominated system of patronage. Donawerth does not mention Weiner's work.

34. Santina M. Levey, *An Elizabethan Inheritance: The Hardwick Hall Textiles* (London: National Trust, 1998), 36, 69.

35. Shell, *Elizabeth's Glass*, 112.

36. Susan Snyder, "Guilty Sisters: Marguerite de Navarre, Elizabeth of England, and the *Miroir de l'âme pécheresse*," *Renaissance Quarterly* 50 (1997): 443–58.

37. David Kastan, "An Early English Metrical Psalm: Elizabeth's or John Bale's?" *Notes and Queries* 21 (1974): 404–5.

38. For a discussion of Bale's printing of Askew's examinations, while in exile in Wesel, see Elaine Beilin, *The Examinations of Anne Askew* (New York: Oxford University Press, 1996), xlv–xlix. The printer of both volumes was Dirik Van der Straten, who employed a revised version of the type used for the Tyndale Bible. In his commentary on Askew's answers to Henry's bishops' questions, Bale reserves some of his most energetic fulminations against their too-Catholic insistence on priestly authority in the eucharist. Female authority is, in a sense, the polar opposite of priestly Roman Catholic authority: hence, perhaps, Bale's sympathy for the writing of low-born Anne and teenage Elizabeth. Excerpts from Anne's examinations are reprinted in the *Monument of Matrons*, so Anne's work circulated along the same lines as Elizabeth's.

39. D. B. Updike, *Printing Types: Their History, Forms, and Use* (Cambridge, Mass.: Harvard University Press, 1922), explains the difference between roman and black letter (or "English") type: "The Humanist writing was round, and was a revival of the old Carolingian minuscule hand as then understood. The Gothic or black letter hand was pointed and was a survival of the Gothic minuscule of the Middle Ages." The latter's association with "Englishness" made it an appropriate choice for Bale's anti-Roman attack.

40. Pierre Ronsard, *Oeuvres complètes*, vol. 2 (Paris: Marcel Didion, 1948), 13, 39–75. The whole volume was dedicated to Elizabeth.

41. Susan Doran gives a detailed outline of Dudley's reasonable, if ultimately unsuccessful, plans in *Monarchy and Matrimony: The Courtships of Elizabeth I* (London: Routledge, 1996), 47–66.

42. For a discussion of Dudley's elaborate designs on Elizabeth in the

Kenilworth pageants of 1575, see Susan Frye, *Elizabeth I: The Competition for Representation* (Oxford: Oxford University Press, 1993), esp. 70–71. Frye describes the cancelled masque of Diana and Juno which resurrected the marriage proposal at even this late date. Anne Lake Prescott argues that the Cancellar 1568 print might better suit publication later in 1569 — but it would have been impossible after 1570, when Elizabeth had been excommunicated. Prescott does not mention the similar Alphabet Cancellar had prepared for Leicester. Whatever faction supported its publication would have had to be pro-Catholic (which could have been the Hapsburgs, the Valois, or — with whatever sincerity — Dudley himself). See Prescott, ed., *Elizabeth and Mary Tudor*, xi.

43. Helen Hackett, *Virgin Mother, Maiden Queen: Elizabeth I and the Cult of the Virgin Mary* (New York: St. Martin's Press, 1995), argues that the full-blown cult surrounding Elizabeth's virginity only became paramount after the threat of the Anjou marriage had passed in 1579, and that representations of the queen still were open to the possibility of her marriage even after that date. Philippa Berry, *Of Chastity and Power: Elizabethan Literature and the Unmarried Queen* (London: Routledge, 1989) also argues for a nuanced, decade by decade chronology for an evolving discourse of chastity throughout Elizabeth's reign.

44. Summit, *Lost Property*, 161.

45. Louis A. Montrose, "The Fantasies of Elizabethan Culture," in *Rewriting the Renaissance: The Discourses of Sexual Difference in Early Modern Europe*, ed. Margaret Ferguson, Maureen Quilligan, and Nancy Vickers (Chicago: University of Chicago Press, 1986), 80–81. It may be useful to point out that the three roles of maiden, matron, and mother correspond closely to the roles of daughter, wife, and mother of the incest metaphor in the *Glass* (thus leaving out only the notion of "sister").

46. Cited in Hackett, *Virgin Mother, Maiden Queen*, 124–25.

47. *Elizabeth I: Collected Works*, ed. Leah S. Marcus, Janet Mueller, and Mary Beth Rose (Chicago: University of Chicago Press, 2000), 59.

48. Jonathan Goldberg, "Fatherly Authority: The Politics of Stuart Family Images," in *Rewriting the Renaissance: The Discourses of Sexual Difference in Early Modern Europe*, ed. Margaret W. Ferguson, Maureen Quilligan, and Nancy J. Vickers (Chicago: University of Chicago Press, 1986), 3–32.

49. *Collected Works*, 314.

50. *Collected Works*, 263.

51. Jonathan Goldberg, *James I and the Politics of Literature* (Stanford, Calif.: Stanford University Press, 1989), 15–16 discusses the procedure by which James transformed himself into Elizabeth's child.

Chapter 3. Sir Philip Sydney's Queen

1. Sir Fulke Greville, *The Life of the Renowned Sir Philip Sidney* (London: Henry Seile, 1651), 53–65; hereafter cited in the text.

2. Pierre Bourdieu, *Outline of a Theory of Practice*, trans. Richard Nice (Cambridge: Cambridge University Press, 1977), 12. Frank Whigham, *Ambition*

and Privilege: The Social Tropes of Elizabethan Courtesy Theory (Berkeley: University of California Press, 1984), 4–5, argues for the "double adaptation of Bourdieu's formulation" in order to fit it to the social practices of Elizabethan England. First, honor was a "notion specific to the ruling elite, not shared by all males (different from Bourdieu's undifferentiated societies); and second, honor was no longer merely a question of birth, but could be "achieved as well as ascribed."

3. Philip Sidney, *The Prose Works of Sir Philip Sidney*, ed. Albert Feullerat, 4 vols. (Cambridge: Cambridge University Press, 1969), 3: 128; hereafter cited as *Works*.

4. Wallace MacCaffrey, *Queen Elizabeth and the Making of Policy, 1572–1588* (Princeton, N.J.: Princeton University Press, 1981), 295–96.

5. John Osborne, *Young Philip Sidney, 1572–1577* (New Haven, Conn.: Yale University Press, 1972), 475–500.

6. Neville Williams, *All the Queen's Men: Elizabeth I and Her Courtiers* (New York: Macmillan, 1972), 232.

7. Susan Doran, *Monarchy and Matrimony: The Courtships of Elizabeth I* (London: Routledge, 1996), 252 n.

8. *Works*, 3: 51.

9. *Works*, 2: 216. David Kalstone notes that it is difficult to understand the queen's rejection of Therion the Woodsman, *Sidney's Poetry: Contexts and Interpretations* (New York: W.W. Norton, 1965), 46. Sidney may have been counting too heavily on a rather more masculine response from Elizabeth when he asked her to elect as husband for the Lady one who, in the Lady's words: "withall . . . growes to such rages, that sometimes he strikes me, sometimes he railes at me." In fact, it not really difficult to see how a woman would choose to reject a physically abusive suitor. For a discussion of Sidney at the Elizabethan court, see Louis A. Montrose, "Celebration and Insinuation: Sir Philip Sidney and the Motives of Elizabethan Courtship," *Renaissance Drama* n.s. 8 (1972): 3–35, esp. 22 for comment on "The Lady of May" as Sidney's attempt to "explore the foundations and limits of royal power, and to promote the rights and interests of men of his own status vis-à-vis the crown and peerage." See also Alan Sinfield, "Power and Ideology," *ELH* 52 (1982): 259–78, for a discussion of Sidney's class position "at a point of structural confusion."

10. Alan Hager argues in *Dazzling Images: The Masks of Sir Philip Sidney* (Newark: University of Delaware Press, 1991), 55 that Sidney turns Elizabeth's dynastic progeny into her "posterity," that is, the loyal subjects of the realm: "the idea of the queen bearing children thus gradually dissolves in favor of rearing the good children of loyal subjects." As we have seen, Elizabeth herself made her subjects her children—in this sense Sidney is merely appropriating again her own metaphorical language of multiple familial positions.

11. Bourdieu, *Outline of a Theory of Practice*, 15. The specific content of the honor challenge as Greville reports it would seem to insist upon male virility, in the process somewhat eliding the female function of reproduction in marriage. It is probable that Oxford originally intended the epithet "Puppy" to insult Sidney in terms of his own achieved status of masculinity—any family insult ("race

of dogs") would have been less important. Sidney's unanswerable riposte—if dogs beget puppies, then *men* beget children—insists that all the world already knows that he, Sidney, is a man (and in so saying he proves it); Sidney was higher born on his mother's than on his father's side and so could claim some nobility through his mother. Yet Sidney here—one might say unconsciously—emphasizes the shared biological substratum rather than the class difference.

12. For a discussion of the problems Elizabeth faced as a female prince see Allison Heisch, "Queen Elizabeth and the Persistence of Patriarchy," *Feminist Review* 4 (1980): 45–56.

13. MacCaffrey, *Queen Elizabeth and the Making of Policy*, 265–66.

14. *The Correspondence of Sir Philip Sidney and Hubert Languet*, trans. Stuart A. Pears (1845; rpt. London: William Pickering, 1971), 187.

15. *Correspondence*, 170.

16. Richard C. McCoy, *Sir Philip Sidney: Rebellion in Arcadia* (New Brunswick, N.J.: Rutgers University Press, 1970), chap. 1, outlines the general tensions between Sidney and Queen Elizabeth. See also A. C. Hamilton, *Sir Philip Sidney: A Study of His Life and Works* (Cambridge: Cambridge University Press, 1977), 27–28.

17. Leonard Tennenhouse, *Power on Display: The Politics of Shakespeare's Genres* (New York: Methuen, 1986), 25.

18. Blair Worden argues in *The Sound of Virtue: Philip Sidney's Arcadia and Elizabethan Politics* (New Haven, Conn.: Yale University Press, 1996), that both versions of the *Arcadia* consider in detail the problems of the Elizabethan succession. While not all the parallels he adduces are persuasive, Worden does usefully call attention to the context of contemporaneous political theory and practice, both in England and on the continent, with which Sidney was obviously familiar and within which it is right to see Sidney maneuvering. Of particular interest is his suggestion that the introduction of Cecropia as the threatening agent in the revised *Arcadia* owes something to the increasing threat posed by Mary Queen of Scots.

19. Osborne, *Young Philip Sidney*, 497.

20. Sir Philip Sidney, *The Poems of Sir Philip Sidney*, ed. William A. Ringler, Jr. (Oxford: Clarendon Press, 1962), 440.

21. Sidney placed such Protestant politics, his "love of the caws," as he put it, above his desire to please the queen, and so to be safe, rich, and graced by her favor. In a most revealing letter, Sidney confesses to his father-in-law Walsingham that his radical protestant activism, his very self, is more important to him than the queen's favor. It is difficult not to conclude that Elizabeth was wise when she refused to reward such lack of devotion:

I had before cast my court of dang[er] want and disgrace, and before God Sir it is trew [that] in my hart the love of the caws doth so far over-ballance them all that with Gods grace thei shall never make me weery of my resolution. If her Majesty wear the fowntain I woold fear considiring what I daily fynd that we shold wax dry, but she is but a means whom God useth and I know not whether I am deceaved but I am faithfully persuaded that if she shold with draw her self other springes woold ryse to help this action. For me thinkes I see the great work indeed in hand, against the abusers of the world, wherein it is not greater fault to have confidence in mans power, then it is to hastily to despair of God work. I think a wyse and constant man ought never to greev whyle he doth plai as a man mai sai his own part truly though othgers be out but if him self leav his hild becaws other marriners will be ydle he will hardli fogive him self this own fault. For me I can not promise of my own cource no nor of the my [ ] because I know there is a hyer power that must uphold me or els I shall falll, but certainly I trust, I shall not by other mens wantes be drawn from my self. . . . I understand I am called very ambitious and prowd at home, but certainly if thei knew my hart thei woold not altogether so judge me. (*Works*, 3: 166–67)

22. Sidney's works went through nine editions in the next century, while Spenser had only three editions and Shakespeare four; of the three, only Sidney was translated into foreign languages, including French, German, Dutch, and Italian. See *The Poems of Sir Philip Sidney*, 440.

23. *Works*, 3: 167.

24. Ronald A. Rebholz, *The Life of Fulke Greville, First Lord Brooke* (Oxford: Clarendon Press, 1971), 211–16 discusses Greville's "self-centered" account and argues that he depresses his worth to elevate Sidney's and with it his own in relation to the age of James.

25. The recent publication of the two versions of the *Arcadia* in accessible paperback format may change our sense of Sidney's achievement from poetry to prose—a distinction, of course, he held to be moot.

26. Jonathan Goldberg, *James I and the Politics of Literature* (Baltimore: Johns Hopkins University Press, 1983), 23–24, traces James's own anti-Petrarchan poetics and contrasts James's and Elizabeth's styles of self-presentation.

27. See Tennenhouse, *Power on Display*, 34, and Louis A. Montrose, "Of Gentlemen and Shepherds: The Politics of Elizabethan Pastoral Forms," *ELH* 50 (1983): 441–48 for comment on the political function of Petrarchism during the reign of Elizabeth.

28. Pierre Bourdieu, "The Economics of Linguistics Exchanges," trans. Richard Nice, *Social Science Information* 16 (1977): 545–68.

29. Margreta de Grazia, "Homonyms Before and After Standardization, *Deutsche Shakespeare Gesellschaft Jahrbuch* (1990): 143–56. De Grazia specifically argues that none of the rhetorical figures which name wordplay of various sorts (syllepsis, antanaclasis, paranomasia, significatio, traductio) describe what we post-dictionary readers and speakers identify as a pun—that is, two separate words that are spelled and spoken identically. Sixteenth-century logic manuals do discuss the homonym but define it as "one word that signifieth diverse things," a very different sense from ours; as de Grazia puts it, "what a prelexical age considers one word, a postlexical age considers two or more words." According to the OED, the term "pun" was first used in 1660.

30. *The Poems of Sir Philip Sidney*, 447. Citations of Sidney's poems are to this edition.

31. *The Poems of Sir Philip Sidney*, 441.

32. Arthur F. Marotti, "'Love Is Not Love': Elizabethan Sonnet Sequences and the Social Order," *ELH* 49 (1982): 396–428.

33. Ann Rosalind Jones and Peter Stallybrass, "The Politics of *Astrophil and Stella*," *SEL* 24 (1984): 53–68. Stallybrass and Jones extend the now classic argument made by Nancy J. Vickers, "Diana Described: Scattered Woman and Scattered Rhyme," *Critical Inquiry* 8 (Winter 1981): 265–79.

34. For a discussion of Laura's uncertain identity, see Robert M. Durling, *Petrarch's Lyric Poems: "The Rime Sparse" and Other Lyrics* (Cambridge, Mass.: Harvard University Press, 1976), iv.

35. Rich was "lackey" to his wife's powerful brother the Earl of Essex, acquiescing in his wife's later long-term liaison with Sir Charles Blount, yet not remaining loyal to Essex's followers when the earl was executed for treason. As Ringler puts it, "He was zealous in religion and affected the air of a Puritan, but like Malvolio he was more of a 'time-pleaser' than anything else" (Ringler, in *The Poems of Sir Philip Sidney*, 445).

36. Marotti, "'Love Is Not Love,'" 406. Marotti points out that poems from the sequence do not appear in contemporaries' manuscript collections until after Sidney's death, while other poems of his come into these miscellanies earlier. Ringler notes that Sir John Harington copied eight poems by Sidney into the collection started by his father. He himself first copied "Certain Sonnets" 3 (on f. 34), and then Song x from *Astrophil and Stella* (on f. 36v). As Ringler notes, Harington apparently did not know that Stella was Lady Rich at the time he first copied the poem because he headed it "Sr Philip Syd: to the bewty of the world^e"; subsequently, he copied *Astrophil and Stella* 1 (on f. 155) and headed the poem "Sonnets of Sr Philip Sydneys vppon to ye Lady Ritch." What seems to have been kept most close while Sidney was alive was Stella's identity. It is fascinating to see Harington hesitate in his designation of Penelope Devereux's relationship to the first poem. Is she its subject ("upon") or its addressee ("to")? Harington's confusion about how to state the relationship of the real historical Stella to the poem (which does not, in fact, address her) aptly demonstrates the unstable position of the female with respect to the male speaking voice in the Petrarchan tradition.

37. Robert Sidney, *The Poems of Robert Sidney*, ed. P. J. Croft (Oxford: Clarendon Press, 1984).

38. Jennifer Summit, *Lost Property: The Woman Writer and English Literary History, 1380–1589* (Chicago: University of Chicago Press, 2000), 165–72, traces the importance of Elizabeth's identification as a poet. The major female-to-female exchange Summit discusses (between Elizabeth and Mary Queen of Scots) postdates Sidney's death, but such dating does not detract from the challenge Sidney's writing would pose Elizabeth as herself a member of a poem-writing courtly coterie.

39. Sir Walter Ralegh's later prominence as favorite owed much to his cultivation of the cult of Elizabeth; his fragmentary "Cynthia" may stand as testimony to his sense (however disproved) that direct address in poetry could win back the queen's favor. Sidney addressed no poem to Elizabeth save for the early "The Lady of May."

40. Osborne, *Young Philip Sidney*, 509–10.

41. Ringler, in *The Poems of Sir Philip Sidney*, 443.

42. Ringler, in *The Poems of Sir Philip Sidney*, 445–46.

43. Both Lady Rich and Frances Walsingham helped Robert Sidney during his period of political unpopularity, when even Essex had dropped his support; see Croft, in *Poems of Robert Sidney*,. 83. As we have seen, Walsingham's father also had a hand in arranging Robert Sidney's marriage with Barbara Gamage against Elizabeth's express wishes. Ringler, in *The Poems of Sir Philip Sidney*, 70–71.

44. A. R. Braumuller, *A Seventeenth-Century Letter-Book: A Facsimile Edition of Folger MS.V.a.321* (London: Associated University Press, 1983), 77.

Chapter 4. Mary Sidney Herbert (with a Note on Elizabeth Cary)

1. Signature at the end of "To the Angell spirit of the most excellent Sir Phillip Sidney," *The Collected Works of Mary Sidney Herbert, Countess of Pembroke*, ed. Margaret Hannay et al. (Oxford: Oxford University Press, 1998), vol. 1, 112.

2. Cited in Jonathan Crewe, *Hidden Designs: The Critical Profession and Renaissance Literature* (New York: Methuen, 1986), 82.

3. Arthur Marotti, "Love Is Not Love": Elizabethan Sonnet Sequences and the Social Order," *ELH* (1982): 396–428; Louis Montrose, "Celebration and Insinuation: Sir Philip Sidney and the Motives of Elizabethan Courtship," *Renaissance Drama* 8 (1977): 3–35, "Of Gentlemen and Shepherds: "The Politics of Elizabethan Pastoral Form," *ELH* 50 (1983): 415–59; Richard McCoy, *Rebellion in Arcadia* (New Brunswick, N.J.: Rutgers University Press, 1979).

4. Pierre Bourdieu's discussion of "symbolic capital" in *Outline of a Theory of Practice* (Cambridge: Cambridge University Press, 1977), 178, seems to be an almost direct description of the kind of prestige Mary and Philip Sidney's poetic productions may have increased: "the patrimony of a family or lineage includes not only their land and instruments of production but also their kin and their clientele . . . the network or alliances, or, more broadly of relationships, to be kept up and regularly maintained, representing a heritage of commitments and debts of honour, a capital of rights and duties built up in the course of successive generations and providing an additional source of strength."

5. For a thorough rebuttal of Aubrey's claims, see Kenneth Thorpe Rowe, "The Love of Sir Philip Sidney for the Countess of Pembroke," *Papers of the Michigan Academy of Arts, Sciences, and Letters* (1939): 579–95, by Hannay in *Collected Works of Mary Sidney Herbert*, 259.

6. For a full discussion of the relationship among the various texts, see *The Countess of Pembroke's Arcadia: The New Arcadia*, ed. Victor Skretkowicz (Oxford: Oxford University Press, 1987), lii–lxxviii.

7. For a discussion of the female readership of the text and its crucial bearing on Sidney's special negotiation of questions of authority, see Mary Ellen Lamb, *Gender and Authorship in the Sidney Circle* (Madison: University of Wisconsin Press, 1990), 72–89. I am everywhere indebted to this pathbreaking study of female authority in the Sidney family.

8. Sir Philip Sidney, *The Countess of Pembroke's Arcadia (The Old Arcadia)*, ed. Jean Robertson (Oxford: Oxford University Press, 1973), 27.

9. Arthur Kinney, "Sir Philip Sidney and the Uses of History," in *The Historical Renaissance: New Essays on Tudor and Stuart Literature and Culture*, ed. Richard Strier and Heather Dubrow (Chicago: University of Chicago Press, 1988), cites Greville as characterizing the second version as "fitter to be printed than the first which is so common" (30).

10. Sir Philip Sidney, *The Countess of Pembroke's Arcadia* (London, 1590), A4: "The division and summing of the Chapters was not of Sir Philip Sidneis dooing, but aduentured by the ouerseer of the print, for the more ease of the Readers . . . if any defect be found in the Eclogues, which although they were of Sir Phillip Sidneis writing yet were they not perused by him, but left till the worke had been finished that then choice should haue bene made, which should haue bene taken, and in what manner brought in. At this time they haue bene chosen and disposed as the ouer-seer thought best."

11. Wendy Wall, *The Imprint of Gender: Authorship and Publication in the Renaissance* (Ithaca, N.Y.: Cornell University Press, 1993), 150.

12. Margaret Hannay, *Philip's Phoenix: Mary Sidney, Countess of Pembroke* (Oxford: Oxford University Press, 1990), 60; Eleanor Rosenberg, *Leicester, Patron of Letters* (New York: Columbia University Press, 1955).

13. Crewe is attempting to make a claim for literary achievement per se in the face of new historicist arguments that Sidney's career was primarily political, see *Hidden Designs*, 88.

14. *Arcadia*, ed. Skretkowicz, lxii.

15. Lori Humphrey Newcombe, *Reading Popular Romance in Early Modern England* (New York: Columbia University Press, 2001), 33.

16. Louis Montrose, "Domestic Domain: Poetry, Property, and the Early Modern Subject," in *Subject and Object in Renaissance Culture*, ed. Margreta de Grazia, Maureen Quilligan, and Peter Stallybrass (Cambridge: Cambridge University Press, 1996).

17. Richard Helgerson, *Self-Crowned Laureates: Spenser, Jonson, Milton, and the Literary System* (Berkeley: University of California Press, 1983), 55, 63–67.

18. Edmund Spenser, *The Yale Edition of the Shorter Poems of Edmund Spenser*, ed. William A. Oram et al. (New Haven, Conn.: Yale University Press, 1989).

19. Wall, *Imprint of Gender*, 154.

20. Cited in Gary F. Waller, *Mary Sidney, Countess of Pembroke: A Critical Study* (Salzburg: Institut für Anglistik und Amerikanistik, 1979), 277.

21. Mary Sidney Herbert, *The Collected Works*, ed. Margaret P. Hannay, Noel J. Kinnamon, and Michael G. Brennan, 2 vols. (Oxford: Oxford University Press, 1998); hereafter cited in the text.

22. Sidney Herbert, *Works*, vol. 1, 100.

23. Sir Philip Sidney, *The Poems of Sir Philip Sidney*, ed. William A. Ringler (Oxford: Oxford University Press, 1962), 173–74.

24. Edmund Spenser, *Spenser's Minor Poems*, ed. Ernest de Selincourt (Oxford: Oxford University Press, 1960), 372.

25. Lamb, *Gender and Authorship*, 117.

26. Aemilia Lanyer, *The Poems of Aemilia Lanyer*, ed. Susanne Woods (Oxford: Oxford University Press, 1993), 28.

27. Pamela Benson, in a lecture delivered at the Renaissance Society of America, Chicago, April 2001.

28. Isabella Whitney, *A sweet nosgay, or pleasant posye* (London: R. Jones, 1573).

29. Jonathan Goldberg, "The Countess of Pembroke's Literal Translation," in *Subject and Object in Renaissance Culture*, ed. Margreta de Grazia, Maureen Quilligan, and Peter Stallybrass (Cambridge: Cambridge University Press, 1996), 321–36, challenges such critical dismissal in a discussion of Pembroke's translation of Petrarch's *Triumph of Death*.

30. Barbara Lewalski, *Writing Women in Jacobean England* (Cambridge, Mass.: Harvard University Press, 1993), 190–94.

31. Mary Sidney Herbert, *Works*, vol. 1, 153–54.

32. Dympna Callaghan has interestingly argued that Cary outlines the difference between Salome and Mariam as one of racial bifurcation, Cleopatra representing a derogated racial other in the face of Mariam's "white" purity. See "Re-Reading *The Tragedie of Mariam*," in *Women, "Race," and Writing in the Early Modern Period*, ed. Margo Hendricks and Patricia Parker (London: Routledge, 1994), 163–77.

33. Margaret Ferguson, "Running on with Almost Public Voice," in *Traditions and the Talents of Women*, ed. Florence Howe (Urbana: University of Illinois Press, 1991), 37–67. Ferguson has revised and considerably extended her earlier discussion of the important and complicated relations between private speech and written publication in Cary's play. See *Dido's Daughters: Literacy, Gender, and Empire in Early Modern England and France* (Chicago: University of Chicago Press, 2003), 284–97.

34. Compare the reaction of Shakespeare's Juliet. Although at first enraged at Romeo for killing her cousin Tybalt, ("Beautiful tyrant, fiend angelical!" (III.ii.75), she quickly asserts her priorities: Nurse: "Will you speak well of him that killed your cousin?" Juliet: "Shall I speak ill of him that is my husband?" (96–98). Nevertheless, it is imagining this murder of her cousin that torments Juliet (at some length) just before she brings on her false death in order to avoid being traded by her father to Paris. In horror, she thinks of waking in the vault, "Where for this many hundred years the bones / Of all my bury'd ancestors are pack'd, / Where bloody Tybalt yet but green in earth / Lies fest'ring in his shroud" (IV.iii.40–44)

35. *The Tragedy of Mariam with the Lady Falkland her Life*, ed. Barry Weller and Margaret Ferguson (Berkeley: University of California Press, 1994).

36. Milton in *Samson Agonistes* may well be remembering Cary's play, especially when he makes the biblical concubine into a *wife*. Delilah's transgressive desire for a life as a public figure among the Philistines demonstrates how problematic the codes for behavior make any political speech by a woman who is first and foremost a wife.

37. For a fuller discussion of the connections between speech and silence in these two plays, see Maureen Quilligan, "Staging Gender: William Shakespeare and Elizabeth Cary," in *Sex and Gender in Early Modern Europe*, ed. James G. Turner (Cambridge: Cambridge University Press, 1993), 208–32.

38. Samuel Daniel, in a poem written as a letter from Octavia to Antony, has Octavia call Cleopatra "incestuous," as indeed she doubtless was, married by Pharaonic convention to her brother and sleeping with the adopted son of her earlier lover Julius Caesar, with whom she had a son, Cesario. "A Letter from Octavia to her husband Marcus Antonius into Egypt," in *Certaine Small Poems lately Printed* (London, 1605), A4.

39. *Tragedy of Mariam*, 39.

40. Elaine Beilin, *Redeeming Eve: Women Writers of the English Renaissance* (Princeton, N.J.: Princeton University Press 1987), 171.

41. Weller and Ferguson print *The Lady Falkland, Her Life, by One of her Daughters*, which details her suffering for her religious conversion, with *Tragedy of Mariam*, 183–275.

42. Just as Shakespeare's Antony cannot stop the autonomous Cleopatra from speaking, even to utter his last words: Antony: "I am dying, Egypt, dying. / Give me some wine, and let me speak a little." Cleopatra: " No, let me speak . . ." (IV.xvi.45–45)

43. See Chronology in *Tragedy of Mariam*, 180.

Chapter 5. Spenser's Britomart

1. For one of the most recent discussions of Britomart as a character with a potential "interior self," see Julia Walker, *Medusa's Mirrors: Spenser, Shakespeare, Milton, and the Metamorphosis of the Female Self* (Newark: University of Delaware Press, 1998).Walker guesses that the writing of actual women may provide a fuller sense of the female self she sees to be only potentially present in texts by males (193). That writing, as I argue, instead insists on how unmodern Elizabethan senses of personhood are; we have misread male self-fashioning as being modern before its time.

2. For a fascinating discussion of the woman warrior in Tasso, see David Quint, *Epic and Empire: Politics and Generic Form from Virgil to Milton* (Princeton, N.J.: Princeton University Press, 1993).

3. For a now classic discussion of Spenser and Elizabeth, see Louis Montrose, "The Elizabethan Subject and the Spenserian Text," in *Literary Theory/ Renaissance Texts*, ed. Patricia Parker and David Quint (Baltimore: Johns Hopkins University Press, 1986), 303–40.

4. Maureen Quilligan, "The Comedy of Female Authority," *ELR* 17 (1988): 427–41.

5. Linda Gregerson, *The Reformation of the Subject: Spenser, Milton, and the English Protestant Epic* (Cambridge: Cambridge University Press, 1995).

6. The mirror phase is an event in the child's development which precedes a sexual identity. Why Spenser—and Milton mirroring him—should choose to make the scenes so central to the question of selfhood concerning females is interesting. Sexual difference, instantiated by the Oedipal narrative, is clearly at the center of both.

7. Gregerson positions two texts in a useful conjunction and marshals an exceedingly sophisticated set of terms for talking about the subject. Yet while

she is everywhere sensitive to issues of gender, both in history and in the texts she reads, her theory seems to make it oddly difficult to ask why reformation subject formation takes place in mirrors into which *female* protagonists look, in these male-authored texts (93–95). Gregerson finally notes that the postlapsarian subject is female (197).

8. In *Milton's Spenser: The Politics of Reading* (Ithaca, N.Y.: Cornell University Press, 1983), I broached the issue of the female reader's relationship to Book III of *The Faerie Queene* in a chapter titled "The Female Reader." That argument has attracted many useful disagreements; in what follows I am indebted to David Lee Miller and Harry Berger (in particular) for the seriousness with which they objected to my suggestion that a woman might read the text differently. See David Lee Miller, *The Poem's Two Bodies: The Poetics of the 1590 Faerie Queene* (Princeton, N.J.: Princeton University Press, 1988), and Harry Berger, "Actaeon at the Hinder Gate: The Stag Party in Spenser's Garden of Adonis," in *Desire in the Renaissance: Psychoanalysis and Literature*, ed. Valeria Finucci and Regina Schwartz (Princeton, N.J.: Princeton University Press, 1994), 91–119. The case of the female reader of Spenser's Renaissance text is less purely theoretical now, because we have a contemporary woman reader in Mary Wroth. For a discussion of her rewrite of the Amoret episode, see Chapter 6.

9. C. S. Lewis, *The Allegory of Love: A Study in Medieval Tradition* (1936; reprint Oxford: Oxford University Press, 1986), 332.

10. Laura Mulvey, *Visual and Other Pleasures* (Bloomington: Indiana University Press, 1989); Nancy Vickers, "Diana Described: Scattered Woman and Scattered Rhyme," in *Writing and Sexual Difference*, ed. Elizabeth Abel (Chicago: University of Chicago Press, 1982) articulates the function of the Petrarchan blazon to dismember and master poetic competition by mastering the female body. Patricia Parker, "Suspended Instruments," in *Literary Fat Ladies: Rhetoric Gender Property* (London: Methuen, 1987) analyzes the threat to that mastery in the Bower of Bliss. Spenser's echoing allegorical structure would allow the Venus and Adonis moment to reprise the earlier episode and to achieve similar purposes.

11. Robert Ellrodt, *Neoplatonism in the Poetry of Spenser* (Geneva: E. Droz, 1960), 71–90. For a more recent and thoroughgoing discussion of the Ficinian pretexts to the Garden of Adonis, see Jon A. Quitslund, *Spenser's Supreme Fiction: Platonic Natural Philosophy and "The Faerie Queene"* (Toronto: University of Toronto Press, 2001).

12. Lauren Silberman, *Transforming Desire: Erotic Knowledge in Books III and IV of "The Faerie Queene"* (Berkeley: University of California Press, 1995), 46–48 describes the paradoxical notions of safety and risk embodied in the problematic image of the boar; the joke on stamina can be found in her earlier dissertation. See also my "The Female Reader," in *Milton's Spenser: The Politics of Reading*, chap. 3. In a note, Roche wryly remarks that the landscape is a landscape as well as anatomical metaphor. Shakespeare, of course, also turns Venus's body most explicitly into a landscape in *Venus and Adonis*.

13. Harry Berger, "'Kidnapped Romance': Discourse in *The Faerie Queene*," in *Unfolded Tales: Studies on Renaissances Romances*, ed. George Logan and Gordon

Teskey (Ithaca, N.Y.: Cornell University Press, 1989), questions the friendliness of Spenser to his female readers. In "Actaeon at the Hinder Gate," Berger further demonstrates the unavoidable menace to the male viewpoint in a gendered reading of the Garden of Adonis. This second response to my earlier argument has deepened and extended my own understanding of Spenser's tactics. What follows is, in part, a further response to his reinterpretation of my position. David Miller's sense of Arthur's "castration" however, suggests just how endangered the male genitals are in the poem (which had been my original point—the male viewpoint must necessarily feel the danger of Actaeon's position). It is only the female reader who will not feel threatened, but perhaps heartened, by this image of unending erection and intercourse. (Berger found Silberman's and my suggestion "exhausting" to contemplate.) Miller reads the absence of the male genitals as the fundamental unnameable presence that subtends the entire narrative (Silberman had made the boar into the detached phallus just as the cave beneath the Mount is the female womb written into the landscape). For Miller the Garden of Adonis is the point at which "Spenser's allegory appropriate[s] feminine procreativity on behalf of a patriarchal symbolic order" (28).

14. Gordon Teskey, *Allegory and Violence* (Ithaca, N.Y.: Cornell University Press, 1996), 18–19.

15. Susan Frye, *Elizabeth I: The Competition over Representation* (Oxford: Oxford University Press, 1993), 124–35, argues for Spenser's complicity in Busirane's rape of Amoret.

16. Harry Berger, *Revisionary Play: Studies in Spenserian Dynamics* (Berkeley: University of California Press, 1988), 179.

17. Cited by Lisa Freinkel, *Reading Shakespeare's Will: The Theology of Figure from Augustine to the Sonnets* (New York: Columbia University Press, 2001), 161.

18. James Broaddus, *Spenser's Allegory of Love: Social Vision in Books I, III, and V of "The Faerie Queene"* (London: Associated University Presses, 1995), 62–66 argues very closely that the birth of the twins is designed to be as positive a vision of female sexuality as possible.

19. David Miller, *The Poem's Two Bodies* argues that the Error episode is a key for reading the procreative energies represented in Book III, the Garden of Adonis being "an allegory of natural reproduction" (274), where the male genitals are "absent," but they appear in the "phallic circle which gathers fecundity back into the Logos" (264). The anamorphic topography of the cave underneath the Mount of Venus, Miller also confesses, requires that the boar "is inside Venus herself as she 'takes her fill' of sweetness from Adonis." If the boar does not now represent the male member, then it must somehow be a child.

20. John Watkins, *The Specter of Dido: Spenser and Virgilian Epic* (New Haven, Conn.: Yale University Press, 1995) 171 argues that Britomart repudiates a too narrow Virgilian view of antieroticism when she rejects the definition of love represented by Busirane's tapestries; Watkins suggestively points out that the "ideal shews," which do not frighten Britomart, are very much like the *pictura inani* Aeneas views before capitulating to desire for Dido.

21. Sheila Cavanagh, *Wanton Eyes and Chaste Desires: Female Sexuality in "The Faerie Queene"* (Bloomington: Indiana University Press, 1994).

22. Although her ultimate point is different from mine, Silberman also understands that Britomart points up the "contradictions" of Satyrane's tournament and the basically homosocial economy of the joust, with its "indefinitely repeatable choice between fundamentally similar antagonists" (105).

23. Gregerson, *Reformation of the Subject*, 31, n28.

24. Orgel cited in Valerie Traub, *Desire and Anxiety: Circulations of Sexuality in Shakespearean Drama* (London: Cambridge University Press, 1992), 93.

25. Silberman, *Transforming Desire*, 30–33.

26. Ariosto, *Orlando Furioso*, 2 vols., trans. Barbara Reynolds (Harmondsworth: Penguin, 1977).

27. Traub tracks the difficulty of finding evidence of female same-sex erotic activity in the period; it only becomes "visible" when it mimics heterosexual (penetrative) sexuality. She traces the way in which the mode of chaste friendship becomes bound to the far more threatening idea of the tribade later in the seventeenth century. See *The Renaissance of Lesbianism in Early Modern England* (Cambridge: Cambridge University Press, 2001).

28. Karma Lochrie usefully outlines the important place of female agency (excessive desire) in the discourse of medieval sodomy; she hypothesizes that there are few instances of condemnation of female same sex desire in the literature not because people didn't acknowledge that women engaged in sexual activity with each other, but because there were so many other modes of controlling female sexuality; indeed, female agency is involved in the control of male sodomy because it is so insistently the one sexual desire that needs control. See "Presumptive sodomy and Its Exclusions," *Textual Practice* 13 (1999): 295–310.

29. Kathryn Schwarz, *Tough Love: Amazon Encounters in the English Renaissance* (Durham, N.C.: Duke University Press, 2000), 44–45 understands stories about Amazons as a means for understanding the instability of patriarchal modes of discourse about proper female domesticity.

30. Miller, *The Poem's Two Bodies*, 279.

31. Plutarch, *Morals*, trans. Sir Thomas North (London: Thomas Wight, 1603), 1292.

32. Schwarz, *Tough Love*, 174.

Chapter 6. Mary Wroth

1. Helen Hackett, *Women and Romance Fiction in the English Renaissance* (Cambridge: Cambridge University Press 2000, pp. 164–66 discusses the "convenient correspondence between romance conventions and circumstances of Wroth's life," which was so strong that Hackett asks, "How could Wroth *not* have written a romance?"

2. Lorna Hutson, *The Usurer's Daughter: Male Friendship and Fictions of Women in Sixteenth-Century England* (London: Routledge, 1994) "Sidney's knights are not heroes as Tyler's Trebatio is, because of being fantastically tall and strong, but because . . . their minds are prepared for any eventuality by the exemplary reading of histories" (97).

3. Fredric Jameson, *The Political Unconscious: Narrative as a Socially Symbolic Act* (Ithaca, N.Y.: Cornell University Press, 1981), 118.

4. See Maureen Quilligan, "On Epic: Slavery and Gender in the Renaissance Epic," *South Atlantic Quarterly* 100 (2001): 15–39.

5. Howard Bloch, *Etymologies and Genealogies: A Literary Anthropology of the French Middle Ages* (Chicago: University of Chicago Press, 1983), 211.

6. Elspeth Kennedy, "The Knight Reader of Arthurian Romance," in *Culture and the King: The Social Implications of the Arthurian Legend: Essays in Honor of Valerie M. Lagorio*, ed. Martin B. Schichtman and James P. Carley (Albany: State University of New York Press, 1994), 70, offers proof that romance had an actual effect on some knights' understanding of chivalry.

7. Sarah Kay, *The Chansons de Geste in the Age of Romance: Political Fictions* (Berkeley: University of California Press, 1995): "However ironic, the dreamy successes of romance heroes stress the potential for male bonding, and play down the consequences of inter-male strife. . . . Inter-male violence is the repressed of romance; in this way we see quite clearly to what extent the *chansons de geste* function as its political unconscious" (24–25).

8. The inclusion of the sonnet cycle *Pamphilia to Amphilanthus* at the end of the text of the romance makes Wroth the first female author in English in that (Sidneian) genre as well. Lady Elizabeth Cary had published her closet drama, *Mariam, Faire Queen of Jewry*, in 1613, and Aemilia Lanyer had published her long poem on Christ's passion and Eve's defense of women, *Salve Deus Rex Judaeorum*, in 1611.

9. I am indebted to Gwynne Kennedy, who argued in a brilliant graduate paper that the fundamental subject of Wroth's romance is the traffic in women.

10. Josephine A. Roberts quotes some of the contemporary notices of Wroth's writing in *The Poems of Lady Wroth* (Baton Rouge: Louisiana State University Press, 1983), 7–26. P. J. Croft, in Appendix C to *The Poems of Robert Sidney*, ed. Croft (Oxford: Clarendon Press, 1984), lists Wroth's verbal echoes of her father's poems in Appendix C.

11. Shannon Miller, "Constructing the Female Self: Mary Wroth's *Urania*," in *Renaissance Culture and the Everyday*, ed. Patricia Fumerton and Simon Hunt (Philadelphia: University of Pennsylvania Press, 1999), 144.

12. *The First Part of the Countess of Mountgomery's Urania*, ed. Josephine A. Roberts (Binghamton, N.Y.: Center for Medieval and Early Renaissance Studies, 1995), cvi.; hereafter cited in the text.

13. Margaret Hannay discusses Van de Passe's portrait of Mary Sidney Herbert as a potential title page, in "The Countess of Pembroke's Agency in Print and Scribal Culture," in *Women's Writing and the Circulation of Ideas: Manuscript Publication in England, 1550–1800*, ed. George L. Justice and Nathan Tinker (Cambridge: Cambridge University Press, 2001), 21. For a discussion of Crispin and Willem Van de Passe's engravings of the Stuarts, see Jonathan Goldberg, *James I and the Politics of Literature: Jonson, Shakespeare, Donne, and Their Contemporaries* (Baltimore: Johns Hopkins University Press, 1983), 89–101.

14. An early catalogue of the Van de Passe family engravings (which misses Simon's frontispiece for the *Urania*) is D. Franken, *L'oeuvre gravé des van de*

Passe (Paris: Rapilly, 1881). A more complete accounting can be found in Sidney Colvin, *Early Engraving and Engravers in England, 1545–1695* (London: British Museum, 1905), 159–61. For further discussion of frontispieces in general (neither of which mentions the title page to *Urania*), see Margery Corbett and Ronald Lightbown, *The Comely Frontispiece: The Emblematic Title-Page in England, 1550–1660* (London: Routledge, 1979), and Alfred Forbes Johnson, *A Catalogue of Engraved and Etched English Title-Pages . . . to 1691* (Oxford: Oxford University Press, 1934).

15. Wendy Wall, *The Imprint of Gender: Authorship and Publication in the Renaissance* (Ithaca, N.Y.: Cornell University Press, 1993), 336.

16. Lady Mary Wroth, *The Countess of Montgomeries Urania* (London: John Mariott and John Grismond, 1621), 48.

17. The only other title page by Simon Van de Passe which uses any columnar framing device was his frontispiece for Roger Bacon's *Instauratio magna* (1620), which, like Hole's vision for *Poly-Olbion*, imaged a seascape between the architectural features.

18. Aaron Rathborne, *The Svrveyor, in Foure Bookes* (London: W. Stamsby, 1616), 175ff.: "The Legall Part of Surveying Arguement of the fourth book I would not bee mistaken, or haue it vndertood; that I here vndertake (as a Lawyer) to instruct or teach the rules of Institutions of the Law (being out of mine element) but as a Surueyor, briefly and truely to expresse and deliuer herein what I hold fit and meete for a Surueyor to know and vnderstand. As first what a Mannor is, and the seuerall parts and members thereof, with the appendants therevnto: Next, the perquisites, casualties and profits of Court, and their seuerall natures: then the diuersitie of estates, with any Lands or Tenements may bee holden, occupied, or enioyed; and the seuerall tenures depending on those estates; with the Rents and seruices incident and belonging to those tenures: Also what reprises, paiments, and deductions may bee issuing out of a Mannor."

19. Richard Helgerson, *Forms of Nationhood: The Elizabethan Writing of England* (Chicago: University of Chicago Press, 1992), 117–22, 139–47.

20. Commentary on the portrait is vast: Roy Strong, *The Cult of Elizabeth: Elizabethan Portraiture and Pageantry* (London: Thames and Hudson, 1977); Strong, *Gloriana: The Portraits of Queen Elizabeth I* (London: Thames and Hudson, 1987); Andrew Belsey and Catherine Belsey, "Icons of Divinity: Portraits of Elizabeth I," in *Renaissance Bodies: The Human Figure in English Culture, c. 1540–1660*, ed. Lucy Gent and Nigel Llewellyn (London: Reaktion, 1990).

21. For a superb summary of the arguments so far, see Valerie Traub, *The Renaissance of Lesbianism in Early Modern England* (Cambridge: Cambridge University Press, 2002), 133–37. Traub's notes are very full, but a key set of texts are Joel Fineman, *The Subjectivity Effect in Western Literary Tradition: Essays Toward the Release of Shakespeare's Will* (Cambridge, Mass.: MIT Press, 1991), 228–29; Susan Frye, *Elizabeth I: The Competition for Representation* (Oxford: Oxford University Press, 1993), 102–3.

22. As Peter Stallybrass and Ann Jones have pointed out, the portrait was often a picture of the costume, not the sitter. See Ann Jones and Peter

Stallybrass, *Renaissance Clothing and the Materials of Memory* (Cambridge: Cambridge University Press, 2001).

23. Traub, *Renaissance of Lesbianism*, 152.

24. Reinhard Bentmann and Michael Muller, *The Villa as Hegemonic Architecture* (1970; Atlantic Highlands, N.J.: Humanities Press, 1992), 81 (see also Figure 8).

25. Ben Jonson, *The Poems of Ben Jonson*, ed. George Johnston (Cambridge, Mass.: Harvard University Press, 1962), 76.

26. Jonson may not have known that the walls of Penshurst were built during the 1388 Peasants' Rebellion, for he compliments their low, unmartial nature (whereas they were made to keep out attackers who went on foot, not horseback). The Sidney country seat is an exemplar of all that is happy, where all labor is erased and all natural plenty makes itself available to aristocratic ease.

27. Ben Jonson, *The Workes of Benjamin Jonson* (London: William Stansby, 1616).

28. Kelly Boyd McBride, *Country House Discourse in Early Modern England: A Cultural Study of Landscape and Legitimacy* (Aldershot: Ashgate, 2001), 78.

29. Susan Frye, "Maternal Textualities," in *Maternal Measures: Figuring Caregiving in the Early Modern Period*, ed. Naomi J. Miller and Naomi Yavneh (Aldershot: Ashgate, 2001), 224–36.

30. Don Wayne, *Penshurst: The Semiotics of Place and the Poetics of History* (Madison: University of Wisconsin Press, 1984), 118.

31. Mark Girouard, *Life in the English Country House* (New Haven, Conn.: Yale University Press, 1978).

32. The windmill has two separate functions as outlined in Arthur Henkel and Albrecht Schone, *Emblemata: Handbuch sur Sinnbildkunst* (Stuttgart: Metzler, 1967), 1240–42: either as an emblem of inappropriateness, with a man trying to move a windmill with hand-operated bellows, or as an image of sloth, the passive waiting for fortune to grind one's corn. Neither seems at all germane to the *Urania*; the use of the windmill to image idleness appeared in Geoffrey Witney's *A Choice of Emblems* (1586). I am grateful to John Mulryan for these citations.

33. I am indebted to Michael Vennera, who first suggested the windmill's possible reference to *Don Quixote*.

34. I am indebted to David Kastan for pointing out this connection.

35. For a detailed discussion of Wroth's Cervantes-like realism and irony, see Hackett, *Women and Romance Fiction*, 174–77.

36. Sir Philip Sidney, *The Countess of Pembroke's Arcadia*, ed. Maurice Evans (Harmondsworth: Penguin, 1988).

37. For a discussion of the Countess of Pembroke's part in the publication of the *revised Arcadia*, see A. C. Hamilton, *Sir Philip Sidney: A Study of His Life and Works* (Cambridge: Cambridge University Press, 1977), 169–72.

38. For a discussion of Sidney's rewrite of the opening of Montemayor's *Diana* in the scene with Strephon and Claius, see Hamilton, *Sir Philip Sidney*, 126–29.

39. Wroth, *The Countess of Montgomeries Urania*, 1.

40. Webster plays a very different variation on the female voice in an Echo

scene when he has Echo speak from the tomb of, and in the voice of, the slain incest-inscribed Duchess of Malfi, whose remarkable agency persists even after death when she tries to warn her unsuspecting (exogamous) husband of her jealous brother's murderous rage:

Antonio: 'Tis very like my wife's voice.
Echo: Ay, wife's voice.
...
Antonio: Necessity compels me.
Make scrutiny throughout the passages
Of your own life, you'll find it impossible
To fly your fate.
Echo: O fly your fate!
Delio: Hark! the dead stones seem to have pity on you,
And give you good counsel.
Antonio: Echo, I will not talk with thee,
For thou art a dead thing.
Echo: Thou art a dead thing.

    41. For a discussion of the problematic status of Echo for producing the effect of female agency, see Gina Bloom's subtle analysis of Sandys's translation in "Localizing Disembodied Voice in Sandys's Englished "Narcissus and Echo," in *Ovid and the Renaissance Body*, ed. Goran V. Stanivukovic (Toronto: University of Toronto Press, 2001), 129–54. See also Josephine A. Roberts, "The Phallacies of Authorship," in *Attending to Early Modern Women*, ed. Susan D. Amussen and Adele Seeff (Newark: University of Delaware Press, 1998), 451–42, for a discussion of Anne Vavasour's use of the figure of Echo.

    42. Wroth is also continuing contemporaneous Scots and continental romance tradition, which had become something of a prose fashion at James's court. See *Poems of Lady Mary Wroth*, ed. Roberts, 28–29.

    43. Compare Ferdinand's baroque keen in *The Duchess of Malfi* that the image of his sister's making love to another man will "stick" in his memory, "Till of her bleeding heart I make a sponge / To wipe it out."

    44. What Wroth has done is to literalize not only the "flames" of passion that "burn" a lover's heart, but also the elaborately celebrated body parts from the tradition of the blazon Spenser himself mocks, for instance, in the scene with Serena and the cannibals in Book VI of *The Faerie Queene* (VI.ix.39). For a discussion of the blazon as implicit dismemberment, see Nancy Vickers, "Diana Described: Scattered Woman and Scattered Rhyme," *Critical Inquiry* 8 (1981): 265–79.

    45. The story of Argalus and Parthenia, the first new story Sidney interpolated into his revised *Arcadia*, tests male versus female constancy. The story of Parthenia's disfigurement may be a reference to Sidney's own mother's tragic facial scarring by smallpox; her case was so severe that Lady Sidney secluded herself from court. Parthenia's magical healing may represent the son's wish to erase his mother's pain—as well as, of course, to provide the exemplary test case

of Argalus's constancy when he refuses to accept a perfect lookalike who is not in fact Parthenia herself. For an argument assuming this familial referentiality in the Argalus episode, see Hannay, *Philip's Phoenix*. The possibility that Sidney's episode is a familial roman à clef (a possibility that could have been assumed, if anywhere, within the Sidney family) would have provided added authority for Wroth's autobiographical account of her own experiences in the story of Lindamira in the *Urania*, especially as her story begins with an apparent description of her parents'—Robert Sidney and Barbara Gamage's—courtship. For a discussion of the parallels see Roberts, *Urania*, 30–31.

46. In the first prose romance written in Italy (ca. 1558), also titled the *Urania*, by Giulia Bigolina, the heroine is cross-dressed. As Valerie Finucci points out in her introduction to her modern English translation, Bigolina was following the convention for sixteenth-century Italian romances. Bigolina's text was not printed until the twenty-first century, so it is unlikely that Wroth would have known of it; the coincidence of title and genre reveals how inevitable the choice must have been for two female authors. The coincidence makes all the more striking Wroth's decision not to have her heroine cross-dressed.

47. Rosalind mocks the practice in *As You Like It*—a play which some have suggested might have been performed at Wilton for William Herbert. If so, Shakespeare like Jonson might be commenting on what was known to be a Sidney-Pembroke pastoral pastime.

48. Roberts, *Urania*, 5.

49. Catherine Belsey, *The Subject of Tragedy: Identity and Difference in Renaissance Drama* (London: Methuen, 1985), 149–50.

50. Wroth comments on this gender-blind power when she notes in passing that "Parents have (were it not for Christianity, I should say), a cruel and tyrannical power over their children" in the choice of marriage partners (35).

51. Roberts prints the poem on p. 217; for the argument as to identification, see 43–44.

52. Gary Waller, *The Sidney Family Romance* (Detroit: Wayne State University Press, 1993), 109.

53. Roberts, *Urania*, xxxiii.

54. Lori Humphrey Newcombe argues that Ovid suggests that Pygmalion may have regretted the loss of his masterpiece "'If that which is lost be not found': Monumental Bodies, Spectacular Bodies in *The Winter's Tale*," in *Ovid and the Renaissance Body*, ed. Stanivukovic, 239–59.

Chapter 7. Shakespeare's Cordelia

1. Raphael Holinshed, *Holinshed's Chronicle as Used in Shakespeare's Plays*, ed. Allardyce Nicoll and Josephine Calina (1927; New York: E.P. Dutton, 1937).

2. Samuel Johnson, *Johnson's Shakespeare*, ed. Arthur Sherbo (New Haven, Conn.: Yale University Press, 1968), 704.

3. Jonathan Dollimore, "King Lear and Essentialist Humanism," in *King Lear*, ed. Harold Bloom (New York: Chelsea House, 1987), 83.

4. Janet Adelman, *Suffocating Mothers: Fantasies of Maternal Origin in Shakespeare's Plays* (New York: Routledge, 1992), 128.

5. Richard McCabe, *Incest, Drama, and Nature's Law, 1550–1700* (Cambridge: Cambridge University Press, 1993), 179.

6. Stanley Cavell, *Disowning Knowledge in Six Plays of Shakespeare* (Cambridge: Cambridge University Press, 1987), 70.

7. William Shakespeare, *The Complete Works*, Compact Edition, ed. Stanley Wells and Gary Taylor (Oxford: Clarendon Press, 1988). All citations of Shakespeare's plays are to this edition, which uses an unusual form of scene numbering in *Pericles*.

8. Contrary to today's attitudes toward incest, it seems that common English people of the sixteenth and seventeenth centuries did not regard incest with horror. Very few instances of it appear in the records of church courts and parishes, and when they do, the punishments are very light, at least compared with the capital penalty required by new laws in the middle of the seventeenth century: it usually comprised simple public penance in the parish church or other public place. It was punished no more harshly than other sexual crimes such as adultery or fornication. See John Addy, *Sin and Society in the Seventeenth Century* (London: Routledge, 1989), 181–83. Eight instances of incest recorded in the diocesan records of Kent for the years 1559–65 show excommunication as the worst recorded punishment: Arthur J. Willis, *Church Life in Kent, being Church Court Records of the Canterbury Diocese, 1559–1565* (Lambeth Palace Library). In one case both father and daughter are excommunicated, but that may simply be for having failed to appear to receive and do penance (entry 463, p. 57); this case was heard by the archbishop. The word "dying" appears in the context of the daughter's presentation and admission to having borne a child by her father, but Willis prints a question mark, querying whether this refers to the mother or child. In another case, a twelve-year-old daughter is brought by her mother to court to accuse her father, but she confesses only that he kissed her. He is allowed to do penance by paying a fine. In yet another case a man does penance on four Sundays for having committed "fornication" with his wife's sister and is "certified"; it is simply noted that the woman in question, "who has not yet given birth, is at Netherfield in Sussex." The records of the court of Arches at Lambeth palace (which only begin in 1660, as volumes for earlier years were burned in the great fire of London) and which list appeals from all dioceses in England, include twenty cases of "nullity of marriage" by reason of "incest," most commonly marriage of a man with his deceased wife's sister, and less commonly his deceased brother's wife. In only two of the nine cases which include the record of a sentence, the woman is excused from punishment, usually a fine of between 5 and 15 pounds sterling. In one case the couple are not fined at all, probably owing to the fact that they have had two children and that they pled ignorance, or so it is recorded in the very rare instance of "personal answers" included in the file; their marriage was "broken" and they were divorced.

Two notorious cases of incest made it into print in the seventeenth century: John Atherton, *The Life and Death of John Atherton, Lord Bishop of Waterford and Lysmore . ; .. who for Incest, Buggery, and many other . . . crimes . . . dyed a shamefull death . .. and was hanged on the Gallows Greene at Dublin*, (London, 1641) and Thomas Weir, *An Account of the Trial of that most wicked Pharisee Major Thomas Weir, who was Executed for Adultery Incest, and Bestiality* (London, n.p., 1678). The doggerel poem does not tell us what happens to Atherton's wife's sister (Atherton is pardoned), but we are told in lurid detail about Weir's own sister's lack of any remorse for her sin. He was burned and she was hanged. In general, then, the woman bears equal punishment, as in *Pericles*.

9. John Gower, *Confessio Amantis*, book 8, 302–17, in *The English Works of John Gower*, ed. G. C. Macaulay (1901; Oxford: Early English Text Society, 1969), 394.

10. Mary Douglas, *Purity and Danger: An Analysis of Concepts of Pollution and Taboo* (1966; London: Routledge, 2001).

11. Robert Greene, Thomas Kyd, and Thomas Lodge, *The True Chronicle History of King Leir and his Three Daughters, Gonorill, Ragan, and Cordella* (London: John Wright, 1605), sig. A2ᵛ; hereafter cited in the text.

12. Lynda Boose, "The Father and the Bride in Shakespeare," *PMLA* 97 (1982): 325–47.

13. I take the details of St. Marina's legend from Christine de Pizan's telling of it in *The City of Ladies*, the translation of which was printed in 1521, so that Shakespeare could have known a version of it.

14. See Phyllis Rackin, "Androgyny, Mimesis, and the Marriage of the Boy Heroine on the English Renaissance Stage," *PMLA* 102 (1987): 29–41; Stephen Orgel, *Impersonations: The Performance of Gender in Shakespeare's England* (Cambridge: Cambridge University Press, 1996); and Peter Stallybrass, "Transvestism and the 'Body Beneath': Speculating on the Boy Actor," in *Erotic Politics: Desire on the Renaissance Stage*, ed. Susan Zimmerman (New York: Routledge, 1992), 79. Stallybrass's speculations about what the audience might have thought it saw in seeing Desdemona's dead body at the end of *Othello* are germane to the issue of the theatrical display of St. Marina's newly female corpse. If the St. Marina legend resonates at all behind the revelation of Marina's identity, it poses interesting questions about the boy actor's body beneath hers.

15. Leonard Tennenhouse, *Power on Display: The Politics of Shakespeare's Genres* (New York: Methuen, 1986).

16. Walter Cohen's note to this moment is instructive: "the possible sexual complications here, including incest, can be highlighted in performance by doubling the part of Marina with that of Thaisa." Cited in Stephen Greenblatt, Walter Cohen, Jean Howard, and Katharine Eisaman Maus, eds., *The Norton Shakespeare* (New York: Norton, 1997), 2771 n9. Susan Frye, "Incest and Authority in *Pericles, Prince of Tyre*," in *Incest and the Literary Imagination*, ed. Elizabeth Barnes (Gainesville: University Press of Florida, 2002), 39–58, argues that Shakespeare's version radically increases the complicity of Antioch's daughter.

17. John Cunliffe, *Influence of Seneca on Elizabethan Tragedy* (Hamden, Ct.: Archon Books, 1965), 85.

18. Sir Philip Sidney, *The Countess of Pembroke's Arcadia*, ed. Victor Skretkowicz (Oxford: Clarendon Press, 1987), 183.

19. George Gascoigne and Francis Kinwelmersh, *Jocasta, a Tragedy*, in *Four Old Plays*, ed. Francis J. Child (Cambridge: G. Nichols, 1848), 253.

20. Robert S. Miola, *Shakespeare and Classical Tragedy: The Influence of Seneca* (Oxford: Oxford University Press, 1992), 1.

21. Seneca, *Seneca his tenne tragedies* (London: Wright, 1605).

22. Bruce R. Smith, *Ancient Scripts and Modern Experience on the English Stage, 1500–1700* (Princeton, N.J.: Princeton University Press, 1988), 211.

23. Miola locates the difference between Shakespeare and Seneca in terms of "kindermord": in *Lear* "Shakespeare pointedly opposes an antitypal scene which features a romance reunion instead of a tragic separation. He presents a quiet, utterly moving reconciliation between parent and child" (168). Miola does not discuss Seneca's *Thebais*, which at least begins with Antigone's attempt to effect a reconciliation between parent and children.

24. I am profoundly indebted to Adelman's psychoanalytic reading of the play in *Suffocating Mothers*, chap. 5, 107.

Epilogue: Milton's Eve

1. Minaz Jooma, "The Alimentary Structures of Incest in *Paradise Lost*," *ELH* 63, 1 (1996): 25–40.

2. Maureen Quilligan, *Milton's Spenser: The Politics of Reading* (Ithaca, N.Y.: Cornell University Press, 1983).

3. For further discussion of the conversation about labor, see Maureen Quilligan, "Freedom, Service, and the Trade in Slaves: The Problem of Slavery in *Paradise Lost*," in *Subject and Object in Renaissance Culture*, ed. Margreta de Grazia, Peter Stallybrass, and Maureen Quilligan (Cambridge: Cambridge University Press, 1995), reprinted in *Paradise Lost: Contemporary Critical Essays*, ed. William Zunder (London: St. Martin's Press, 1999), 170–94.

4. Maureen Quilligan, *The Language of Allegory: Defining the Genre* (Ithaca, N.Y.: Cornell University Press, 1979), 181–82.

5. Victoria Kahn, "Allegory, the Sublime, and the Rhetoric of Things Indifferent in *Paradise Lost*," in *Creative Imitation: New Essays on Renaissance Literature in Honor of Thomas M. Greene*, ed. David Quint, Margaret Ferguson, G. W. Pigman, II, and Wayne A. Rebhorn (Binghamton, N.Y.: Medieval and Renaissance Texts Society, 1992), 150, argues that "signs, including prohibitions and laws, are not simply a consequence of the fall, but the precondition of any genuine ethical choice."

6. Susan Gemelli Martin, *The Ruins of Allegory: "Paradise Lost" and the Metamorphosis of Epic Convention* (Durham, N.C.: Duke University Press, 1998), 179.

7. Quilligan, *Milton's Spenser*, 112–18, 124–28.

Index

Acknowledgments

Scholarship is a collective effort. By this I mean not merely the mutual help scholars offer each other, their aid testified to in footnotes, but the effort to collect, to bring together the disparate wisdoms scattered variously throughout many lifetimes of reading and teaching. The footnotes I provide are the barest recognition of my indebtedness to the writings of other scholars; it is impossible to cite the conversations, in and outside of class and at various symposia, the phone calls, the lunches and dinners, email messages, and bibliographic notes that go into gathering the material for a book. I will try here to note a few of them.

Ann Rosalind Jones first told me I was writing this book when she asked me if I were writing a book on incest. I said, "No, I am not," but then I realized I was. So I need to thank her. Eric Cheyfitz gave me an important bit of bibliography after a seminar at Penn organized by Peter Stallybrass on Marcel Mauss's *The Gift*. It was Annette Weiner's *Inalienable Possessions*. I got the book from my colleague and next-street-over neighbor in Philadelphia, Margreta de Grazia, who had bought it for another purpose. I don't think I ever gave her back the copy. I traveled to New York City to meet Professor Weiner, then dean at New York University, specifically to ask her about "real" incest in the theory. She graciously responded: "Well now, that's a very good question." I heard Karen Newman give a talk on the need to discard theorizing about traffic in women at a panel organized by Margie Ferguson. Her talk made me realize that incest was a key theoretical issue and that the traffic in women might need to be revisited.

But, of course, I was working on this book even before I found its proper theoretical foundations. I had been trying to teach Mary Wroth's *Urania* in graduate seminars at Penn and at the Folger Shakespeare Library. In one of those classes I learned from Gwynne Kennedy that the fundamental subject of Wroth's romance was the traffic in women at the early Stuart court; Kennedy's dissertation has seeped so deeply into my consciousness that I am incapable of ascertaining exactly where her work intersects with mine. I have a serious suspicion that Bruce Boehrer's work on monarchy and incest occupies an even deeper foundational place. I do know for sure that had it not been for the anonymous reader of Bruce's book manuscript who suggested Jack Goody's argument about incest and the medieval church, I would probably not have found that pivotal argument. Michael Vennera first saw the windmill on the frontispiece to the *Urania*—I had never even seen it there before. Vin Nardizzi alerted me to the importance of Judith Butler's *Antigone* to my project. And these are just the students whose specific contributions I can remember. I know I owe a general debt of gratitude to Kim Hall, Wendy Wall, Juliet Fleming, Julie Solomon, Jennifer Morrison, Susan Iwaniscwu, Greg Bredbeck, and Jeff Masten, who have taught me far more than I could ever hope to teach them.

There is a whole cadre of people whose entire profession is to help scholars. Martin Kaufman, Keeper of Western Manuscripts at Duke Humphries Library at the Bodleian, showed me the embroidery-covered book eleven year-old Elizabeth Tudor made. He spread it out for me among its tissue papers, opened as many pages as I asked for, and allowed me to touch it. He gave me, as librarians are supposed to do, a lot of bibliography for the volume. And he pretended all the while that I might know—or come to know—more about it than he.

A half world away at the Huntington Library in San Marino, California, Susie Krasnoo and Romaine Ahlstrom helped to make available the largest books I have ever read, spread out for me on two whole tables in the reading room so that I could compare all the frontispieces and emblems which made their way into Chapter 6. Without the amazing resources of the Huntington, I could never have begun to make the argument I have about the title page to Wroth's romance, and I will be forever grateful for the sublime moments I spent there in autumn 1999.

Rather different versions of some of the chapters have appeared in print over the past years; I am grateful to the following people and presses for permission to reuse some of the material they published:

"Sidney and His Queen," in *The Historical Renaissance*, ed. Richard Strier and Heather Dubrow (Chicago: University of Chicago Press, 1989), 171–96.

"The Anthropology of Intertextuality: Mary Wroth and the Family Romance," in *Unfolded Tales: Essays on Renaissance Romance*, ed. Gordon Teskey and George Logan (Ithaca, N.Y.: Cornell University Press, 1989).

"The Constant Subject: Instability and Authority in Wroth's Urania Poems," in *Soliciting Interpretation: Literary Theory and Seventeenth-Century English Poetry*, ed. Elizabeth Harvey and Katharine Maus (Chicago: University of Chicago Press, 1990), 273–306.

"Staging Gender: William Shakespeare and Elizabeth Cary," in *Sex and Gender in Early Modern Europe*, ed. James G. Turner (New York: Cambridge University Press, 1993), 208–32.

"Incest and Agency: the Case of Elizabeth I," in *Genealogies*, ed. Valeria Finucci and Kevin Brownlee (Durham, N.C.: Duke University Press, 2001).

The final group of people who need to be thanked and simultaneously indemnified against all responsibility for the errors in the pages are my patient prepublication readers. First, Jonathan Crewe and Leah Marcus, readers for Penn Press; Jerry Singerman and Alison Anderson, excellent editors at Penn Press. And second, those people who read the material as my friends: Margreta de Grazia, Annie Jones, Priscilla Wald, Laura Edwards, and Anne Allison. I leave my last thanks for Michael Malone, for his careful editing, great good humor, and enduring patience.